A Mosaic of Indigenous Legal Thought

This book offers an Indigenous supplement to the rich and growing area of visual legal scholarship. Organised around three narratives, each with an associated politico-poetic reading, the book addresses three major global issues: climate change, the trade in human body parts and bio-policing. Manifesting and engaging the traditional storytelling mode of classical Indigenous ontology, these narratives convey legal and political knowledge, not merely through logical argument, but rather through the feelings of law and the understanding of lawful behaviour produced by their rhythm. Through its own performativity, therefore, the book demonstrates how classical Indigenous legal traditions remain vital to the now pressing challenge of making peace with the earth.

Dr C. F. Black, Adjunct Senior Research Fellow, Griffith Center for Coastal Management, Griffith University, Australia.

Discourses of Law
Series editors: Peter Goodrich, Michel Rosenfeld and Arthur Jacobson
Benjamin N. Cardozo School of Law

This successful and exciting series seeks to publish the most innovative scholarship at the intersection of law, philosophy and social theory. The books published in the series are distinctive by virtue of exploring the boundaries of legal thought. The work that this series seeks to promote is marked most strongly by the drive to open up new perspectives on the relation between law and other disciplines. The series has also been unique in its commitment to international and comparative perspectives upon an increasingly global legal order. Of particular interest in a contemporary context, the series has concentrated upon the introduction and translation of continental traditions of theory and law.

The original impetus for the series came from the paradoxical merger and confrontation of East and West. Globalization and the internationalization of the rule of law has had many dramatic and often unforeseen and ironic consequences. An understanding of differing legal cultures, particularly different patterns of legal thought, can contribute, often strongly and starkly, to an appreciation if not always a resolution of international legal disputes. The rule of law is tied to social and philosophical underpinnings that the series has sought to excoriate and illuminate.

Titles in the series:

The Land is the Source of the Law
A dialogic encounter with Indigenous jurisprudence
C. F. Black

Shakespearean Genealogies of Power
A whispering of nothing in *Hamlet, Richard II, Julius Caesar, Macbeth, The Merchant of Venice*, and *The Winter's Tale*
Anselm Haverkamp

Visualizing Law in the Age of the Digital Baroque
Arabesques and entanglements
Richard K. Sherwin

Novel Judgments
Legal theory as fiction
William Macneil

Sex, Culpability and the Defence of Provocation
Danielle Tyson

The Scene of Mass Crime
Peter Goodrich and Christian Delage

Wickedness and Crime
Laws of homicide and malice
Penny Crofts

Shakespeare's Curse
Björn Quiring

Exemplarity and Singularity
Thinking through particulars in philosophy, literature, and law
Edited by Michèle Lowrie and Susanne Lüdemann

Law and Enjoyment
Power, pleasure and psychoanalysis
Daniel Hourigan

Genealogies of Legal Vision
Edited by Peter Goodrich and Valerie Hayaert

Masculinity and the Trials of Modern Fiction
Marco Wan

A Mosaic of Indigenous Legal Thought
Legendary tales and other writings
C. F. Black

Forthcoming:

Crime Scenes
Forensics and aesthetics
Rebecca Scott Bray

The Rule of Reason in European Constitutionalism and Citizenship
Yuri Borgmann-Prebil

Varieties of Liberalism
Nineteenth-century contract between literature, law and history
Anat Rosenberg

The publisher gratefully acknowledges the support of the Jacob Burns Institute for Advanced Legal Studies of the Benjamin N. Cardozo School of Law to the series *Discourses of Law.*

A Mosaic of Indigenous Legal Thought

Legendary tales and other writings

C. F. Black

LONDON AND NEW YORK

First published 2017
by Routledge
2 Park Square, Milton Park, Abingdon, Oxon OX14 4RN

and by Routledge
711 Third Avenue, New York, NY 10017

First issued in paperback 2018

Routledge is an imprint of the Taylor & Francis Group, an informa business

© 2017 C. F. Black

The right of C. F. Black to be identified as the author of this work has been asserted by C. F. Black in accordance with sections 77 and 78 of the Copyright, Designs and Patents Act 1988.

All rights reserved. No part of this book may be reprinted or reproduced or utilised in any form or by any electronic, mechanical, or other means, now known or hereafter invented, including photocopying and recording, or in any information storage or retrieval system, without permission in writing from the publishers.

Trademark notice: Product or corporate names may be trademarks or registered trademarks, and are used only for identification and explanation without intent to infringe.

British Library Cataloguing in Publication Data
A catalogue record for this book is available from the British Library

Library of Congress Cataloging in Publication Data
A Mosaic of Indigenous Legal Thought
Library of Congress Cataloging in Publication Control Number: 2016025764

ISBN 13: 978-1-138-60615-9 (pbk)
ISBN 13: 978-1-138-22384-4 (hbk)

Typeset in Baskerville
by Wearset Ltd, Boldon, Tyne and Wear

To my children, Ashley, Maleah and Kapun

Contents

Acknowledgements   xi

PART I
Visualizing Indigenous jurisprudence   I

1 A poem: the originals   3

2 Video clip   5

3 Visualizing Indigenous jurisprudence through a
   diverse range of narratives   6

4 The influential theories   10

5 Retribalizing the tales   12

PART II
Climate change   15

6 A poem: becoming history   17

7 Some words   18

8 The Wind Watchers' tale: skinned alive   21

9 A poem: so very different from us   42

10 Native women and healing the neglected rights of the
   land   44

x   Contents

PART III
The trade in body parts   57

11   Some words: the story of Wibari   59

12   The Wind Watchers' tale: Wibari and the Rogue
     Protectors   61

13   A poem: an ode to the children of Guatemala   110

14   Modern cannibalism: the trade in human body parts   111

PART IV
Bioinsecurity   129

15   Some words   131

16   The Wind Watchers' tale: Bringers of the Red Dust   132

17   A poem: in search of immortality (an ode to the
     scientists)   154

18   The insidious disease of bioinsecurity: bats and
     badgers at large!   155

PART V
Last words   173

19   A poem: to the little people   175

20   In conclusion: some reflective thoughts   176

Acknowledgements

This book has been a long time coming into being because the stories came first, as if they were scouting out the territory to be crossed. On that journey, many people have come and gone, including my mother. In her place, I have witnessed the arrival of another grandchild – a future custodian of traditional lands of the Kombumerri and Munaljahlai peoples. I also wish to acknowledge the traditional custodians of the lands on which I wrote part of the book: Montreal, Canada and Efate Island, Vanuatu. The contributions of the inhabitants of those lands have been significant in many ways, which are mentioned in the book. My three trips to South Africa have also been influential. However, there are others who have been a constant presence and influence throughout that time, including Shaun McVeigh for his intellectual guidance, Christine Zuni Cruz, Beth Rose Middleton, Glenda Donovan, Donna Weston, Kine Camara, Robin Trotter, Kirsten Anker, Honni van Rijswijk, Olivia Barr, Val Napoleon and Rodolfo Cruz for their comments and editing. I am also indebted to the people who influenced my stories: Waneek Horn-Miller, Rita Mazzocchi, Ralph Regenvanu, Delene Cuddihy Patricia McGarr and Rodger Tomlinson. Special mention must go to my young reader, Jan Mihal, whose comments have been invaluable. As always, I am grateful to my editor, the fine-tuner of my thoughts, Sue Jarvis. I am deeply appreciative of the support provided by the Northern Institute, Charles Darwin University, Griffith University Centre for Coastal Management and the Australian government's Endeavour Scholarship program. And finally, I cannot begin to express how grateful I am for the constant support of my family.

– C. F. Black, 2016

Part I

Visualizing Indigenous jurisprudence

Chapter 1

A poem

The originals

The originals,
they came long before us,
seeking out food and shelter,
harbouring their own ways of thinking,
their own ways of knowing the land.
So very different from us.

They held their nightly feasts
in places unseen by us.
They shared their knowledge
and built their towers of mud and clay
or burrowed deep underground.

Those on high chirped and discussed
the pervading winds
and the knowledge borne
by the spirits of the winds of the West.
They took their direction from the Unseen
and knew of places that we could not see
So very different from us.

As they spread with ease
and gentleness across the land,
their direction guided
by a collective unknown.
Their expectation was much
and their lives were devoid of stuff.

They fought and breed at the speed
that Nature preordained.
And so the balance came
and went and so did they.

No need of despair
that they no longer bore
nor breed.
So very different from us.

Their intention was not
to rule the world
for they barely noticed it
as their lives passed
with speed and intent.
Intent borne of survival
and rapture in the moment.
So very different from us.

Chapter 2

Video clip

As we are all basically cyber-connected through our handy mobile phones, it would not seem out of order to ask the reader to watch this short video clip of Marshall McLuhan before reading on, as it will contextualize my book and also show just how far we are behind in our understanding of the present world of technological development and control of the way we do things.

https://www.youtube.com/watch?v=viuIKgjLnDE

Chapter 3

Visualizing Indigenous jurisprudence through a diverse range of narratives

The manner in which primitive, tribal people understood the world and the way we must now understand the world are identical. We stand at the dawn of a new creation, for we can no longer process our experience into predetermined categories of explanation; we require a generalised approach to life which can give us meaning that transcends the immediate intake of data.

– Vine Deloria Jr[1]

But now, gazing across a landscape that has shown us the consequences of the Cartesian model as it has played out from early to late modernity, it has become apparent a new paradigm is needed. We have come full circle and the renewal of the very impulse that gave birth to modernity, in the face of comparable epistemological crises, now calls for an integral rhetoric that complements the virtues and counters the defects of critical reason with the sublime elegance and binding power of ethical wisdom.

– Richard Sherwin[2]

Although we know a tremendous amount about the nuances of cognitive processing, that knowledge does not go all the way toward explaining human behavior. In fact, emotion turns out to be an enormously powerful predictor of behavior, especially in the area of politics and policy.

– Jennifer Lerner[3]

This book offers a timely departure from the standard form of Indigenous legal argumentation within the discourses of laws and returns to the 'old' for guidance on preparing text that may transition into the visual vortex now surrounding us with meaning. The exponential speed and volume of data upon us each day call for a different approach to understanding the world, as do the ways in which connectivity is eroding traditional power structures.[4]

Google alone is teaching us new ways of understanding our knowledge – the shift from the knowledge worker to the smart creative typifies the new employee in the internet century.[5] This book is written for the smart creative – that person whose understanding of the world is lateral and diverse. Google rose as the shift from the dominance of the supplier moved to that of the 'informed' consumer: a consumer whose world is saturated with visual stimuli cached in tantalizing storylines. A consumer with an expectation that they must be entertained on the one hand, but choose the meaning they wish to draw from the information being offered on the other. The legal world is also subject to this fundamental power shift in meaning-making. We can no longer dictate who or what is an expert because the internet century is one of speed and constant change in social norms and geopolitics. Just as the nineteenth-century male legal theorist is now suspect in a world in which women and 'the other' have a voice and a right to practise their laws, so too is the manner in which we present knowledge. Therefore, this book offers a mosaic of writings that are more aligned to a matrix structure, and encourages the reader to connect with the stories and other writings in order to form their own opinions. The intention is not to offer a complete thesis on one subject, but rather to present a new paradigm as suggested by Sherwin – one built on Deloria's call for a generalized approach to life – which can give us a meaning that transcends the immediate intake of data. Furthermore, it is designed to align the reader's feelings about a topic rather than suggest that they try to 'take in the immediate data' on the subject being discussed, because:

> when law migrates to the screen it lives there as other images do, motivating belief and judgement on the basis of visual delight and unconscious fantasies and desires. This condition of ontological and ethical uneasiness threatens the legality of law's claim to power.[6]

Sherwin cautions that new factors have begun to influence judgement and belief and, as neurologists have discovered, it is emotions and experiences that shape decision-making; this points to the importance of storytelling, which I suggest is an important skill in the new paradigm. Just as legal judgments often come down to who tells the most compelling story, the same principle applies in the visual world.

The mosaic is therefore made up of a group of loosely interconnected themes and characters, meant to stimulate the reader to make connections to their own understandings of law and lawful behaviour in the Indigenous world and the world around them. This book does not guide or encourage the traditional ways of critical thinking, but instead follows the path of the traditional story and offers an opportunity for the reader to consider an issue by reading my account, in both narrative and rhetoric form, of how I came to an understanding of it. Just as anthropomorphic tales are not written for critical analysis, the mosaic of works can be said to be a series of journeys or songs through which the reader may move at their own pace. Like all journeys/songs, some are of interest and others are not. This certainly applies to the following works. I am not setting out a definitive account of any particular issue; rather, I invite the reader into the world of my moral compass and the ways in which I find meaning. I therefore take the reader on a journey/song to make their own connections, and to evoke their own emotions and experiences, which may help to formulate their own decisions and to guide their moral compass in these times of exponential growth of data and visual stimulation. My approach is a response to Sherwin's argument that 'motivating belief and judgement on the basis of visual delight and unconscious fantasies and desires' requires a new approach to Legal Studies.[7] This book offers a matrix of writing to bring forth the jurisprudence of 'feeling the law' or song of the law, as well as returning to a 'tribal way' of understanding Indigenous legal thought.

Building on that jurisprudence, this book is held together thematically by three anthropomorphized animal tales, which make up the *Legendary Tales of the Wind Watchers*. Each tale develops a narrative loosely centred on a major global issue. Those three issues are climate change, the trade in human body parts and bio-policing. The intention is not to turn the global issue into the central theme of each story, but rather to influence the interaction of the characters in the stories and also in the other writings.

Interwoven through the themes are a series of subtexts that are impacted by these global dilemmas, together with a smattering of poetry. Once again, the poetry is highly visual, and is an emotive response to the issues dealt with in the writings that follow each tale. The three themes, and the decision to write on these subjects, were introduced into the text through an engagement with Indigenous players from North America, Africa and Australasia while carrying out visiting fellowships, as well as stemming from long-term friendships.

Each story is woven to demonstrate how interactions I experienced while undertaking a series of visiting fellowships led me to write the tales and the subsequent discourse. In other words, the themes are situated within an Indigenous engagement with life. The book is about what concerns me the most in these tumultuous times – in particular, our youth. I therefore developed the character of the Wind Watcher in each tale; however, this character is more a pivotal point for collective action rather than an individual superhero saving the day, for each tale is about being part of a team to overcome adversity. There are overarching themes with which the Wind Watcher identifies, but not in an overt way; rather, the process involves coming to their own personal understanding of the role of a Wind Watcher. It must be remembered that the stories were evoked by context and the human interactions I encountered in the differing landscapes.

Notes

1 Deloria Jr, V., *Metaphysics of Modern Existence*, Harper and Row: New York, 1979: 145–146.
2 Sherwin, R., *Visualizing Law in the Age of the Digital Baroque*, Routledge: Oxford, 2011.
3 Gavel, D., 'Jennifer Lerner on emotions and decision making', *Harvard Kennedy School*, 22 April 2015. www.hks.harvard.edu/news-events/publications/insight/management/lerner, accessed 4 April 2016.
4 Johnson, S. 'Where good ideas come from', 17 September 2010. https://www.youtube.com/watch?v=NugRZGDbPFU, accessed 12 April 2016.
5 Schmidt, E., and Rosenberg, J., *How Google Works*, John Murray: London, 2014: 17.
6 Sherwin, *Visualising Law*. ii.
7 Ibid.

Chapter 4

The influential theories

> Cut off from its figurative, poetic roots, blinded by lack of a pragmatic ethical phenomenology, justice recedes from view. In its place, legal forms endlessly proliferate: guidelines and principles, policies and regulations, rules and metrics – overwhelming in their disparate array.
>
> – Richard Sherwin[1]

The back-story to this book was my engagement with the scholarship of Richard Sherwin's *Visualizing Law in the Age of the Digital Baroque*,[2] especially after viewing his Vimeo presentation at the *Visualizing Law in the Digital Age* conference.[3] I was excited about what I saw as a kind of surrealism, which I thought would open up an opportunity for shaping a text that would be more suitable for both Indigenous readers and today's cyber-youth.

I was looking for a shape that would allow for a transitional guide from the written to the visual – a sort of Indigenous *Hitchhiker's Guide to the Galaxy*[4] that would incorporate essays, tales, poetry and links to visuals through a mosaic of texts. This search led me to *The Gutenberg Galaxy: The Making of Topographic Man*,[5] written by communication theorist Marshall McLuhan – a writer who specialized in the 'non-linear form of writing which re-elaborates the alphabetic form so as to give the written page a tactile and multi-sensory dimension'.[6] *The Gutenberg Galaxy* was an attempt to take the reader out of the safe linear world and into a mosaic of ideas in a series of essays that allowed the replacement of logical thought with free association and the artistic, visually controlled juxtaposition of ideas.[7]

Native American scholar Vine Deloria Jr nicely links McLuhan's views with Indigenous ontology:

> We view a universe of our own creation that has transcended its cultural and intellectual roots in Western society and now seeks to bind all societies together instantaneously. The best comparison McLuhan can make between our world and any other is to the world of tribal people.[8]

McLuhan's ideas are aesthetically crafted into the video *McLuhan's Wake*,[9] for he was trying 50 years ago to alert us to the powerful impact the visual would have on our society, its values and institutions. In other words, he pre-empted the need for an appreciation of visual jurisprudence. He talked about the age of the electronic media – the forerunner of the digital age that would sweep us into a vortex that would reshape the individual from an isolated bookworm into part of a global village of cyber-interconnection. McLuhan further warned that we would willingly give up our private information to powerful advertising gurus, who would understand us better than any philosopher. We are now all caught up in the great vortex of the internet. Furthermore, McLuhan saw a retribalizing of humanity brought on by this great vortex. Fundamental to surviving the great vortex was to study the patterns; fundamental to Indigenous law is the understanding that we are all patterned into the cosmos and its great vortex of life-giving energy.

Notes

1 Sherwin, R., *Visualizing Law in the Age of the Digital Baroque*, Routledge: Oxford, 2011: 5.
2 Ibid.
3 Sherwin, R., 'Presentation by Professor Richard Sherwin', 21 October 2011. https://vimeo.com/36349457, accessed 12 October 2013.
4 Adams, D., *The Hitchhiker's Guide to the Galaxy: The Original Radio Scripts*, Pan: London, 2003.
5 McLuhan, M. (ed.), *The Gutenberg Galaxy: The Making of Topographic Man*, University of Toronto Press: Toronto, 1962.
6 Lamberti, E., 'Not Just a Book on Media: Extending the Gutenberg Galaxy', in McLuhan, M. (ed.), *The Gutenberg Galaxy: The Making of Topographic Man*, University of Toronto Press: Toronto, 1962: xxix.
7 Scheffel-Dunand, D., 'The Invisible and the Visible: Intertwining Figure and Ground', in McLuhan, M. (ed.), *The Gutenberg Galaxy: The Making of Topographic Man*, University of Toronto Press: Toronto, 1962: xlviii.
8 Deloria Jr, V., *Metaphysics of Modern Existence*, Harper and Row: New York, 1979: 145–146.
9 *McLuhan's Wake*, YouTube video, https://www.youtube.com/watch?v=A9y-ZAIdxrE, accessed 7 April 2015.

Chapter 5

Retribalizing the tales

> After Thought-Woman, the spider
> named things and
> as she named them
> they appeared.
> She is sitting in her room
> Thinking of a story now.
> I'm telling you the story she is thinking.
> – Paula Gunn Allen[1]

As though waiting for me to remember the Originals – that is, the animals and plants that came well before the humans, which are therefore the natural mediators to teach humans how to act lawfully in a great cosmos of interlinking species and land/seascapes – the tales began to push forth their presence. As Kathleen Kemarre Wallace begins her story of the Emu man ancestor:

> Everyone can learn from stories; this one is about listening, learning and respecting the culture we share. It is about the knowledge of our ancestors, speaking to us through ampere, art, dance, song and stories. This story used to be told to us by our grandparents. It shows us the importance of respecting our culture and its laws.[2]

Anishinabek legal scholar John Borrows (Kegedonce) reminds us in many of his legal texts and visuals that it is the animals that led the Anishinabek into understanding lawful behaviour.[3] In his book *Drawing Out the Law: A Spirit's Guide*,[4] Borrows brings together a mosaic of oral tradition, pictographic scrolls, dreams, common law case analysis and philosophical reflection to speak to Anishinabek law in the contemporary world. There are very few Indigenous legal scholars who see the value of using animals as a way of teaching ethical behaviour, let alone applying it to larger global issues. Yet is it not the animals that taught us our Indigenous laws? Are we not defined by our totems, and are not our social relations and marriage laws historically woven together by powerful animal ancestors?

As well as Borrows, there are other Indigenous writers focusing on this area. One is Pueblo academic Paula Gunn Allen, who brought forth the importance of the power of animals – especially as creator beings. Gunn Allen grew up on the Laguna Pueblo in New Mexico. Her fellow country-man is Greg Cateje, who wrote *Native Science: Natural Laws of Interdependence*, which also references the important role of animals in understanding the world. His account, however, is one of a Native Scientist. He writes:

> In the Native way, there is a fluid and inclusive perception of animal nature that makes less of a distinction between human, animal and spiritual realities. These realities are seen as interpenetrating one another. This a view held in common with evolving descriptions of reality in quantum physics.[5]

In such accounts, Indigenous scholarship becomes the literary critique of the stories that may position the animal as law bearer.

Each tale in this book came out of an experience in the various places mentioned earlier – in North America, Africa and Australasia. From those countries, I experienced world events and met amazing people, who in turn evoked the characters in the book. But the characters I met could not help but remind me of the animals I also met along the way. For example, the vulnerability of a potoroo and other small marsupials of Australia reminded me so much of the vulnerability of the people around me at the time of the 2008 Global Financial Crisis. The marsupials embodied their feelings rather than their personalities. Likewise, the harbour seals embodied the vulnerability of Native women at a time where there is a looming tipping point of climate change. The intelligence of a hyrax I saw one day on YouTube embodied the courage of two female African (Senegalese and Eritrean) lawyers, who were willing to lay down their lives for the rights of women in their countries as well as for the rights of the poor.

This book contains those tales, and in the reading of the tales, I hope the reader will be transformed. It will not be a transformation of a Buddhist awakening or a Christian experience of being born again. However, just like the animals in the story, you will come to understand that you are not alone in the world – that other beings inhabit the same space and are watching you. These are the Watchers of humans. They watch what we do. In most cases in the West, they must continuously readjust to cater for our carelessness. For a Watcher does not race out and say 'stop in the name of our animal rights'; rather, they observe and learn and adjust – and in many cases die due to our greed and torture.

For every minute of the day, some animal is committed to a Messianic role in which it must give up its life so that we humans will be well. How many of us give thanks daily to the animals that suffer immense torture and pain so that drugs can be designed so that we can live our consumer lives with all their vagaries? And perhaps most evil of our ways is the avoidance of death – as though only we privileged-nation humans have the right to choose when we will die. Animals must die so that we can have that privilege. This is the great folly of our belief in just how important the human species is and why it should be saved by drugs. I personally think there should be a day of gratitude and celebration for all those animals that have fallen unwillingly so that we may be safe. So that we can go to war and kill each other over oil and our national ideologies of how life should be lived. And so we continue to gorge ourselves and live unhealthy lives, yet expect animals to give their lives so that a wonder drug will cure the results of our over-indulgence. When will we learn that the fauna of this great blue globe we inhabit are here to teach us the lessons of lawful behaviour?

The tales are there to facilitate learning through osmosis rather than critical analysis, thereby encouraging the reader to take hold of their animal nature, which has been reduced by the mechanized thinking of rationalism and played out through superheroes such as the battle-clad Superman or Wonder Woman. The book espouses the benefits of ditching these individualistic superheroes and turning instead to 'the native' in all cultures, where stories are told of the great deeds of animals, thereby raising one's animal self to its totemic self – which is full of the possibilities of goodness/evil, courage/cowardice and moral fortitude. As the catch-cry goes, 'become your own legend' through your animal of choice – the one that best reflects your inner nature. It is through knowing your own story, and the lawful behaviour that governs that story, that real heroism and meaningfulness manifest; in turn, this guides your moral compass.

Notes

1 Gunn Allen, P., *The Sacred Hoop: Recovering the Feminine in American Indian Traditions*, Beacon Press: Boston, 1992: 123.
2 Wallace, K. M. and Lovell, J., *Listen Deeply Let These Stories In*, IAD Press: Alice Springs, 2009: 75.
3 Schmidt, J., 'John Borrows: Drawing Out Law', lecture, 18 January 2016. http://jeremyjschmidt.com/2016/01/18/john-borrows-drawing-out-law, accessed 7 March 2016.
4 Borrows, J., *Drawing Out the Law: A Spirit's Guide*, University of Toronto Press: Toronto, 2010.
5 Cateje, G., *Native Science: Natural Laws of Interdependence*, Clear Light: New Mexico, 2000: 150.

Part II

Climate change

Chapter 6

A poem
Becoming history

And what of this I write,
like a river flowing at a fast rate,
for world events are moving at such a pace
to keep up one must refer to the day's dictate;
for long gone is the need to contemplate,
speed is upon us and so are events
as the tipping point has arrived
and we must run to keep pace with Nature
as she rises to tell us we have too much stuff.
So reader beware I am writing for the day
which will become part of history
as my words flow across the page.

Chapter 7

Some words

I dreamt of my muse, which was a seal spirit, when I was undertaking post-doctoral research in Montreal, Canada. As soon as the seal spirit appeared, the story began to be tapped out upon my laptop and a tale began to unfold of seals in distress and being stalked by a psychotic polar bear that enjoyed skinning the seals alive, rather than eating them. I soon found the old adage to be true: Life imitates Art rather than Art imitating Life. For no sooner had I began to write than I started to come across reports of the sudden disappearances of seals en masse and, in late 2010, a strange phenomenon in which seals in both northern England and to a lesser degree Canada washed up on the shores with a strange corkscrew skinning pattern. They had been partially 'skinned alive' and not eaten in any form; the cutting was a precision cut, as though by some industrial encased cylinder.[1] Scientists believe boats associated with the building of the Sheringham Shoal wind farm may explain the death of 50 seals whose bodies washed up on the Norfolk coast.[2]

The seals had been skinned alive by a military-industrial complex that does not care who or what it destroys – unless it is caught out. Giant wind turbines and solar panels spread like diseases bent on feeding the military-industrial complex's demand for energy. It is a demand for security in supply, but no security is offered to the small beings who have lived longer on this Earth than any humans, and who are now being destroyed by these so-called 'clean, green energy' machines. But there is nothing particularly clean or clever about millions of solar panels scarring the desert floor, or skinning seals alive. A civilized society would appreciate the need for a change in values and consumption, not for a shift in the source of energy. And who is leading the call for a more civilized approach?

Step aside *Sea Shepherd* – the seals can handle it!

Had the following incident not been aired on one of Australia's most respected investigative programs, *The 7.30 Report*,[3] I would not have believed it. Instead, it provided me with the character of Galeen. What better character to craft in order to epitomize my own ancestor Galeen[4] than one of these feisty heroes of the sea. The story is told in such a way to indicate that the environmental boat the *Sea Shepherd* need not be called to the rescue, as the seals of the south are making their own mark:

MARK RYAN, TASSAL: Yeah, we've had a guy who's needed 30 stitches in his calf because a seal had attacked him from behind and then we've had night-watchmen where they've have been chased up on top of their wheelhouse.

JOCELYN NETTLEFOLD: Such showdowns are increasing, particularly in Victorian and Tasmanian waters. In the past decade, the Australian fur seal population has risen from about 80,000 to 90,000 and colonies of New Zealand fur seals are booming in South Australia and in the west.

BOB PENNINGTON, AUST SEAFOOD INDUSTRY COUNCIL: In 20 to 30 years, the numbers of seals will double or treble.

JOCELYN NETTLEFOLD: It's not just the numbers that have the fishermen worried, it's the difficulty they have trying to keep seals away from fish stock. According to Mark Ryan, chief executive of Tassal, an Atlantic salmon producer, seals are becoming harder to outwit.

MARK RYAN: They've got a skull and brain size exactly the same as an Alsatian – and Alsatians are quite a smart animal – and they learn new tricks and they teach the pups those tricks, so each year you've got to go that one step further to stop them from getting into your pen.

DAVID PEMBERTON, BIOLOGIST: Basically, it takes something like four years for seals to find a fishery. When they find it, learn about it, they hammer it.

JOCELYN NETTLEFOLD: Tassal spends up to $10 million a year on seal management, including hundreds of relocations.

Fishermen in the southern seas are indignant that seals have the audacity to think they own the fish. Not only do they think this, but they act on it by boarding the fishing vessels and promptly chasing the fishermen up the masts to seek safety. One must remember that a southern seal is the size and body weight of the best of our Olympic swimmers. These Olympians know their jurisdiction and power. Like Captain Jack Sparrow in *The Pirates of the Caribbean*,[5] they swagger with audacity and panache into the catch and select the best to savour. Tasmania's Parks and Wildlife Department does its best to round up the criminals and herd them back to the depths of the Southern Ocean, but it would appear there are the Geronimo-like recalcitrants – as they call them – who just won't learn, and so return to harass the fishermen. These seals not only return but, to the horror of the fishermen, appear to train their young to use the same tactics.

These *Sea Shepherd*-like tactics adopted by the seals are met with the same disapproval as the Japanese whaling research ships. One cannot help wonder about the fishermen who, on the one hand, see nothing wrong

20   Climate change

with fishing the seas for the corporate dollar while complaining bitterly about the bigger vessels that fish the place dry, yet can find no empathy for the seals. Perhaps if the fishermen had known the creation story of Sedna – the goddess who guards the seas of the Arctic – they would have been more sympathetic towards the seals.

I tell the creation story of Sedna in the section on Native Women, but in the following tale the power of Sedna will become evident through the voice of Kanuk the Windwatcher. It is also a curious fact that in 2004 NASA named a small planet in the coldest known region of our solar system Sedna.[6] As though this honouring of the sea goddess Sedna also influenced those down on planet earth, the humans got busy and made up their own narratives about the great changes in the ocean through the climate change blockbuster *Day After Tomorrow*[7] and Michael Crichton's best seller, *State of Fear*[8] in that very same year. In other words, the return of Sedna's twin in the outer galaxy had come back to remind us that if the great oceans are not cared for Sedna will cause havoc for humans.

The seals' tenacity and courage is evident – and perhaps that is why the seal came to me in my dream. In that dream, the seal's determined face showed me it was courageous and that I should pay attention and remember what I had dreamt. Traditional stories remind us of the bravery of animals and other species. They remind us that animals care for and defend their young. They know the male of the species can be a deadly predator in his own right. And so I dare to declare that security of a community should be the female realm – and the dominion of an older woman at that! The seals remind us of the need for endurance and discipline, but also carry the stories of how our 'older brothers/sisters' – the animals – teach us how to be human.

Notes

1 Sims, P., 'Scientists Baffled by Mysterious "Corkscrew" Deaths of Seals Off British Coast', *Daily Mail*, 18 August 2010. https://www.sott.net/articles/show/213651-Scientists-baffled-by-mysterious-corkscrew-deaths-of-seals-off-British-coast, accessed 20 November 2015.
2 Bugler, T., 'Wind Farm Clue to Horrific "Corkscrew" Seal Deaths', *Daily Mail*, 23 August 2010. www.dailymail.co.uk/news/article-1305402/Wind-farm-clue-horrific-corkscrew-seal-deaths.html#ixzz1VufMQpFZ, accessed 20 November 2015.
3 Nettlefold, J., 'Fishermen Want Seal Population Culled', *ABC Program Transcript*, 9 November 2004. www.abc.net.au/7.30/content/2004/s1239682.htm, accessed 20 November 2015.
4 Galeen, or Kadeen, was one of my Kombumerri Australian Aboriginal ancestors; he was considered a great warrior.
5 *Pirates of the Caribbean* film series, Disney, 2003.
6 NASA, *Mysterious Sedna*, 2004. http://science.nasa.gov/science-news/science-at-nasa/2004/16mar_sedna/.
7 *Day After Tomorrow*, Twentieth Century Fox, 2004. Dir: Roland Emmerich.
8 Crichton, M., *State of Fear*, HarperCollins: New York, 2004.

Chapter 8

The Wind Watchers' tale

Skinned alive[1]

Nukard the Wind Watcher

He ran across the ice, as fast as his great paws would carry him; close on his heels was Cartier the torturer. Cartier was determined to catch Nukard and make him fight. But Nukard did not want to fight Cartier. As far as Nukard was concerned, Cartier was no longer a polar bear; he had become something else – he had become human! Cartier lunged with great speed behind the Wind Watcher, calling out to him.

'Stop, stop! Fight me you fool! What are you scared of?' he yelled as he tried to gain on the Wind Watcher. But as he knew full well that it would not be long before the wind would begin to blow and slow him down.

Whoosh! A great gust of wind hit Cartier in the side and sent him sliding across the ice.

'Damn you trickster, that's not fair! You coward! Fight me!' he yelled again as he tried to regain his footing on the slippery ice. But Nukard was not listening; he was now moving like the wind, becoming the great Wind Watcher and disappearing, as though caught up in a tempest of ice, which dissolved his form into a shadowy reflection of something off in the distance – a distance too far for Cartier to reach.

Cartier relented and slowed down, then turned and grunted with a deep guttural noise. He moved heavily, showing his further annoyance, as the gust of wind now seemed to be taking pleasure in belting against his thick white coat.

'Piss off, Wind! You and that coward Nukard have won, so leave me alone', he growled again, and swung his paw in the air, trying to hit what could not be hit. But the wind had no intention of leaving him alone; if anything, it appeared to delight in torturing him with its razor-sharp icicles that were wrapped up in its ferocity. The wind tore at him so viciously that droplets of blood began to appear on his facial fur. This was not the first time Cartier had been tormented by this particular wind. It had come many times since he had begun to hang around the great ship that had intruded into their icy paradise.

The seals from the North

'Look, Buzzy! Look at those strange seals!' cried Augy the squirrel. 'They all look so shabby and poor. Who are they?' questioned Augy as Buzzy the bumblebee landed on his head. Augy was a watchful squirrel and had a panoramic view from his ancient oak tree that stood on a hill overlooking the St Lawrence River. He often scurried up the great oak to watch the goings-on in the river. He was used to seeing seals passing through the causeway, but this time he was puzzled by what he saw. The poor creatures looked hungry and tired; their fur was lacking the usual silvery lustre.

'It's criminal, Buzzy', Augy said, as he scurried to a higher branch and his little friend buzzed up beside him as her iridescent blue body glistened in the morning sunshine.

'It is as though some great crime was taking place and the evidence was now floating into the great and beautiful St Lawrence River', said Augy excitedly as he moved further out onto the branch. He loved this river because it had power. In some ways, it was unconquerable – Augy was sure the great river would have the last say if anyone tried to tame it.

'They may succeed for a while', he called out confidently to Buzzy, who was flying around his head as he bounced further out onto the branch, 'but the river would eventually take back her freedom'.

'Yes, the river is a strong and fearless female making her mark on the landscape, cutting out her own path and changing it at will. And the worst of her power has yet to be seen, for she could slow her waters right down to a trickle, if she felt so inclined', he laughed and looked up at Buzzy, without noticing the precarious position he had now put himself in. Buzzy was moving higher to try to encourage Augy to follow her up the tree, rather than to bounce further out onto the end of the branch, but to no avail, as Augy was now in full swing, pontificating on the wonders of the mighty river.

'The worst this lot has seen is her ability to stubbornly ice over until she was rock hard. But the old stories had told of a time when she was really angry at the animals and she ran dry. That would make those silly humans think twice, with their great dams and locks. Those silly constructions were built on the assumption that her waters would flow forever. But what if she dried up? Ha! What then? Would the humans then suffer the great die-off that occurred in the times when animals ruled the world?' he cried out in a loud voice and jolted his body as he said it, which in turn made his branch snap. Before he knew it, he was spiralling down, down, down through the branches below until he hit the ground. He then staggered to his feet.

'I really must pay more attention', grumbled Augy to Buzzy, who could not help laughing as she watched Augy stagger away from the tree and over to a soft clump of grass.

Napoleon leads the Arctic harp seals

The exhausted Ring Seals from the north were led by Napoleon. She was an old matriarch with a gash in her neck that had healed over time, leaving a deep scar. She had barely escaped with her life when attacked by Cartier the polar bear. Cartier was an infamous bear who did not follow the normal routine set down for the polar bear, but had begun a new pattern – an evil pattern. This was a pattern formed from spending too much time around the new arrivals in the crystal-blue waters of the Arctic. He had seen the arrival of the large grey ship and watched the sailors throw their rubbish overboard, which attracted his curiosity. He had become fascinated with them, and would watch them for hours as they moved around the ship. So it was not long before he was picking up the worst of their traits. This had turned Cartier into a sadistic creature, who now terrorized the seals of the north. He had always been a successful hunter, but now he had learnt a new way of hunting. He didn't just kill the seals; he had now learnt how to torture them.

This kind of terror had never been known before in these times. Yet some had said it had happened before – a long time ago, when there were no ships or humans. But Napoleon was not going to wait around to find out whether this was true; she knew she had to care for the coming generations and so had demanded that the young female seals follow her to safety. The males were left behind to try to defeat Cartier.

Cartier the sadistic

Nukard finally stopped running and resumed his gentle pace along the ice until he came to a stop at the edge of the ice and looked into the seawater below. 'I can't keep running; it will only make Cartier more determined. I have to think of a new tactic', thought Nukard, as he looked at his image in the water. Nukard was a Wind Watcher and a powerful storyteller. When he told stories, things happened. They somehow appeared to come through into reality. This had made Nukard more reserved as he became older. He knew very well he could tell a story and dispel Cartier from their icy paradise, but that would not help find the source of Cartier's evil ways. He paced backwards and forwards as polar bears do, and he thought about Cartier. He was deeply disturbed by the change in his behaviour. He was also concerned by the arrival of the great grey ship. As far as he could remember from the stories of his tribe, there had only been a few large ships to make it through to their distant land of ice. Mostly it was men in kayaks. Nukard paced even more quickly as his mind churned over these strange goings on. He knew the ice was melting, and he and his fellow bears were getting hungry. It was a hunger that he feared would turn more of the bears into Cartier clones.

He stopped his pacing as a seal's head popped out of the water. Like lightning, his great paw swung with lethal accuracy and knocked the seal unconscious. He then bit its head and killed it instantly.

'A death more worthy of the very species which kept the great polar bears of the Arctic alive', thought Nukard.

Nukard had often told the young bears that without Sedna's favourite – the seal – they would starve to death, as they could not sustain their great body weight on smaller prey. Seals were very important, and must be respected for giving their lives to keep the bears alive. Yet here was Cartier encouraging other bears to treat them like some plaything to torture and do to as they pleased.

'They would incur the wrath of Sedna, if she found out', grumbled Nukard. 'What a stupid statement!', he thought. Of course, Sedna already knew what was happening and the melting of sea ice was the proof. He had seen the great caravan of female seals leaving. Not only were the seals leaving, but the whales no longer came close enough for them to catch them, nor did the other mammals. In fact, he had noticed over the years that fewer and fewer mammals seemed to be being born. Was Sedna resurfacing, and taking back her own?

Seals of the South

Napoleon and her tribe swam slowly but surely into the St Lawrence River, which drew the curiosity of the silky spotted Harbour Seals and particularly that of Neeky. She was the fastest seal in the river and had engaged in many a brave deed. Neeky had a longer body than most, and was therefore a stronger swimmer. Her silky coat glistened in the sun when she jumped up on the rocks to view the arrival of the straggly ones. She came from a long line of heroines. Her mother had been responsible for many brave acts to save her fellow seals and her sister was a healer.

She jumped down from her rock, swam cautiously over to Napoleon and welcomed her and her people, then asked what had happened to them. Napoleon told her of the dangerous circumstances in the north and how things were changing, and explained that the females had particularly felt vulnerable as their birthing caves of ice were melting and being invaded by the polar bears. But there was also a new threat. A large ship had arrived in their territory, full of humans. This had all become too much for Napoleon, so she had decided that all the females had to leave for their own safety, if the tribe was to survive.

'Don't worry, Napoleon, your tribe can stay with us, but when you are strong we will travel back with you and help you fight the bears. And as for the humans, we know how to stay out of their way', said Neeky confidently, as she did a back-flip in the water.

Wind Watchers' tale: skinned alive   25

'I don't think you quite know what I am talking about, Neeky. They are not just eating us – they are torturing us!' said Napoleon emphatically, as she dived down after Neeky. 'There are also many strange things happening with the weather, which is making it worse. I don't think you realize what it means. The great ship and the strange weather are sending the bears crazy. We don't know how to deal with this mayhem. Do you, Neeky?' challenged Napoleon, as she swam up to Neeky's face.

'I mean, has your world been turned upside down in your lifetime? We just can't go back and fight. We have to learn to adjust to the changing conditions as well. For all these signs tell us Sedna is returning, and we cannot just go out and fight to the death when the greater power of Sedna is calling all the shots. All we can do is try to read the signs before we are consumed by the chaos that Sedna brings, which seems to include the bears going virtually mad', cried Napoleon and she swam up to the surface, in dismay at Neeky's naivety. She then lifted her head above the surface of the water and called out to Neeky once again.

'Well, Neeky, have you ever suffered through the wrath of Sedna?'

'No, Napoleon, I haven't', answered Neeky apologetically, for Neeky was not egotistical – just enthusiastic. She then sunk under the water and began to swim around in circles as she thought about the plight of Napoleon and her people. Neeky's life had been quite secure for a seal. Indeed, she and her clan had experienced many a scrap with the humans, their boats and the pollution they left behind, but nothing resembling Napoleon's distress. And then there was the wrath of Sedna – something that did not bear thinking about. Sedna was the great power that gave life and took life away. No one worshipped Sedna; they just wanted to stay out of her way – or at least appease her if things started to go haywire. Neeky's old stories told of the wrath of Sedna, which particularly affected males. Her grandmother had told her of ancient times when Sedna's twin, who was said to live on the outer edges of the galaxy, would come to Sedna's aid if she called. The last time she called her twin, all the seas rose. This changed the whole landscape and ways of doing things. The males did not cope with this change, as it brought scarcity, so they slipped into cannibalism and started eating the young.

Many years before, the old female seals had foretold that this change was coming again. They had seen the return of Sedna's twin in their visions, but no one really listened as they could not see proof. Now, though, they could – and it was moving at a great speed, particularly after the arrival of the great grey ship. The old females had said that was a warning that something bad was about to happen.

Neeky again swam down to the depths of the St Lawrence and thought about the story of Sedna. As she swam down, she thought to herself, 'We need help, but we need very powerful help; we need fearless seals to help us and I know just the ones we need!' Neeky swirled and darted to the

26 Climate change

surface. 'We need seals who are used to chaos, humans and strange weather. Who better than the Southern Seals! Yes nothing stranger and braver than the seals from the land Down Under.' Nothing was normal in their lives as far as Neeky was concerned.

So Neeky resurfaced and swam immediately to Napoleon's side. 'In the Southern Ocean there live many a fearless seal. I have never seen seals like them, and they live in the strangest land. They would know how to cope with these violent polar bears; they are not frightened of anything – not even humans! They actually attack the humans! They are used to strange things, I assure you', said Neeky as the others moved in closer to hear about these strange seals from the far-off Southern Ocean.

Neeky then climbed up onto a rock so that the others could hear her story.

'Many moons ago, I travelled to a strange land full of strange animals. I travelled there with a group of other seals for a competition with the Seals of the South. It was a place full of deadly poisonous snakes and spiders and the birds were so noisy. But the strangest thing was that none of the animals that lived on the land seemed to be dangerous. If anything, they were a quiet lot. Most of them were soft, furry marsupials that only came out at night – that is, other than the strange kangaroos that just hopped all over the place and took no notice of the dangers or the noise.'

'During the day, the skies came alive and were full of wondrously col-oured birds, which made the biggest noise. If they weren't laughing, they were shouting out like there was a competition to see who had the loudest voice. No wonder the animals mainly come out at night. So this was indeed a strange land: soft, furry marsupials, vicious snakes and noisy birds. It made me very nervous, and I was glad I was out on the rocks on the shoreline.'

'And then there was the heat – it was so hot! One friend came from *Munaljahlai* country, which means "hard baked land". All I could think about was how easy it would be to die of thirst. Not like our snow-covered land, where it may get cold, but you always have water and you can even build a shelter if the snow turns to ice.'

'But that hot dry land and its great winds of red dust were very scary indeed. The winds would scream at me when I tried to sleep on the rocks, like it was telling me to get out of the country, which I promptly did. I didn't want to be there anyway, and was happy to blame the wind for leaving, as the koalas and kangaroos had been so nice to us. Such gentle marsupials who were always patting us when we came up on the shore to make sure we were happy. But I was happy to leave that land from Down Under. Those southern seals were just too tough, and they beat us in the competition', chuckled Neeky.

'And, as I said, they aren't even frightened of humans – they are so tough. They were even known to take on humans and board their boats and take their fish. Their leader, Galeen, said they had a right to do so, because it was their territory and that humans belonged on land with the kangaroos and had no right to steal their fish. They knew the humans valued one particular fish, and they took great delight in taking that fish and throwing it into the air, biting it and then spitting it out. This made the humans go crazy, shouting and screaming at the seals. The seals thought it a great joke. And so we Seals of the North were happy to leave that place, but the southerners told us if we ever needed help just to call them through our dreams and they would come to our aid. And now I will dream and call them to aid us!' said Neeky triumphantly.

This was all too much for the Seals from the North, who would never take on the humans, let alone board their boats!

'Actually', mused Napoleon, 'I think they are so brave because their neighbours on the land sound like a crazy lot; no wonder they weren't scared of humans! A land full of vicious snakes, loud-mouthed birds and timid nocturnal marsupials sounds pretty upside-down to me. No wonder it is called the land from down under – you would have to go down under the water just to keep your sanity!' This comment made everyone laugh. They then all agreed that Neeky should dream up her friend Galeen, and ask the Southern Seals to help them in their battle with the polar bears and the strange ship.

Tales of old

As the great Nukard surveyed the ice, he noticed that the wind had changed again. This was the fifth change since sunrise and the sun was not yet at its zenith. These sudden changes were very disturbing. They were making it hard for the polar bears to hunt. This wind was a maddening one, full of disturbing spirits – whispering sounds that made the polar bear think there was a whale calling out nearby. These were dangerous times for polar bears, surrounded by false voices.

Nukard moved slowly along the ice floor, as he didn't know for sure whether the ice would take his weight. The thickness of the ice had changed. He had to try to move into his intuition as his old tracking knowledge was of little use in these new times of thinning ice. He would have to adapt, and no longer expect things to be the same. Daily life would now bring new challenges, ones not heard of for many moons. He would have to consult old Zack to find out whether there were old stories of ancient times when things might have been like this. Were there stories of times when the ice had thinned and wind had played tricks? How did the old ones survive? What did he have to learn to teach the young ones so that they could survive?

And the ship – what was this ship? Had ships been here before? And why was Cartier going crazy from being around them? He had so many questions. Zack would know why Cartier seemed mesmerized by these strange humans. It was as though their magic had stolen his very soul.

28   Climate change

In an Arctic cave

Hidden in one of the seals' ice birthing caves was Cartier. He was polishing off his latest victim. He just loved to do this skin-stripping exercise and listen to the little seals scream out in pain. He no longer practised Sedna's law, by which the seal must first be killed quickly and skilfully. Instead, he tried his hardest to keep the seal alive so he could enjoy the pleasure of its pain. Cartier had learnt this behaviour from watching the humans. He had long been looking for something that would validate his sense of difference. Deep in his soul, he knew he was different. He had been born with a third ear, which made him different, but he didn't know how to turn that oddity into a sign of power.

Yes, Cartier was marked out by life. He was proud of his third ear because he could hear more than others. His mother had told him so, and he believed that he had stronger powers than the others, but he didn't quite know how to express them. However, that had all changed the day the large grey ship had slowly sailed into the harbour. There was a lot of noise coming from the ship, and also from the shore. A group of humans who looked like seals had gathered around and were shouting and making lots of noise; they seemed to be very annoyed at the humans on the ship. To Cartier, the humans on the ship looked like polar bears in their white uniforms because they appeared to have white skins like him and the humans on the shore appeared to have seal skins, but had human faces and bodies. He was quite taken aback when he saw the first human polar bear. The white colour was unmistakeable. They were human, but seemed to have white skins – the same colour as his coat.

The Admiral

'Shoot them!' shouted Admiral Chaney, 'No one will know in this God-forsaken place – just shoot them. But not the leader! I want him. Bring him to me alive. I want to make an example of him.'

The next minute, Cartier heard shots ring out across the icy terrain like a thunderbolt cracking the ice in two. He immediately turned and hid behind an ice hill, which he then climbed so that he had a better view. From the top, he could see the Admiral and he could see the human seals being dragged towards him. One seal was fighting for his life. This excited Cartier: he enjoyed watching the tussle. Next he heard more shots and he looked across to the shore and he could see that all the other human seals were dead. The human polar bears were now pulling all the bodies towards the sea and pushing them into the water. They dropped with a great splash, one after the other.

His gaze returned to the Admiral who was now hitting the human seal and shouting at him. The human seal shouted back. Cartier didn't understand the humans, so he couldn't work out what was going on. Next he noticed that the Admiral seemed to pull his body to its full height and he pulled a long knife out from his skin. He had seen humans use them when they were skinning animals. Humans didn't have razor-edged claws like him.

The Admiral then began to cut off the skin of the human seal. Oddly, Cartier noticed that there was no noise when the seal lost its skin; all he could see was its pale flesh. But then the Admiral seemed to be using the knife again and he could hear the seal screaming. At first it shocked him, but then he found that he began to enjoy the sound. For, deep inside of him, he could feel the power the Admiral had over the seal: it was palpable and it was enjoyable. He could see how slowly the Admiral was using the knife as he appeared to cut the flesh. This made Cartier very excited, and he moved backwards and forwards on the hill in an agitated manner as he watched the scene. For with each cry of pain from the poor human seal, Cartier was immersing himself in the feeling. It was an aphrodisiac, and it was giving Cartier a lot of pleasure.

However, soon the cries stopped and the seal's head hung down in front of its body. The next minute, he saw the body being thrown overboard. This action deeply excited Cartier. He really enjoyed the climax of the brutality – that sense of the victim being mere trash. He then crouched down and savoured these actions and wondered about this large human polar bear. He was now truly in love with this human. He wanted to be like him. So in the days that followed, Cartier watched the Admiral in the hope that he would do it again – that he would enact this ritual that brought so much energy to Cartier's body.

The coming of the black box

The Admiral was a merciless barbarian who wasn't going to let a few Inuit stop his mission. He was here to 'take over'. No matter who or what lived in this harbour, they would be removed to make room for the new world, a new world full of new technology, a new way of doing things. A secret that had been kept from the world was about to be revealed, and he was the keeper of the knowledge – a knowledge stored in a black box that sat deep beneath the sea on the Continental Shelf. This box emitted sound waves that could disturb the weather of the Arctic and so affect the weather patterns of the world.

It was a human version of Sedna. Sedna controlled the weather when she saw her fellow females being treated badly by their males. She would take back the food and stir up the weather. Now the humans who paid no heed to Sedna thought they could do the same, but they were about to learn that Sedna had a twin and so was twice as powerful. They were mere humans with their toys. Her twin was in the stars and a long way from their

30 Climate change

reach, but the impact of her celestial influence with the other great bodies of the sky was about to be felt, just like a long-range missile, ready to target the enemy. Sedna was moody – she might bring the seas up so far and then drop them again, as though playing with the fears of humans. There was no guarantee of her pattern, as it all depended on how matted her hair was. This kept the humans on the back foot.

Calling Galeen

Neeky then began to dream. She entered the dream world and travelled until she came to the south and called out to Galeen, the strong and handsome golden brown fur seal. Neeky had no trouble remembering what he looked like. She was quite taken by the lustre of his coat and his humorous ways. Galeen soon appeared in her dreams, for he was also very taken with Neeky. But he had not let her know for they lived just too far away, at opposite ends of the earth, which meant that they could never be together. She then telepathically sent images of Cartier killing the seals through to Galeen's mind. She showed him the scene of the Seals of the North floating exhausted down the river. Galeen didn't need to think things through; he immediately began to round up his crack team of seals. This was the team of mighty seals that boarded fishing vessels and kept the fishing fleets in a state of anxiety.

The arrival of the Seals from the South

A few months later, into the river came the Seals from the South.

'They're coming, they're coming!' called out Augy, the squirrel, from his high vantage point in the great oak to Buzzy, the metallic-coloured bee, who was busy pollinating the flowers that had just bloomed near the oak tree.

'I've seen a huge school of them jumping and dancing around in the water. And I'll tell you something really strange. They are headed by the ugliest seal I have ever seen. If you ask me it's not a seal but a crocodile or monster from the deep. But the other odd thing is that it has the same markings as the harbour seals. It must be one of their ancient ancestors returning to help', said Augy as he scratched his little furry head. 'Mind you, Buzzy, I think I would rather take my chances on my own rather than relying on that big brute, no matter how much he looks like the locals', he said, as he peered down from a large branch. Augy had learnt his lesson and was not taking any chances on a slimmer branch this time.

Galeen and Mr Leo Pard

Galeen swam up the front of the herd of seals but just slightly in front of him – in that male territorial way – was Mr Leo Pard. Mr Pard was a leopard seal from the Antarctic seas. He was a powerfully built seal with a massive, bone-crunching jaw. His slight edge did not worry Galeen, as he wanted to give his ally as much leeway as possible. He had made a dangerous pact with this monster, who he saw as a psychological match for the sadistic Cartier.

Neeky felt she had no need to fear this rather brutal-looking mammal because Galeen was just behind him. However, she did wonder what kind of seal he was as he was not from her part of the world, yet the markings on his coat were the same as hers. Being the generous soul she was, she assumed Mr Pard was some kind of long-lost relative.

'Surely it could not be one of our ancestors?' shouted Neeky to Napoleon, who had swum up beside her. 'We never looked that ugly. And look at those teeth!'

'I sure hope Galeen knows what he is doing bringing that sea monster here', said Napoleon cautiously. 'Hey, Napoleon, maybe Galeen brought him because he is so ugly, to scare the polar bears off. Wouldn't it be funny if Cartier died of fright?' laughed Neeky, as she did a back-flip.

This joke renewed Napoleon's energy, and gave her a sense of the future that she had lacked in recent times. On seeing this monster, she could feel a winning streak coming her way.

Galeen's choice of Mr Pard

Galeen had studied Mr Pard for many years. He often watched the big seal and had taken notice of his behaviour. He found him fascinating, as he was very different from most leopard seals. He was more cautious and patient. He was also observant, and his hunting skills were very different as he was a cannibal and so had a diet of seal. He had learnt the art of war during his early years and had many a scar to show for his indiscretions, as his fellow leopard seals were as merciless as himself and just as egotistical. He had therefore trained himself never to lunge without due cause or without careful planning. Mr Pard, however, had also found as he got older that he was becoming more pedantic about what he ate and therefore chased. He did not just eat to consume, but rather chose the juiciest of seals and penguins. He liked his meat just so – not too blubbery and not too lean. Yes, Pard had found a kind of pleasure in developing a more discriminating palate. It was part of being an apex predator. In his mind, killing was an art. Just hunting for the sake of eating was boring. He couldn't abide his fellow seals, who were consuming just for the sake of putting something into their mouths. This was not how Mr Pard saw himself as he gazed at his reflection in the icy hills that surrounded him in the isolated Antarctic Ocean. Consumption must be an art form, otherwise one's habits could become sloppy, which in turn trickled down to one's other survival skills – not to mention one's fighting skills.

32   Climate change

The relationship between Mr Pard and Galeen was an interesting one. Pard tolerated Galeen – or at least allowed him to live – because he was amused by his antics. He had found that Galeen had a way of tapping into his 'taste' for entertainment and excitement: being an apex predator was at times quite boring. As for Galeen, he liked to watch the Big Fella, as he called him. Galeen always enjoyed something that involved risk taking. So when Neeky asked for help, he thought the only choice was the Big Fella, whom he knew could surely have no equal in the world of ice. So when Galeen put forward the proposition to travel to the Arctic, Pard did not hesitate to agree, feigning that he was only coming for the challenge, rather than the possibility of a new species to add to his diet.

The introduction of Mr Leo Pard

As Galeen swam up with Mr Leo Pard, the other Northern Seals ducked for cover behind any rock they could find, for they did not want to go underwater – that would mean missing the introductions. Neeky swam up gingerly to greet Galeen and his great ugly friend. 'So good to see you, Galeen, and I see you have brought reinforcements', she said shyly as she indicated to Mr Pard.

'Let me introduce Mr Leo Pard. He is an acquaintance of mine, and was fascinated by your plight. He thought he might come for a bit of a change of scenery', said Galeen cheerfully.

'Pleased to meet you, Miss', said Mr Pard as he eyed off Neeky's strong and rather delicious-looking body. 'I hope I can be of service', droned Pard, for Pard had a dreadful-sounding voice as well as carnivorous-looking teeth.

'You know, Mr Pard, you look just like us and we are going to treat you like an uncle who has come to help us. But I tell you, Uncle, what a big nose you have, and what big eyes you have, and what a big mouth you have!' said Neeky in wide-eyed fascination.

'All the better to eat you with!' said Mr Pard playfully, and opened his great mouth, which revealed powerful teeth that sent shudders down the backs of all who looked on. All the seals headed to the bottom of the river at a great speed.

Galeen fell about laughing. 'Mr Pard ain't no kindly uncle when he gets going. Even I am scared to death of him – so, kid, pay him some respect', said Galeen with a glint in his eye. 'Don't get too friendly, and keep your distance.'

The attraction

Galeen noticed that Neeky had no idea of the danger. He wondered whether he should warn her that Pard was a cannibal. But then he realized that she would actually enjoy being exposed to such danger. Indeed, Galeen had wondered whether he was somehow a masochist by exposing both himself and the others to such danger. But then he reasoned that life is a risk. Alive today, someone's meal tomorrow – you were hardly going to call foul after you were dead and your remains were rumbling around in Mr Pard's stomach!

So he decided all he needed to tell her was that Pard had a violent temper and that he would not be responsible for Pard's actions if the seals did not heed his warning. After all, they had asked for the help and he had brought along the perfect foil. One hunts predominantly above sea level, and the other below. One is from the north and the other from the south. To Galeen, they were a mirror image of each other.

Neeky found herself strangely attracted to this strange but familiar being. She felt instinctively that he was a predator, and a cannibal at that! She could actually see her own flippers going down his gullet in her mind's eyes. But somehow this did not lead her to resist his attentions; if anything, it drew her closer to him. Was it the sense of danger? Was she excited in some way by fear? Was her courage madness hidden in good deeds? She shook her head in confusion and let her body sink below the surface.

She looked across at Galeen and for some reason he seemed ordinary beside Mr Pard. Yes, handsome and strong and sleek, but somehow safe and – well, boring. Why boring? She was shocked to think she thought this way.

Napoleon was watching Neeky from a safe distance, but could see by Neeky's body language that she was attracted to the beast. As for his handsome companion, Galeen, Neeky seemed not to have noticed him after the initial greeting. So Napoleon swam up to Neeky after Pard had moved along with Galeen.

'You find Galeen boring and Pard exciting, do you?' whispered Napoleon into Neeky's earhole. 'Common problem with females! They just can't be satisfied with something that is too easily gained. That is until they nearly die at the hands of the danger.' Napoleon remembered her own deadly attraction to Cartier. 'Then Mr Boring is all you will want. But I know with you, Neeky, that no amount of good advice is going to stop you from placing yourself in the line of danger.' She sighed and swam away, but then stopped and turned back as she felt the urgency to get the message through to Neeky before this very dangerous beast killed her friend. So she swam up beside her once more.

'Neeky, try to think of it in this way: Nature has its own way of sorting us all out. Nature puts before us unsuspecting attractions that have the potential to kill us, if not wound us badly for life. Most just can't resist the attraction and so die; however, while some of us survive, we are marked for life. This can lead to a life of timidity or, for the lucky few, they become

34   Climate change

wise leaders. But even they live with a partly crushed soul', Napoleon counselled.

But then she suddenly changed the mood by saying, 'But my dear, if you don't want to end up on his dinner menu, I think you need to learn how to channel that desire for risky behaviour into something more appetizing that suits your tummy and not his!'

They laughed a deep belly laugh, because they were both scared out of their wits, as they now knew they had a cannibal and predator among them – one who needed to be channelled away from them and onto the sadistic polar bear.

'How could Galeen put us in such danger?' Neeky asked Napoleon.

'Clever if you ask me', replied Napoleon. 'He knows we need someone who can see inside the bear's head, and who better than a fellow predator? I do wonder how Galeen keeps him from eating him.'

The first sighting of Cartier

Napoleon, accompanied by Neeky and a few other Northern Seals led the Southern Seals and Mr Leo Pard up the river and on out into the great ocean. After they arrived in the Arctic harbour where the grey ship was anchored safely to protect it from the prevailing weather, they slowly swam past the ship and past a series of icebergs. Finally they came to the iceberg on which Cartier was busy at his tortuous deeds. Cartier did not notice the herd of bobby heads that had entered the nearby open water. However, not one of the bobbing heads missed Cartier and his blood-stained face, and the harrowing sound coming from his poor victim. They all pulled back and moved over to a large iceberg nearby.

'He's big!' said Galeen, who had never seen a polar bear in his life. Neeky came up beside him and looked. She had never actually seen a polar bear either. 'Wow, he is big!'

Napoleon felt the bravado seeping out of her two heroes and immediately said, 'Yes he is big, but remember a small bug up his nose can kill him in a matter of days.' The two turned and looked at Napoleon. 'What?' they said in unison. Then, before she could answer, another deathly howl came from the poor seal he was torturing.

Mr Pard meets Cartier

In the meantime, Mr Pard had left the others and swum to a different vantage point to assess Cartier. Mr Pard's eyes narrowed as he watched Cartier. Like the others, Mr Pard had never seen a polar bear, so was also suitably impressed by the size and agility of the great animal. He took in Cartier's body language to get an idea of where his strength lay. But as he watched closely, he realized Cartier was becoming very excited by the torturing rather than the possibility of a meal – and there was something else.

'He's an egotist and a careless egotist at that. How immature! He will be easy to kill', smiled Mr Pard to himself, as he sank back below the water. He felt very confident that he could trap Cartier. He could also see that Cartier would be too preoccupied to notice if he swam under the iceberg. Mr Pard couldn't get over how thin the ice was and the fact he could easily see Cartier above him. Even though he was enjoying this ease, it also made him realize that something was changing in these waters, which made him think more carefully about his own habitat.

Mr Pard then swam back to a safe distance and deliberately made a noise so that Cartier would see him just before Mr Pard sank underwater. Cartier heard the loud splash to his north. He saw Mr Pard off in the distance. He wasn't quite sure what he was looking at, because he had never seen a leopard seal. He could see it had the same-coloured coat as a seal, but it was too large; therefore it must be a human seal. He ignored the sound and returned to his pleasure, but something was wrong. He had an uneasy feeling, like he was being watched. He threw down the carcass in disgust and began to stride towards the unknown visitor. He knew it wasn't Nukard or another polar bear, or even a human seal, but someone else – someone who knew what he was doing. He didn't like this feeling. It made him very uncomfortable and spoilt his pleasure. As he came to the edge of the ice, he could now see that the visitor was indeed a seal, but a very large one – bigger than anything he had seen before. He was alarmed by this sight, as he could sense the danger in the creature. A sense of caution ran through his fur. He slowed his pace and narrowed his eyes. Who was this invader, who dared to come into his territory and disturb his pleasure?

At that moment, Mr Pard felt Cartier's intense gaze. To feed the gaze, he surfaced and opened his great ugly mouth and revealed his crocodile-like teeth. Cartier stopped in his tracks and took a step back. 'What! That is not the mouth of a seal! What the hell is it?' thought Cartier as he steadied his nerves.

Mr Pard kept his eyes sharply tuned to Cartier's body language to detect any sudden change of behaviour, and sure enough he received the reaction he wanted. 'Hmm, that was easier than I thought', said Mr Pard, as he turned and swam at a great speed before Cartier could regain his composure. Mr Pard mused to himself as he swam away, 'Looking at the way this ice is thinning, I don't think the seals have got long to wait before all the polar bears drown. He looks strong, but he is not a sea mammal, and must surely rely on the ice being firm. But then that is not my concern. Now, how shall I play it with this feisty fool?'

Mr Pard noisily rose on the other end of the iceberg, which gave Cartier a fright. He spun around and ran at Mr Pard, who immediately ducked and swam as deep as he could go. Mr Pard was a powerful swimmer and could dive great distances below the sea due to the size of his lungs. He could see Cartier following him, but at a much slower pace. He had no doubt he could leave the great white beast behind. As he sank deeper and left the exhausted Cartier to resurface, he was surprised to see Neeky off to one side. 'What is she doing down here – it is so deep.' Then he saw her disappear into a cave.

He immediately decided to swim over to investigate. However, as he began to come closer to the cave, the water became murkier to the point where he couldn't see far in front of him. It was so murky that he felt he would lose his way if he did not pull back immediately. But the murky water appeared to follow him. He turned and swam quickly to get away from the murky swirl, but it was hot on his tail and he swam even faster until he reached the surface. Little did Mr Pard know that Napoleon had entered the cave before Neeky. She was taking Neeky to the cave of her ancestors, a place protected by the sea spirits. The murky swirl was in fact nothing less than the guardians of the ancestral cave.

Mr Pard was now totally disorientated and didn't realize that he was about to surface. Wham! He was knocked momentarily unconscious by Cartier. But Cartier did not take Mr Pard's weight into account as he tried to pull him ashore. This gave Mr Pard time to regain consciousness and assess the situation. Mr Pard jerked downwards, away from Cartier's powerful grip, for a polar bear's grip in water is not the same as it is on land. Mr Pard was able to slip away and again swam with great speed, but this time back to Galeen and the others rather than into the murky depths.

Cartier was furious, but a bit relieved as all he really wanted to know was what the creature felt like, and its strength and speed. Now he could plan his attack carefully, as this was a new kind of prey. He decided he would visit the human polar bears again to see whether he could gain some clues on how to deal with this new enemy.

The kill

Mr Leo Pard returned to the others quite shaken up but he hid his discomfort well and the others had no idea Mr Pard had nearly met his end, let alone was confused by the murky waters that followed him to the surface.

'Well, what do you make of him, Pard?' asked Galeen.

'A dangerous fool. Give me time and I will finish him off', said Mr Pard confidently.

Galeen was about to contradict him when it struck him that Mr Pard had every right to be so confident. Why shouldn't he be able to finish him off? After all, that's why he had brought him along: he was an apex killer. However, thought Galeen with unease, once he had made the kill, would he then turn on them?

Wind Watchers' tale: skinned alive 37

Mr Pard swam around the iceberg on which Cartier was resting. He swam as quietly as possible, as he knew he had to wait until Cartier came into the water where he would be defenceless against Pard's speed as well as his strength. Cartier, on the other hand, knew he must not enter the water while the great seal was nearby. If only he could get the seal onto the land, he would then be able to overpower him and skin him alive.

The days passed and the sun became much more intense. The ice began to melt, so life for Cartier became more precarious. As for Pard, the thumping of Cartier's paws on the ice was a welcome sound as it made it very easy to track him.

Then it happened. Cartier heard a plop and saw a seal surfacing through a hole in the ice. He ran at great speed and lunged into the hole to grab the seal, but as he landed the normally solid ice gave way and Cartier fell through into the arena of death. His foe was just off to the right; he spun round and headed for the polar bear at torpedo speed.

His target was Cartier's hind leg, for Pard had worked out that Cartier's white coat would be thick and not easily penetrated. So he had taken this into consideration and knew his best tactic was to drown Cartier by dragging him to the depths of the ocean.

As he reached out to bite his back leg, Cartier swung around and kicked Pard in the snout. This knocked Pard off balance, which gave Cartier time to escape and swim frantically back to a firmer part of the edge of the hole. He quickly began to scrabble up the slippery ice using his razor sharp claws to dig into the ice.

But Pard was much faster than Cartier expected, and before he knew it his hind legs were being assaulted. He tried to kick Pard again, but Pard had learnt his lesson and kept his body to one side, pulling Cartier sideways. Cartier then swung his great paw with its razor-sharp claws and sent the razors across Pard's face. Blood spouted into Pard's right eye, but he was not going to let go of his grip. Instead, he just jerked even harder on Cartier's legs, which threw Cartier off balance. He fell back into the water with a great splash. It was a splash of death, for now Pard had him and it was only a matter of time before he finished his mission. Pard's powerful body was then able to drag him deeper and deeper into the icy depths, past the great underwater ice caverns. As he dragged Cartier down into the depths, the bear struggled desperately. It was a stupid act on which Pard had counted, for that would mean the bear would run out of air quickly and drown. And so he did. At that moment of death, Pard could feel the sudden lightness in his catch. He then let go of his grip and Cartier's body floated in the murky water.

Pard enjoyed the clean kill. He hated the messy business of attack and ripping skin and blood all over the place. He had thought Cartier a messy creature. Messiness in his kills told Pard he would be messy in his own defence, and indeed he was. Most brutes are messy, always relying on their great weight and strength rather than their intelligence in planning. He

38 Climate change

resented the fact Cartier had clawed his face and eye, so disfiguring him. Yet it was this that gave Pard the extra strength to yank Cartier, for he was an insanely vain mammal.

After dislodging his super-strong jaws from Cartier's body, he let the water cleanse the fur and blood from his mouth. His eye was streaming with blood. He swam around until his eye stopped bleeding and then triumphantly swam to the surface.

Neeky's lust

Neeky and the other seals had watched the battle on the surface and then dived into the water to watch the final demise of Cartier. Like everyone else, Neeky had held her breath at each violent blow, but deep inside her she could feel another sensation rising: the more Mr Pard violated the polar bear, the more sexually excited she became. She was ashamed of her feelings but could not control her new desire for Mr Pard. She felt she could not resist this seal anymore, and if he wanted her after the battle she would be his.

As Mr Pard swam towards the gathered seals hiding behind the ice hills he thought, 'Weak wretches, can't fight their own battles. I will extract a price for this whether they like it or not.' He then noticed Neeky rising from the crowd and making her way towards him.

'Yes that nice fat one – she will make a tasty dinner', said Pard with glint in his good eye.

Galeen instantly felt the danger, Neeky was reading Pard wrong. She thought he was welcoming her, but Galeen knew the look of a leopard seal predator. How could he stop her when she was so wilful? He knew he could not just call out to her, for she was moving too fast across the water. What could he do?

Little did he know that Napoleon had already sensed the danger and had dived down under water and swum at breakneck speed to the iceberg on which Pard was now sitting. Napoleon didn't need anyone to explain what was happening; she had been in Neeky's flippers before. She had, in her younger years, been fascinated with humans – and particularly one human whom she thought was her friend, but instead had turned out to be an explorer looking to slaughter her for her skin. He was not after her to feed his family; he just wanted to make a quick buck and had lured Napoleon into a sense of safety and then had turned on her and tried to axe her to death, but she had been too quick for him. She was the fastest seal in the herd, and that had saved her life. She escaped with a nasty gash, which she wore for the rest of her life. So she instinctively knew when a female seal was being lured into a trap; it came from experience, and no one needed to say it or call out – she could just feel the same sensations like a tune flowing through the air, a familiar ghastly tune of death. Napoleon swam even faster as these memories flooded through her mind.

'Pard, you were wonderful!' cried Neeky, just as she reached Pard. She then threw herself towards his body to show her availability, but just as she did this, Pard opened his great jaws and grabbed her and threw her to the ground so he could get a grip on the back of her neck. However, that very moment Napoleon surfaced and yanked Neeky by the flippers out of Pard's way. She then dragged Neeky through the water as fast as she could. Once again, her agility and speed had saved a life. She dragged Neeky to the iceberg where Galeen was waiting to assist.

Napoleon dragged Neeky's body to the surface and rolled her onto an iceberg. Neeky lay there breathing shallowly, unable to take in what had just happened. Galeen and his fellow seals kept their distance and their counsel. Tears were falling quietly from Galeen's eyes.

Mr Pard was stunned. He was also furious, and roared, which made his eye bleed. In his pain, he made his way to a lone iceberg to vent his anger. He would plan his attack on these stupid seals, and the fat juicy female would be his first. But that was tomorrow's task. Now he must sleep and allow his eye to heal.

Nukard the Watcher

Nukard watched all of this from a distant iceberg; once again, he wondered how Sedna was influencing these events. At that very moment, the upper heavens opened and the Sun sent forth a barrage of solar flares. Their powerful radiation sent forth a blaze of energy that within a mere eight minutes disabled hundreds of satellites, which then began to spin out of control across the sky. Cities and towns across the great north were disabled, including the great grey ship.

The alarm was sounded, but instead of a siren it was the clanging of a saucepan, for all the electronic equipment on the ship had stopped, and with that all military capabilities. The Admiral came to the deck to give orders but found his men running around like rats, desperately trying to make things work. At first the Admiral thought it would only be temporary, but just like his men he felt something deep within his bones – a sudden rush of arctic wind – and he knew this was not temporary; if anything, it was fatal. The mighty ship was now nothing more than a floating sardine can in which many of his men were trapped. The electronic doors and rooms at the lower decks were impassable. The ship began to move from its mooring as there was no longer anything to hold it to the shore.

The Orca

As this calamity unfolded, danger lurked in the waters near the sleeping Mr Pard. Just as he had watched Cartier, he did not realize he was being watched himself. His self-assurance had blinded him to the possibility that

40 Climate change

he could also be someone's prey. It was the glare from the sun on the ice that now blinded his one good eye.

A pod of orca whales had spotted Mr Pard when he entered their territory. The orcas are a highly intelligent mammal, and do not waste their time on emotions to satisfy the individual; rather, they take great pleasure in the collective and their ability to coordinate and move as one with deadly precision. The Admiral and his men had often watched the pod and declared their admiration for their precision timing.

It was particularly satisfying to the orca when the matriarch found them a new challenge and here, sitting on this iceberg, was the perfect target. The matriarch had wanted them to practise more as they were soon to head south, and therefore would have to feed on other whales. They needed to hone their skills, and this seal seemed unusually large and therefore ideal.

In the meantime, Mr Pard had suddenly woken to the sounds of whistles and spouts from the matriarch who had come up to take in the leopard seal's positioning, size and weight. He lurched up and quickly spun around. He was surrounded by the Killers. What could he do? He frantically tried to think what to do but those Killers began to move the iceberg. He knew he was doomed.

The Killers moved the iceberg with ease, as they were not only strong in body weight but aligned telepathically. The iceberg moved out into the ice flow and gave the Killers plenty of room to carry out their manoeuvres. The matriarch then signalled and in unison the five males moved towards the iceberg and generated a wave that would push Pard to one end of the iceberg and hopefully straight into the matriarch's mouth.

This was achieved with seamless ease, and Pard rolled, like so many of the little penguins he had consumed over his life, into the mouth of the great Killer.

As Galeen and the other seals watched this deadly attack, they were all taken aback as the Matriarch did not consume Pard, but rather held him in her mouth. She then turned to her side and threw him the air and he landed on the back tail of one of the five, the male then threw him over to the next and so on. Neeky was horrified at what she saw and turned to Galeen in disgust. 'They are as bad as Cartier – they are torturing him.'

'No they are not, Neeky', said Galeen knowingly. 'They are merely practising for bigger game. I have seen them do this in the Southern Ocean; it helps them practise their timing and precision for the larger game they will be seeking in the bigger ocean'.

'I would say Pard died of fright the minute his body made contact with the teeth of that big female. So put it this way: Pard has had a better death than Cartier or any of his victims.'

Eliminating danger

As Nukard watched the Orca make hay with Pard's body, he turned and looked back at the ship, which was meeting a similar end. The Admiral desperately called out to the port side for help, but there was an uncanny silence. 'How could this place just suddenly be deserted?' His eyes searched desperately for humans, but all he could see was a group of men running off in the distance. It was the Inuit leaving what was basically a sinking ship. It was as though they had a head start – as though they had planned this technological breakdown.

'What could have caused this break? Surely it won't last', he called to Lieutenant Floyd, but Floyd just stared blankly at him. They both knew what it could be, as the scientists had long warned that solar flares could start up at any moment and knock out the satellites. But they had not heeded the warning, as they had too much confidence in their own abilities.

'Don't worry, Floyd. A rescue ship or plane will soon arrive when they realize we are not in contact', said the Admiral with an air of authority.

'That's as long as they aren't also without power. If it's those darn sun flares we are done for, Admiral', said Floyd. The Admiral slapped him across the face and Floyd reeled backwards. Floyd came straight at him and socked him in the jaw, which sent the Admiral reeling into a circle of rope. He found himself stupidly sunk into a barrel of rope with his legs up in the air. Floyd burst out laughing and then glared at him and said, 'Don't hit me you over-sized polar bear. You are no longer in charge, because you haven't got a ship – all you have is a floating sardine can. There are men trapped below and those Eskimos have taken all the sleds and the dogs, everything! And they won't be back to help us thanks to your sadistic behaviour.'

Floyd then stepped forward, pulled the Admiral to his feet and threw him against the railing. 'I advise you to jump, Admiral, before the men find a way out of the sardine can, because it is you who is going to be the next person to be tortured for getting us into this mess.'

The Admiral looked down at the swirling sea and drew back, but just as he did this Floyd lunged at him and pushed him overboard.

Once again, Nukard was watching from a vantage point. 'Hmm' he thought as he watched the Admiral screaming as he fell into the deathly sea. 'Species, no matter what they are have a way of disposing of those that put them in danger. Perhaps Sedna is now about to dispose of more of us than we think.'

Note

1 This was first published in the *Tribal Law Journal*, vol. 16, Spring 2016 (University of New Mexico School of Law). Reprinted with permission.

Chapter 9

A poem

So very different from us

And the whispers began;
they became louder as the months passed
and the seasons turned sour.
The slush and mud lapped on the shores
and the frozen winds swept the land of all vegetation.
Tempered only by moments of searing heat
– merely an hour or two – vaporized into thin air as
if a moment of madness had taken hold while
shivering in the cold.

Those whispers were not sweet, but told stories.
Stories which were not about us or our like,
but others, others who should not be remembered,
but merely subjects of compassion as they passed
through time in their millions.
Or was it billions?
Surely not, surely there weren't that many of
them ... those others.
So very different from us.

And that's how it happened, those stories.
They began to change.
They were no longer about us,
but about them;
those others, those billions of others,
so very different from us.

They came like thieves in the night those stories.
We didn't see them coming,
but we did wonder why the characters in the stories
were so very different from us.

The stories told of places we thought of
as poverty stricken and devoid of
civilization and love.

They said these places were full of something else.
Something which put love first and possessions last.
Ritual was said to heal while vaccinations
were something of the past.
Land was said to teach
while technology was for the fool,
so very different from us.

We didn't like these stories.
We didn't want such stories,
which made us feel like dogs
all locked up in kennels,
stacked a mile high in cities of distrust.
Penned into fear to make us obey,
our masters of corporate greed
and self-delusional affluence.

But like a spreading pandemic
the stories moved across the land
and infected all in their way
until the day when we found
that we were poor and the poor were rich.
We had so much stuff,
but they had so much more,
so very different from us.

Chapter 10

Native women and healing the neglected rights of the land

First words

This story reaches into Indigenous minds and hearts, and draws from this well a song rather than a discourse. So expect that feelings, rather than Western logic, will be drawn from that well. Be mindful that what follows is meant to flow, ensuring that the reader remembers the heart and soul of the lost women as the climate tips all around the globe. So do not be dismayed that I begin with stories from the nations of the Arctic rim, for it is through comparison that disguised violence is revealed, in order to understand whose life is worth remembering and whose life does not register as lost. Nor should you be dismayed when I call out large captains of industry through mythical analogy, for once again it is the ancient I wish to recall. I then take us over the border to Mexico, where a restorative justice solution will be expounded.

Introduction

A polar bear has mauled a 17-year-old British boy to death in the Arctic and injured four other British tourists from Eton College ... after several were spotted near Longyearbyen. BSES Expeditions, based in Kensington, West London, organizes scientific expeditions to remote areas to develop teamwork and a spirit of adventure. The company was founded in 1932 by a member of Captain Scott's final Antarctic expedition of 1910–13.[1] Inuit scholar Gordon Christie asserts:

> A century after excitement peaked around the race to the North Pole and the drive to navigate the Northwest Passage, the Arctic has re-entered the imagination of those living below the 60th parallel. As temperatures dramatically rise, the focus now shifts to 'opening up' the region, with debates swirling around questions of jurisdiction, travel and shipping, security resource management, and environmental protection.[2]

What does this opening up of the explorer's delight mean, other than imaginings of new frontiers as vivid as those of the great explorers, searching out lands that were never lost; discovering what was always known? Let us not tarry on such questions of past injustices, but rather look for a restorative clue, as the youth of the bastion of the explorer caste are once again being sent out to discover the already known, through school expeditions into the vast ice-lands of Svalbard,[3] the homeland of the 'Doomsday' Seed Vault,[4] dragon protected. Like all good 'caring' dragons, the Eye of Sauron[5] of technology – Microsoft founder Bill Gates – has gathered the golden seeds of the world crops, leaving behind many that have since been infected by sterile GM crops that were cultivated by his fellow 'caring' dragon, Monsanto.[6]

The question looms in my mind,

> Why have a Doomsday vault and yet make the whole populous dependent on technology vulnerable to solar flares that take a mere eight minutes to touch down on Earth and disrupt a nation's electrical grid? Even if the flares hit in far-off Siberia, the knowledge of such an impact would have a ripple effect that would cause havoc throughout Western market economies, which cannot operate without 'certainty'.

However, let me return to Earth and the previously mentioned young explorer caste, and examine their relationship with those close to the Earth: Horatio Chapple and his friends – always well fed and well-armed, ready for war with earthly Nature:

> A spokeswoman for the governor of Svalbard said explorers usually set up trip wires that fire off a rocket if animals enter the camp ... it is believed the expedition group undertook firearm training prior to the incident.[7]

Rocket-ready, with trip-wires and arms training before setting off into the frozen north? Little has changed since the sea last froze out their forefathers. Just like their heroic predecessor, Admiral Horatio Nelson, the young Eton-educated 'Horatios' of the world become the captains of industry and the admirals of the high seas of the military-industrial complex. However, in the modern account, the disfiguring of Horatio Nelson by war's manifesto is revisited in the mauling by a polar bear and the ripping of the very identity from their young Eton faces.[8] The unfortunate beast was duly sentenced to death for his sin of starvation. For the opening up of the Northwest Passage brings the reality of climate change and its refugees in search of food.[9] The covenant with the Arctic has been broken, so the sins begin to surface around its border nations, like some ancient Goddess wrecking revenge upon humanity.

46   Climate change

The death of these youthful explorers follows the rise of a new type of killer: Anders Behring Breivik, the Norwegian crusader bent on cleansing the homeland of the migrating hordes from the Middle East and North Africa, forgetting his own people's recent arrival as an invader of the Saami homelands. This crusader is influenced by men of war: Crusader King Richard the Lion Heart, leader of the Knights Templars in battle against the great Muslim warrior, Saladin. Breivik, killing for his own torturous pleasure and sense of superiority, reaffirmed his own anti-Muslim political beliefs and sense of Templar honour.[10]

Breivik should not be dismissed as a deranged mass murderer, alienated from society, but rather viewed as a man with a manifesto, a bomb and a blog. A man who writes a 1,500-word manifesto in which others see merit.[11] He sees himself as a man with an ethic; a crusader's code of honour that only the Japanese of the Mishima ilk could appreciate,[12] telling the world of his admiration for the ethnic purity of Taiwan and Japan, and for leaders[13] such as Australia's former Prime Minister, John Howard, and Catholic Cardinal George Pell. Such luminaries caught up in such media debacles as the infamous 'children overboard' episode[14] in Howard's case and the Catholic Cardinal's[15] resistance to dealing with child abuse cases unfortunately lead one to question whether they were not sending subliminal messages tilted towards ethnic cleansing of the vulnerable.

Breivik's tortuous pleasure came from killing 69 politically orientated youth (a further eight individuals were killed in a city bomb blast), whom he saw as a necessary example to other youth who may be tempted to travel down the road of political folly. As though to reinforce this warning, he dressed as a policeman and coaxed some of them to come to him. He then proceeded to slaughter them, thereby clearly signalling to the youth that neither the politicians nor the authorities could protect them.[16] For whom then does the bell toll, as the slaughtered youth's bodies are strewn around the edges of the island? We are all equally implicated, for we all pursue consumer bliss.

Native women

> Over the past 20 years, approximately 500 Aboriginal women have gone missing in communities across Canada. Yet government, the media, and Canadian society continue to remain silent.[17]

The implication in the case of the Native women and their many disappearances and murders – no media splash, no nation reflecting on its neglect of dead youth – is that to reveal the truth of the cruelty of the legal neglect towards such women would deem the Rule of Law inadequate, if not lawless.[18] The snow and the tyranny of distance have allowed for the cover-ups in the frigid Canadian north. *The Highway of Tears* was infamously named for its roll call of murdered and missing women.[19] But the Arctic is melting, and indeed the time of hiding would appear to have come to an end as the Arctic melts and begins to reveal that which is hidden – bodies of Native women, those silenced voices of the Land. Nature's own unable to conform to consumer bliss, no regular wage or superannuation piling high on mining investments.

So what is the restorative tale we need to tell? What is the ancient or the old spring to which we need to return and listen as it bubbles past? What stories give us a clue? To find the answer I travel south to the American addict's watering hole – Mexico. The south so long silenced by mindless media hype, as though nothing else exists in Mexico other than drug barons and whores! But the restorative clue can be found among the millions of Mayans of the Zapatista bent, who dared to come to the central plaza of the great city of Mexico and let their cause be known.

Zapatista

I therefore look to the Zapatista for the exemplar of drawing on the ancient springs of how Native women may restore their place and exercise power. And what is this power of which they speak, but total responsibility by one and all – democracy at its best?

> As Subcomandante Marcos explained, there is a time to ask power to change, there is a time to demand change from power, and there is a time to *exercise* power. In the eyes of the Zapatistas, after open betrayals by the entire spectrum of the Mexican political class, this third 'time' was long overdue. The Zapatista communities thus delved into the long process of unilaterally implementing 'autonomy' without any official recognition or legal endorsement.[20]

This exercise of power contradicts the Canadian Aboriginal organizations of economic development, which proudly flaunt their ability to reflect a hegemonic political system that for decades has left Aboriginal women along the roadside while pretending to hear their words, with representatives on the hierarchical design. Not representative! Instead, a mainstream fix, to make things easy for their assimilation into the overall state-approved policy, representing themselves to the dominant power as friendly and ready to communicate. But where does that get them – funds short and policy laden![21] Why are these Chiefs unable to launch their own inquiries into their own reservations where so many have been killed? Why must they wait for the federal government to launch a national inquiry? Why must the UN and Amnesty International be players in this search for justice for these women strewn along the Highway of Tears? Why have a

48   Climate change

National Assembly of Chiefs if they cannot do anything without a tick of approval from the federal government? Perhaps it is a guilty conscience and fear of what may be revealed in relation to the responsibility to women and the Land, for such killers reside even on the reservations. Once again we must look to the Zapatista for a fix:

> To the contrary, the exercise of this other power put many indigenous communities in direct conflict with the traditional indigenous structure, and the Mexican state would try to domesticate this other power by opening spaces for indigenous participation.[22]

So where does the difference reside?

> The distinction between this 'representative democracy' is not only the rotating function of governance, which prevents the professionalization of political participation and the formation of a political class, but also the relation of government to the community assemblies, which holds the core of decision-making power. The assembly system locates power firmly at the base and precludes the attachment of authority to a position of delegated responsibility – what would enable a command obedience structure to re-emerge. The practice of recognizing and generating power from 'below' structures all the other relations to be mediated and tasks to be completed: 'In sum, to ensure that in Zapatista rebellious territory, whoever rules, rules by obeying.'[23]

In other words, all adults have to pull their weight and be involved. They all have to serve at some time as leaders so no stones can be thrown. People are made to get involved and be accountable for their community for outcomes. Youth also know that they are needed, and that they have a future where even they will get a say. So surely we must ask: Why *have* Indigenous structures emulated dysfunctional, unrepresentative, corporate-driven nation-states – states whose citizens have very low opinions of their so-called political representatives where party allegiance is paramount? And why copy centralized national bodies when this is the antithesis of the traditional mode of politics?

'Now is not your time; it's ours'

We can take a tip from Forrest Hylton's clever title above.[24] His article brings news of the South American native zeal, a zeal I would recommend to Native women who get so terribly lost in lands rich in 'energy security'. Security forces amass to protect the resources, but where is the security for those who live in poverty on these very same lands? What does that say?

What does it not say – especially when you read articles on the Native women's website reminding us that even women in the RCMP are not safe, as their superiors see nothing wrong with private sexual fantasies that copycat the sexual assault committed by the notorious serial killer Pickton, who murdered 49 Native and non-Native women?[25]

Native women as security chiefs

We need to call out the mining beast and its hidden shareholders, safely indulging in their burgeoning superannuation sheets, pretending that they do not know there are human fatalities that fund their retirement cruises. Demand that they take a cut in their share, and pay for the ongoing security provided by Native women on their own cultural terms. Women know how to make a community safe, far better than some outside security body made up of steroid-hyped males, toting guns and plastic badges. Leave the royalties to the tribe, but demand that security is an extra cost, which the government must demand the beast of the land to pay. Like a tax, but a Native women's 'security tax' placed on mining companies and other such concerns. The beast's security budgets are already high, because security is a priority that the rich understand. So what's another cost? It's security after all. We all understand that: just add it to the budget, the shareholders will get the company's drift and then pat themselves on the back.

But let it be run by Native women and allow the security tax to be paid to them. No government interference – just make the government collect the tax. Make the government accountable for its appalling record in making women unsafe. Naomi Wolf, author of *The Beauty Myth*, states that not even middle-class white women can get a fair deal in the courts if they are raped by an academic or judge.[26]

So stand up Native women and lead the way in security, for it is you who know the young and can spot a change in the youth and their despair. Draw from the old wellsprings of lawful behaviour and come up with 'native' ways to trail the youth. And if there is nervousness about such a thought and not enough Zapatista zest, look to your southern sisters and learn from the Australian Aboriginal women on night patrols.

Community night patrols

After becoming frustrated with the amount of alcohol-related deaths and suicides of young people occurring within their communities, strong women of Yirrkala and Marngarr took action to approach the problem. The night patrol operates from late afternoon through to early morning. Women on patrol will collect children and take them home, assist with picking up intoxicated Indigenous men and women,

50 Climate change

and placing them with appropriate family members or places where they are deemed safe. Currently operating from the Yirrkala Women's Resource Centre, the aim is for this service to begin operating from the Special Care Centre.[27]

So be warned, avoid the government dependency trap. This is women's business, and not for men just because they are Native. Their nativeness or joblessness is not their qualification, for there is a need to draw from the ancient springs of the old stories to redefine what security and protection mean and so find a restorative justice clue that empowers and respects the gender divide for healthy, healing reasons. The Highway of Tears is a vast terrain, but then so are the eyes and relatives of Native women. They are the Watchers all along the highway.

These are not the childlike accounts written by anthropologists, unaware that Elders knew more of the galaxy than they ever might. Translating with vigilance the attempts of the Senior Law People trained in classical thinking stemming 60,000 years or more. How else could they speak to the good-willed anthropologist intent on saving the last of the tribal bedtime stories for their children fed on racist notions of a super race, second to none. For indeed none other would want to be like them.

But let me now turn to one of those tales of old that bubbles forth through the crispy ice of the Arctic, while remembering the words of Huhndorf and her native Alaskan chant that natives are not bound by nation-state boundaries but their transnational nature must be recalled.[28] It is a recall that must be afforded old stories as well, for they know no boundaries and so travel around the Arctic rim and the nations that spill forth from the Arctic lip.

The tale I tell is that of the mighty Sedna. I recite what I know of the original story told so long ago. This 'remembrance' is what I know, and by no means the best account. For that you must travel to the far north and hear it as it should be told, by the women of the Arctic. For, if told by men, Sedna is a loser – what else would you expect?

A cosmological story

Sedna is a young woman who cannot decide upon a husband. She is approached on a regular basis, but finds she still can't make up her mind, as life at home would appear to be simple but safe. Let us say she has a comfort zone. However, her father wants his daughter married and off his hands. The father threatens that she must marry the next man who asks for her hand. A handsome man appears and asks for her hand. He tells her father he is a wealthy man and does not live far away. Both are dazzled by the handsome man and the father agrees to her marriage. Sedna happily leaves with the man. He assures their home is close by, and full of food and comfort. She rows the canoe with her new handsome husband. But as the days pass she realizes her new home is not near at all, but far away. Once they finally arrive, she finds the home is nothing more than a bird rookery: she is married to a birdman.

Her miseries begin, as the birdman is inconsiderate and mean. After many months of unhappiness, she calls to her father in her dreams. He decides to visit his daughter and, finding her living in misery, helps her plan her escape. They head for the open sea but it is not long before the birdman finds them and begins to threaten them. As he is a powerful shaman, he raises a thunderous storm. The father soon realizes that his daughter is a threat to his own safety and promptly pushes her overboard. Sedna is determined not to die, and hangs on for dear life to the side of the canoe, but this enrages the birdman and he stirs up an even greater storm. The father tries to sever Sedna's fingers with the paddle in an attempt to rid himself of this life-threatening situation. Sedna falls to the ocean floor, together with her severed fingers. However, she does not die; she transforms herself into the all-powerful sea goddess Sedna. And so both the birdman and father learn that they must rely on her good nature for their future existence and livelihoods.

Thus it is told that when men abuse women, Sedna rises up and takes back her beloved fingers, which have now become the bounty of the ocean – her fingers are the seals. The only way for the famine to be aborted is if the men ask forgiveness by sending a shaman to the bottom of the ocean to tend to Sedna. He must comb her hair and un-knot all the barnacles and other sea creatures from it, thereby demonstrating masculine caring and tenderness. Upon receiving such tenderness, she then returns the mammals and the birthing seasons start to return to normal.

The heroine

As mentioned before, Sedna is not a victim but rather a heroine travelling along the road of a 'Hero's Journey'. It is an important story for women, giving graphic details of the tortures many women experience from men who are meant to be their protectors. However, it is also an empowering tale that tells of a near-fatal experience, which would normally cultivate a sense of victimization and a hatred of males, exacerbated by the Western legal process and a future dependency on the 'system' to heal the dysfunctional female victim – both of which lack cultural appropriateness and, as said before, efficacy. Unfortunately, Native women's organizations dependent on government funding and the whim of the political process for their continued funding, often finding their 'fingers/funding' cut off by the very system that takes such a paternal attitude towards them.[29]

52 Climate change

Legal storytelling under whose law?

But do not think I leave our sisters in the other law by the roadside, for they too have work to be done and leading the charge is Batchewana First Nations academic Cheryl Suzack, who challenges the legal court:

> The legal storytelling movement has made important interventions within law and narrative studies by breaking down conventional understandings of legal reasoning that purport to be neutral and dispassionate and by challenging objective points of view that limit the range of possibility within which legal questions may be raised. 'Outgroup' stories have been embraced for engendering consciousness about subordinated experiences that subvert the self-evidence of 'ingroup' realties, for expressing narratives that conceal the coercive workings of dominant values through claims to objectivity and for voicing perspectives by the socially marginalized that demonstrated 'tactical resistance' to the injustices of legal power.[30]

Behind this division is nothing less than the impetus for moral courage. For the facts have a way of desensitizing, and are like offering up the 'bare bones' as a meal. The diner wonders where the meat is, while the 'chef of facts' merely looks at the diner with disdain. The Rule of Law is so bent on its objective diet that it has become anorexic and unable to feed its young – and especially women, who are still poor before the law, unable to achieve equal pay let alone equal representation. And what is the meat that is missing? It is the moral courage that comes from a story well told. The Natives live for their stories, as they know that stories, more than food alone, will keep them alive. Suzack looks for the narrative to heal as well as reveal. Often the male-dominated epistemologies know how to expose the wound, but have little understanding of how to heal it.[31]

So Suzack offers us up a well-told story from a novel, Eden Robinson's *Monkey Beach*, set in the far north of British Columbia in the land of the giant trees, hugging the coast and forming misty seas. The novel takes the reader on an inner journey with a young female Native who ends up just like the victims of the aforementioned serial killer, Canadian pig farmer Robert Pickton, who was able to boast that he missed killing his 50th victim due to sloppiness. From the late 1990s to early 2002, he ran amok, the nation spending $102 million trying to find him, yet Native women are still scared. The Highway of Tears is still turning up dead bodies and reports of the missing.[32] So much money was spent on this man's trial, yet the news reports read:

> Poverty. Prostitution. Addiction. That trinity made Willie Pickton's murderous spree possible.

Yet it's unlikely that trio and the desperation it engenders will be aired at a judicial inquiry set to begin Oct. 11.

It seems there's no money for delving into the darkest heart of the problem behind not only Vancouver's missing women, but Canada's.

The Pickton inquiry is narrowly and intentionally focused only on determining two things. Why, over a five-year period, did 33 women go missing from Vancouver's infamous Downtown Eastside without police looking for a serial killer? And why, in 1998, did the attorney-general's ministry stay attempted-murder charges against Pickton.[33]

Pickton preyed on poverty, prostitution and addiction, due to the fact that no true authority cares. Suzack[34] gives an analysis of young women in *Monkey Beach*, in which she argues that:

Robinson also sets out to show how these prior encounters contributed to acts of colonial translation that occluded gender knowledge and participated in contemporary forms of cultural disavowal that lead to the subordination of women.

She further suggests:

If they do not conceal their differences to avoid gender persecution, then they live as exiles among their own community members.[35]

This lack of connection is further demonstrated in the government's 2010 decision to disband Sisters in Spirit and shift funding to the Evidence with Action project. In other words, the grass-roots organization that formed due to the heartfelt loss of their sisters is now replaced by a government-sanctioned organization, whose existence depends on government oversight rather than the human-felt need built on personal relationships. The spirit – the family connection – is being severed, just as in the Sedna story. The male 'action/evidence'-orientated title and the Western legal terms of 'evidence' and 'action' take the spirit/relationship out of the women's efforts to support them and turn it into another programme that is judged worthy by its financial accountability, as Suzack has evoked. It reminds one of the father of Sedna, as a representative of the Canadian government thinking only of his own survival, rather than his responsibility to his daughter, the procreator of the next generation. In the case of the government, it is the need to be seen to be accountable for the monies spent from a budget that looks to manage the population on behalf of corporate profiteering. Indigenous people live in the most resource-rich areas, yet as the poorest of populations. As Suzack deduces from Eden Robinson's *Monkey Beach*:

54 Climate change

Robinson seems to suggest that these social justice projects will make little difference if they do not also recognize how and why gender relations matter. Her writing thus takes up the struggle enacted by the 'war between stories': to urge a reconsideration of the elisions authorized by legal representations in order to guide future justice projects, which recognize and affirm the importance of storytelling to gender relations.[36]

Conclusion

And so this story ends, with the fresh waters of Indigenous thoughts and literature recognizing and healing harms anew by looking to the brave Zapatista and remembering the might Sedna brings forth as a restorative muse who calls Native women and federal governments to support a security firm of Native women shaped by their own rules, with shareholders and mining beasts paying the price. Suzack tells this story so well when she calls upon Eden Robinson's tale of youthful exuberance, which leads to a woman being the meat hanging in the Pickton hell-hole. The call is to draw from the old springs of lawful behaviour as Sedna did so long ago, and asks the native women in tandem with their sisters trained in Western law to join together and bring forth a restorative tale that empowers native women.

Notes

1 'Polar Bear Kills British Boy in Arctic', *BBC News*, 5 August 2011. www.bbc.co.uk/news/uk-14415592, accessed 20 November 2015.
2 Christie, G., 'Indigeneity and Sovereignty in Canada's Far North: The Arctic and Inuit Sovereignty', in Cheyfitz, E., Duthu, N.B. and Huhndorf, S.M. (eds), *Sovereignty, Indigeneity, and the Law*, Duke University Press: Durham, NC, 2011: 329.
3 'British Tourist Killed by Polar Bear', *Sky News*, 5 August 2011. http://uk.news.yahoo.com/british-tourist-killed-polar-bear-094654991.html, accessed 20 August 2011.
4 '"Doomsday" Seed Vault', *National Geographic*, 26 February 2008. http://news.nationalgeographic.com/news/2008/02/photogalleries/seedvault-pictures, accessed 20 August 2011.
5 Tolkien, J. R. R., *Lord of the Rings*, Allen & Unwin: London, 1954.
6 Robin, M., *The World According to Monsanto: Pollution, Corruption and the Control of the World's Food Supply*, The New Press: New York, 2011.
7 'Eton Student Killed by Polar Bear in Norway', *Sky News*, 6 August 2011, http://news.sky.com/story/873681/eton-student-killed-by-polar-bear-in-norway, accessed 20 August 2011.
8 'British Tourist Killed by Polar Bear', *Sky News*.
9 Borrows, J., *Recovering Canada: The Resurgence of Indigenous Law*, University of Toronto Press: Toronto, 2002: 13.
10 Thompson, J., 'Breivik Manifesto Praises Australian Conservatives', *ABC News*, 26 July 2011. www.abc.net.au/news/2011–07–26/breivik-manifesto-praises-australian-conservatives/2810730/?site=sydney, accessed 20 August 2011.

11 Hooper, J. 'Ex-Berlusconi Minister Defends Breivik', *Guardian*, 27 July 2011. www.guardian.co.uk/world/2011/jul/27/ex-berlusconi-minister-defends-breivik, accessed 20 August 2011.
12 Wikipedia, 'Yukio Mishima', http://en.wikipedia.org/wiki/Yukio_Mishima, accessed 20 November 2015.
13 Thompson, 'Breivik Manifesto Praises Australian Conservatives'.
14 Manne, R., 'When Trust Goes Overboard', *The Age*, 18 February 2002. www.theage.com.au/articles/2002/02/18/1013132462174.html, accessed 20 February 2015.
15 Jensen, E. and Tibbets, A., 'Pell Accused of Sex Abuse Cover Up', *Sydney Morning Herald*, 7 July 2008. www.smh.com.au/articles/2008/07/07/12152827 50977.html, accessed 20 February 2015.
16 Thompson, 'Breivik Manifesto Praises Australian Conservatives'.
17 Government of Canada, 'Victims Week', www.victimsweek.gc.ca/pub/jenl_1. html, accessed 24 August 2011.
18 'Funding Dispute Missing Women Inquiry British Columbia', *The Canadian Press*, 28 July 2011. www.ctvbc.ctv.ca/servlet/an/local/CTVNews/20110728/funding-dispute-missing-women-inquiry-british-columbia-110728?hub=BritishCo, accessed 20 August 2011.
19 'Missing and Murdered Women: Vancouver's Missing Women Website', http://missingwomen.blogspot.com.au/2012_07_01_archive.html (July 2011 archive), accessed 1 August 2011.
20 Reyes, A. and Kaufman, M., 'Sovereignty, Indigeneity, Territory: Zapatista Autonomy and the New Practices of Decolonization', in Cheyfitz, Duthu and Huhndorf (eds), *Sovereignty, Indigeneity, and the Law*. 514.
21 Black, C. F., 'Maturing Australia Through Australian Aboriginal Narrative Law', in Cheyfitz, Duthu and Huhndorf (eds), *Sovereignty, Indigeneity, and the Law*. 350.
22 Reyes and Kaufman, 'Sovereignty, Indigeneity, Territory': 515.
23 Ibid.: 517.
24 Hylton, F., 'Now is Not Your Time; It's Ours' in Cheyfitz, Duthu and Huhndorf (eds), *Sovereignty, Indigeneity, and the Law*. 502.
25 MacQueen, K., 'The RCMP: A Royal Canadian Disgrace', *Maclean's*, 18 November 2011. www.macleans.ca/news/canada/a-royal-canadian-disgrace/, accessed 20 August 2016.
26 Wolf, N., 'Julian Assange Sex Crimes Anonymity', *Guardian*, 5 January 2011. www.guardian.co.uk/commentisfree/2011/jan/05/julian-assange-sex-crimes-anonymity, accessed 20 August 2011.
27 O'Meally, S. and Barr, A., *Families in Crisis: Implications of Change for Yolngu Living in Remote Arnhemland*, Queensland Government, 2014. https://publications.qld.gov.au/storage/f/2014-01-31T03%3A31%3A24.943Z/omealley-simone-final.pdf, accessed 20 August 2016.
28 Huhndorf, S., *Mapping the Americas Native: The Transpolitics of Contemporary Native Culture*, Cornell University Press: New York, 2009.
29 Hall, N., 'More Groups Bowing Out of Pickton Probe a Blow to Commission, Criminologist Says', *Vancouver Sun*, 10 August 2011. http://endingviolence.org/wp-content/uploads/2014/03/Vancouver-Sun-More-groups-bowing-out-of-Pickton-probe-a-blow-to-commission-criminologist-says-Oct-2011.pdf, accessed 15 November 2015.
30 Suzack, C., 'Law and Literature in *Delgamuukw and Monkey Beach*', in Cheyfitz, Duthu and Huhndorf (eds), *Sovereignty, Indigeneity, and the Law*. 549.
31 Ibid.

32 'Highway of Tears: Preventing Violence Against Women', www.highway-oftears.ca.
33 'Opinion: Pickton Inquiry Problems Underscore Truth'.
34 Suzack, 'Law and Literature': 457.
35 Ibid.
36 Ibid.: 459.

Part III

The trade in body parts

Chapter 11

Some words
The story of Wibari

This was the original tale that was brought by a busybody muse who found me sitting with a vacant mind after completing my doctoral thesis. It was as though it was whizzing across the ethereal plane in search of an empty template, which it could fill in with its thoughts. The template, of course, had to have certain pre-programmed experiences about which it could prompt the victim to type. And so it landed in my mind and began to pester me day and night until I had finished its story. I had no idea what it wanted or where the story would lead, but as I typed away, I found it most interesting as it allowed me to include the adventures of my friends from the great continent of Africa – one a law professor from Senegal, another a Zulu philosophy professor and the third a humanitarian worker in the countries of the Horn of Africa.

It was my friend Kine Camara and her mentor Saliou Kandji who inspired the sense of resilience of the slave to endure. As Professor Kandji argued:

> In addition, in spite of 300 years of economic plundering and socio-cultural destruction, the French language, which was the principal instrument of this enterprise of economic exploitation and cultural adulteration, is still not understood by the majority of the population. It is understood, in various degrees, by only 10 per cent of the eight million inhabitants of Senegal, whose exact frontiers are still unknown![1]

This story did not stay still on the African continent, however, but travelled back in time to a date that seems to fit: 1760. I was not sure why, but it sounded good. It was only when I began the research for the following tale, which deals with the issue of the trade in human body parts, that I realized its relevance. Once I understood that the story was about this appalling trade, how could I not realize then that it was a story of slavery and would end up on the other side of the earth in Richmond, Virginia – that bustling town of greed and despair for so many in the 1760s.

Some may say the story lacks the experience of the Native American people who were also enslaved, but for some reason the Muse wanted this to be an African story rather than paying lip-service to my fellow Indigenous through political correctness. And perhaps this is so, because this is a tale of sorrow – as is the following. It is not one to be tampered with, but rather a deep song of the tragedy of the past that has intergenerational implications. But, like all old stories, they are meant to heal rather than just tell or reveal a past hurt. Indeed, this exploration led me to read the works of Toni Morrison, which in turn brought about a deeper understanding of the experience of the Negro male and his despair – a despair that in some ways is reflected to a certain degree in other cultures that have clashed with invaders of their traditional homelands. This includes the Irish – but not as being invaded by the English, rather as being slaves to the North African traders. I then wondered about how many of us carry the genetic memory of slavery.

But let me not forget the heroine of the tale – Wibari. Wibari is a hyrax, which is a cute, rabbit-like animal that I was surprised to find is actually related to the elephant. This animal was also presented by the Muse, as I had no prior knowledge of it. But its personality soon came through vividly, and if you take the time to research the hyrax, and watch these animals for a while, you will be able to see the depth of character such a little being has brought to our wonderful planet.

Note

1 Saliou Kandji, speaking at the ANAFA conference, 1992, http://afrikibouge. com/litterature/273-saliou-kandji-dans-afrikrcflexion, accessed 20 August 2009.

Chapter 12

The Wind Watchers' tale
Wibari and the Rogue Protectors

Chapter 1: the rats from over the seas

The year of 1760

'Eeekk! The rats, the rats, the chains ... let me go, let me go!' screamed Wibari the hyrax as she woke from her recurring nightmare. She got up and hopped over to her bowl of water and lapped it up eagerly. Wibari was the pet hyrax of a teenager from the ancient land of Siinegana. Her name was Kinni and she lived in the small village of Ndaayaan. Wibari was a beautiful-looking rock hyrax with golden fur. She looked like a rabbit, with a spiky haircut – a very cool-looking animal indeed. Her little button snout, big black eyes and cute little round ears made her too adorable as far as Kinni was concerned; Kinni was therefore very proud to carry Wibari in her basket, wherever she went.

One eventful day, as Kinni set out to visit a village by the sea to buy some fish, a great sense of fear rippled through Wibari's little fur coat. She felt something in her bones that told her this was going to be a very bad day – so bad that her life and Kinni's were in grave danger. But she was a hyrax, so she had no way of warning her human friend of the impending danger.

It was not long before Wibari's fears were confirmed. As Kinni approached the shore, she was shocked to see tall ships on the horizon. Then she realized that village people were running about and crying out for help. A village woman ran past her and told her to run. She immediately turned and began to flee, but instead of escaping she ran straight into the chest of a large man. Wibari knew it was the end for both of them. Suddenly Wibari could feel herself and the basket flying through the air and she heard Kinni screaming for help. Wibari landed with a thump and scurried out of the basket, then ran after Kinni and the huge man. The man dragged Kinni across the sand to a waiting boat. He then shoved her onto the boat and she was immediately tied up by some other men who were loading the little boat with their human cargo, ready for the large ship.

Wibari was desperate; she could not let her friend down. She must save her! So she cleverly hopped onto a little log and paddled out to the boat, then jumped onto the back of the boat, where she hid under some ropes. After much screaming and shouting, the boat began to move. The 'heave ho' of the sailors as they rowed out to the large ship sent a feeling of doom down into Wibari's stomach. She somehow felt that the heaving was a sensation that would become part of the very fabric of her soul.

As they moved along, Wibari looked up to see whether she could see Kinni. She was so relieved to find Kinni had been pushed to the back of the boat where Wibari was hiding. So she tugged at her dress and Kinni looked down. Her expression revealed both surprise and sadness. Big tears welled up in Kinni's eyes and they fell down onto Wibari's face. Poor little Wibari couldn't help herself, and she too began to cry. The two friends just didn't know what else to do. Suddenly the boat jolted to a halt. Wibari and Kinni became desperate, as they both realized that Wibari wouldn't be able to get up onto the ship.

Suddenly Kinni had an idea and signalled quickly to Wibari, 'Climb under my dress and catch hold of the tassels from my waist beads. Hold on tight!' she whispered as she showed Wibari the traditional threads tied around her waist and the tassels of beads that hung from them. She held out two tassels for Wibari to grab with her teeth. Just as Wibari clenched her large teeth around them, a rough-looking man grabbed Kinni and flung her slim body up into the air and onto the deck. He did not notice the little animal hiding under her long skirt. Luckily, Wibari had strong teeth and held on tight even though she did get a bit squashed as Kinni landed. Then Wibari quickly hopped to safety behind a large coiled rope.

Kinni was wrenched to her feet and pushed over to a group of people. She could see from their faces that they came from many of the villages up the coast, but also from the inland territories. All their faces had a look of terror – a terror of the unknown, which would eventually see them land in Richmond, Virginia in America. There they would join the slave population of the living dead that would make America so great.

Just as Wibari gave a sigh of relief and began to catch her breath, she was wrenched from her spot by a set of strong teeth. Before she could make sense of her situation, she was dumped onto the ground in front of a commanding-looking sea rat. Idi was the leader of the pack of rats known as the Ocean Boys. They ran the animal slave trade, specializing in hyraxes. Idi was from North Africa, or so he told the other rats. He fancied himself as an Arabian rat with the luck of a Jinn. But in fact he was just a common bush rat from Mali. He wore a gold chain around his neck with the imprint of a symbol that stood for the hyrax. A Malian goldsmith had made it for him. He worked well with the humans: they tended to their slave business and he tended to his hyrax business, each giving the other their space. The rats stayed out of the humans' bags of grain and other food supplies in return for space on the ship for their hyrax cargo. Of course, the humans allowed them a steady grain supply to keep themselves and the hyraxes alive on the long trip. The rats really didn't care if any of the hyraxes didn't make it, as they always caught more than they needed. It meant the strongest survived; it was a kind of natural selection process. As far as Idi was concerned, if a hyrax could survive the journey, then they were made of the right stuff for enslavement by the American rats.

The hyraxes that were already enslaved below were singing the Great Song to welcome the new hyraxes, but more importantly to calm them down as they came to terms with their prison in the bowels of the ship. Idi was not stupid. He knew what made the world go around and it sure wasn't that Great Song that the stupid hyraxes sung all the time. He never could work out why they kept singing that song; all he knew was that it made them docile, and that was good for his business.

Idi moved around on his podium, which was in fact a large tin can. He wanted to get a closer look at the new hyraxes being pushed onto the ship. He scanned each hyrax face as the poor animal hopped past. He had a sixth sense about whether or not a hyrax would survive – he could tell by the level of terror in their eyes. Real terror would kill a hyrax instantly, but if the hyrax was going to make it, then the terror wasn't taking them over completely and they could survive. Then there were the ones with that look of defiance: they were born to survive – unless they did something stupid, like trying to escape. And then there was this third lot: the singers of the Great Song. A strange lot! They had a blank look in their eyes, a kind of resignation to their fate. He called them the 'Hyraxes of the Song'. It was up to fate, as far as he could work out, whether they survived or not. Fate was their determinant, and the song was their companion along either path. He wasn't into being philosophical or even caring; it was just something he noted.

On the whole, hyraxes were considered the easiest animals to catch and control, even though they were physically bigger than the rats. It was their gentle nature that made them so easy to turn into slaves. Their naivety was their biggest weakness. They just never imagined another animal could enslave them – eat them, yes, but not enslave them. It was not in their mindset. As he strolled past the new slaves, he came to the limp body of Wibari. She looked up at him and seemed terrified.

'Silly female' he thought, 'but what a beauty!' He bent over and felt her hind legs. 'This one is strong and well fed; she will fetch a good price, Zedd, so keep an on eye on her. She's valuable', laughed Idi as he turned to a mean-looking rat that was following him. Zedd was also large and strong and had a thick brown coat. He was also from Mali.

'Just look at the sheen of her coat', admired Zedd, 'You don't get beauties like that too often. I'll keep her away from that inland lot – might put her in with Tellam. Don't want her catching their poxy diseases!'

laughed Zedd as he grabbed Wibari and dragged her to a hole in the cabin wall.

As Idi moved back up to the upper deck, a smile crossed his face as he thought, 'That golden one is certainly going to bring me a nice fat stomach this year, and I'll make that King Rat pay!'

King Rat was from the American seaboard and Idi hated him. King Rat always treated Idi as though he were a slave, as though he was barbaric in some way and as if the King were above the dirty business of slavery. Idi was sure he would outsmart that King one day – and that was going to be the day the King would die!

Idi's thoughts of the King's head rolling off a dock into the water were suddenly interrupted by a scream. Idi's profits were food, but also the game: he loved playing this game of capture, dominance and gain. He got a real adrenalin rush out of it. His crew also revelled in it; they particularly delighted in the initiation bite. This involved the initiation of a new sea rat, which they invariably picked up at each new port. They loved horrifying the hyraxes; nothing gave them more of a thrill than killing or maiming one of them. The new recruit would, upon capturing his first group of hyraxes, have to take one of the hyraxes, as the others were being chained up, and bite its head off. This murderous act kept most of the hyraxes quiet all through the long journey.

'Another one bites the dust', he laughed as he heard the screams from below deck. 'Keeps the slaves cool headed!' He roared even louder with laughter as he placed a rag in the hole in the wall.

The screams from below the deck included Wibari's cries. After being dragged down the hole and pushed into the bowels of the ship, she was confronted by the sight of a large group of hyraxes chained up along the walls. Hundreds and hundreds of hyraxes – she had no idea there were so many in the whole of Africa. She thought that they must have captured every hyrax in existence.

As they were being chained up, there seemed to be a disturbance. She turned around to look and there, rolling towards her, was the head of a hyrax. She convulsed but was given a kick in the butt and told to move along. Wibari vomited as she passed the rolling head, but kept moving although in a daze of despair.

Chapter 2: the secret training of the Wind Watcher

The slave ship was now fully laden and began to pull out to sea. Kinni slunk to the floor like the other slaves and began to cry. All upon the ship knew their fate was now sealed – they were destined for a life-or-death journey to a distant land of unknown terror. She couldn't help the crying; nor could many of the other young women around her. Others just sat in silence, as though struck dumb by some evil spirit. She wondered what had happened to her little friend. She searched desperately with her eyes. Where could Wibari be? Was she under a rope or had she been flung overboard by one of the sailors? Next minute she found herself being pushed down below deck and along to a kind of slot. She was told this slot in the wall was her bed. She was barely able to fit into the two wooden slats on which she was to sleep. There was no head room. As she got up, a large man came along and put a clamp on her leg, which was hooked onto the wall. She tried not to think of this dead weight on her legs, so she distracted herself by thinking about her little friend.

How was it that an animal could care so much as to follow her into such danger? She had never thought of Wibari other than as an extension of herself – something to pet and to make her laugh. She hadn't imagined that anything other than a human could demonstrate such faithfulness. She knew that dogs were said to be faithful, but they had lived with humans for centuries. How could a wild animal have feelings? She then began to remember the stories her grandmother had told her over the years about the bravery of wild animals like the lions and elephants. However, she could not remember any stories about hyraxes. There were stories about the hare and the tortoise, but not about a cute little animal that lived among the rocks and bushes of the highlands. They were too cuddly to be courageous, let alone able to think. Hyraxes weren't even magical like the foxes or snakes, or tricksters like the spider. 'So where does this feeling come from?' pondered Kinni. But soon she was overcome by exhaustion, and even forgot the pain of the great chain around her leg.

In the meantime, Wibari had found herself being pushed through a hole in the wall by Zedd and then up onto a ledge and finally into a cage, which was high away from the other hyraxes. As she hopped into the cage, its other occupant came forward. Zedd slammed the cage door shut and scurried away. The stranger was an older female hyrax with a very shiny dark fur. She was very still, which made Wibari relax.

'I'm Tellam from the rocky outcrops of Timbuctoo', she said. 'You are safe here; the rats will look after you, not like those poor souls down there.'

Wibari looked down from her cage and began to cry at the sight of all the misery.

'It's good to know you have a heart, little one. What is your name?' said Tellam.

'Wibari', the frightened little hyrax replied.

At the moment she said her name, the ship began to lurch and the hyraxes started to sing. Wibari did not know what this singing meant; all she knew was that before she could speak to Tellam, she found herself falling asleep to its gentle rhythm and floated into the land of dreams far from harm's way.

The next day, she woke to the shouting and screeching of the rats ordering everyone around and throwing grain at the frightened hyraxes. Zedd came up to the cage and stuck his long snout through the cage bars. His whiskers touched Wibari's fur, which sent a shudder through her. Zedd laughed at his ability to scare her. Surprisingly, he didn't throw the grain at her, but opened the cage door and spilt some on the floor near her. He knew he could safely open the door because of the fear he could smell on her.

'They must have a wealthy patron on the other end of this voyage, is all I can say', said Tellam as Zedd left. 'To be treated so well by such a thug can only mean there is a healthy profit involved.'

'How do you know that, Tellam?' asked Wibari, as she began to gobble down the grain. She was so hungry!

'I have travelled far and wide in my time, both by paw and cloud, and I know the scent of a profitable trade.'

'What do you mean by cloud?' Wibari said, as she wiped her mouth with her paw and hopped over to be nearer to Tellam.

'Oh, you don't know – yet you have the face of an ancient one. Are you trying to trick me?' Tellam asked suspiciously as she looked into Wibari's eyes.

'No! What would I know? I couldn't even warn my human friend of the danger', This statement brought tears to Wibari's eyes.

'Don't worry, Wibari, your friend is alright. You have more to worry about than your friend. You have to prepare for your own future in the New World. You know you can do that?' said Tellam as she began to stroke Wibari's silky golden coat.

'What is that song they sing, Tellam?'

'It is the Great Song from our land; it is a song that has been sung for centuries when hyraxes are very sad. It is a song that has travelled far across the land and because it is such a healing song, many animals have learnt to sing it in their own tongue', said Tellam. 'We are very lucky that the hyrax slaves around us know the song, for not everyone knows it – especially the young. Only those who have listened to their old people know the song. So Wibari, as the days go by the song will seep into your mind and you will find comfort there.' Tellam looked deep into Wibari's eyes as though searching for something hidden.

'Wibari, we have to make the most of this time of relative privilege. We have to get you prepared', she said.

'Prepared for what?' asked Wibari.

'You are the descendant of a Wind Watcher. The Wind Watcher came in my dreams and told me you were coming and that I must train you as best I could. I can only tell you how to communicate with your ancestors; I cannot tell you how to become a Wind Watcher.'

Wibari looked at Tellam with a quizzical look and wondered how this stranger could know her grandmother was a Wind Watcher, especially as her grandmother had died a few years before.

'My mother told me the hyraxes from the lowlands would come up to the rocky outcrops where they lived to speak to my grandmother. They wanted her help with the wind. They wanted the wind to blow seeds across the grassland so that they would have food', smiled Wibari proudly.

'But when she died, I was so sad that I wandered off and got lost, that is when the human named Kinni found me and made me her pet. Kinni is so very good to me.' This made Wibari cry again.

That night, Wibari began to see fleeting images. After a while, they became more focused. Then she saw her grandmother. At first she could only see an outline of her grandmother. But as she held the image it became clear that she was looking at her. To Wibari's surprise, her grandmother turned and began to hop up the rocks that were now behind her. Wibari realized she was back in her homeland watching her grandmother, just as she had done as a little hyrax.

But just as she was about to call out to her grandmother in excitement that she was back home again, the scene faded and she awoke. It was morning. As she opened her eyes, she again found herself in the filthy ship. After she got over the initial disappointment, she returned her mind to the dream and she was overjoyed as she now knew she would have somewhere safe to escape to each night.

'Tellam, my grandmother came to me and took me back to the rocks. It was wonderful.'

'Lucky! No wonder your fur is golden, Wibari', laughed Tellam.

But then it struck Wibari that sleep was only at night and a bit during the day; the rest of the time was spent listening to the moans of the poor hyraxes below her.

'Tellam, I feel lucky but at the same time I feel so bad about the poor hyraxes below. They are miserable.'

'Just listen to the song, little one. Those down below who know the power of the song are also listening. It is the poor younger ones who do not know the song. So just let the song come into your mind and soon you will be lulled by its power.'

And so the days became bearable, for without the song she would have gone mad – as did many of the young hyraxes who lived in the filth below.

As Wibari focused more and more each night, her grandmother visited her and then became quite insistent that she pay attention to what she was teaching her. First she had to learn the words of the song that everyone was singing. Then her grandmother would teach her other, much more powerful songs. Each night she learnt a song and during the day she would sing the song to Tellam.

Tellam encouraged her to practise the new songs. As she said to Wibari, 'You must surround yourself with songs, they are your protection. You

68 The trade in body parts

can't see songs, but they are as strong as metal, each song is like a guardian, who has come to protect you.'

But Wibari's grandmother was teaching her more than Tellam realized. Wibari's grandmother had warned her Tellam was a *Saltigue* who wanted to be a Wind Watcher and was desperate for Wibari to tell her what she was learning. Her grandmother told her she must not make Tellam suspicious, but act vague and complain she didn't want to do it. Her grandmother would eventually teach her how to open up portholes into other dimensions. Tellam would not be able to enter these portholes.

As the days went by, Wibari was learning how to see the songs as a kind of smoke which she could blow one way or the other. As she blew the smoke, it became cloud-like, and in that form she could have a certain amount of control over it. Her grandmother then showed Wibari how to make the cloud blow into the sails of a ship. She would blow at the cloud and the cloud would produce a wind that pushed the sails in whatever direction she wanted.

Little did Wibari know that she was actually affecting the ship, and that the slave traders were beside themselves with the wind, as it kept turning the ship around. This strange behaviour soon drew the attention of Chudi, the resident witchdoctor of the rats. He knew instinctively it was the work of a Wind Watcher, for he was from the land of the Dogon. The hyraxes that lived with the Dogon were said to be the most powerful Wind Watchers in all of Africa. They were said to be able to cause dust storms that stretched a kilometre into the sky. They rolled across the land like giant tsunamis.

Chudi came down to the hole in search of a possible source of the mischievous wind. He scurried around the hundreds of hyrax, sniffing here there and everywhere, pushing his long snout into the faces and anuses of the hyraxes. This frightened the hyraxes even more, and made many of them quite hysterical. Finally he found he could sense it was a female, a young female; that narrowed it down enough for him to spot Wibari up in her cage. He also noted Tellam, and he could see she was no fool. He needed to get her away from Wibari.

Chudi and Zedd made their way up to the cage and looked at the two females. Chudi ordered that Tellam be put into another cage.

'Get her out of here, Zedd. I want to talk to the Golden one', hissed Chudi.

Tellam resisted, but it was no use, as Zedd would prod and prod until she moved.

Chudi turned to Wibari and sniffed in the air.

'Don't worry about your friend; I am just concerned about the merchandise. We need you to stay healthy; there is a virus running through that dirty lot below. You will bring a better price than your old fat friend there. She has a fine coat but she's a bit old. While you – well, you are just right! So I want you to be kept clean and healthy. We are going to give you medicine, so don't spit it out. It will protect you from the virus', instructed Chudi as he turned to leave. But he spun back and screeched, 'You hear me, drink it!' He then spun around and left.

The next minute, Zedd was back and pushing a bowl of green-looking water towards her. So she drank the sleeping potion. After a short time, she felt very dozy and was soon snoring her head off. The medicine was a drug of nightmares. Her dreams were full of terrifying animals chasing hyraxes. She woke up totally exhausted. The following night, she was too frightened to sleep. But Zedd stood beside her to make sure she drank all of the foul green water. As the nights went by and she kept waking up in horror, she became totally exhausted and just lay around listless in her cage. Zedd reported this, which made Chudi very happy, for this was all he wanted to achieve – a state of exhaustion that would stop her focusing in her dreams and so stop her from directing the wind.

What he did not anticipate was that her exhausted state opened portholes to other dimensions. In those dimensions, she met other strange creatures and also her grandmother, who was younger and stronger and able to speak more directly with her.

'Clever hyrax to open a porthole by yourself', smiled Wibari's grandmother as she appeared before her. Wibari was stunned by the beauty of her grandmother's fur coat. It shone like pure gold.

And so began the education of Wibari the Wind Watcher. Her grandmother explained that she was descended from a long line of Wind Watchers, and their role was to protect the tribe from the destructive elements of the winds. Winds could bring blessings just as easily as destruction. She had to learn to sing to and calm the wind. The wind was her totem and so she must become one with it. Once she was one with the wind, it would obey her call. And when she really knew how to work with the wind she would fill the sails and the ship would sail at great speed to the New World.

'But grandmother, why the New World? I want to go home!'

'It is your destiny, Wibari, you must find your inner strength before you can go home and become a Wind Watcher. Also there are hyraxes in the New World who need your help.'

'When you arrive in the strange land you will be horrified at what you see, and there may come a time when you won't remember anything I have taught you.'

Wibari said that wasn't possible. But then a shudder went through her body and she asked desperately about the fate of Kinni. Her grandmother assured her that Kinni would survive because her grandmother was also a very powerful *Saltigue*, a Medicine Woman, and would protect her.

So Wibari's grandmother taught her how to work with the little winds that blew across the deck of the ship. This was so the rats would not

70 The trade in body parts

become suspicious. Each day when the rats would take the slaves to the surface to be fed and to be allowed some fresh air, she would whistle while she waited. The others took no notice as they were too depressed. Only the Song gave them solace. After a few weeks, Wibari noticed that she could make little whirly winds appear on the deck and dance around the sails and the loose-fitting clothing on the humans. It would dance through their hair but they did not seem to notice.

In the meantime, Kinni had her own awakening to the cloud world. She had lain in her stocks, unable to move. It was only when they were given a bowl of millet porridge in the middle of the day that they were allowed to come up on deck. This was most unusual for a slave ship, as their purpose was merely to move human cargo from one port to another; the greed for money took away their humanity and replaced it with pure evil. This was what the great slave nations counted on: evil men doing their dirty work, while they indulged themselves in fantasies of greatness and intelligence, washing their hands of their own stupidity and inability to create a nation without slavery.

Kinni turned to the woman standing next to her on the deck.

'My name is Kinni; I am from the village of Ndaayaan. You are in the next dock to me, aren't you?' asked Kinni politely.

'My name is Khmet. I am from the northern tribe called the Dogon.'

'Ohh, my grandmother talked of the Dogon. You are said to be great magicians and healers. Are you a magician, Khmet?'

'You are a silly girl; you should not speak of such things. But I will tell you I am a good storyteller and I will tell you stories about the land we are unhappily going to.' They smiled at each other, even though they were both in agony from the chains on their ankles.

To Kinni's surprise, Khmet was very knowledgeable about the future world to which they were travelling. For, just as Wibari's grandmother had helped bring Tellam into her life, so Kinni's grandmother had helped move Khmet into Kinni's life. Khmet was indeed a magician, but Kinni would not learn that until she learned just how bad things could get in the New World.

The next day, when they came to the surface, Khmet began once again to tell her stories of the New World.

'Kinni, you will enter the world of the malevolent spirits', whispered Khmet as she moved closer to her. 'It will be strange and harsh. You will be frightened by these strange humans, and you will not like their smell. Some will be good and some so bad you will know they are the creatures the people of old talked about. Surely when you were little you heard the stories of these strange creatures that were part-human, part-fish?'

This frightened Kinni, as she had heard those tales of how these creatures had eventually become human and that they now roamed the Earth like everyone else. However, she never really believed such stories.

Khmet continued her story. 'They later became fully human. Especially be careful of the tall blond ones with slanted eyes and long fingers; they are the evil ones. They thrive on the fear. They encourage fear and hatred. But worst of all, they make people forget the Great Song and the stories. When people forget the stories and the Song, then they have nothing. Even food is of no use.'

'What, no food?' Kinni felt a pain in her stomach at that moment as she was so hungry. She hated the food they were given on this miserable ship. She missed her grains and fruits from her homeland.

'All ancients know stories are more important than food. It is the stories that give people strength, not food. So when you arrive in this new land, don't forget your stories. You have to tell yourself a story every night. Stay close to your ancestors and they will help you to remember', Khmet warned Kinni.

'You and I will be lucky, as we will be bought by good men, so stay strong and our destiny will be good. Our ancestors cannot change the ways of the world, but they can make it easier for us.'

And, just as Khmet had said, the stories did help Kinni cope with the agony of the chains around her legs and the terrible stench that surrounded her every time she went below decks to sleep.

Even though the Captain allowed them to come to the surface to eat, they still had to return to the filthy conditions in the hull. The ship was full of slaves and there was not enough room to move around, let alone relieve themselves in privacy. The slaves cried, screamed and sang. It was horrendous for Kinni and she was frightened to her core, but the more Khmet told her the stories, the calmer she became. She held onto those stories like they were a rope that would save her from drowning.

And so they sailed for the port town of Richmond in Virginia – one of the many towns which would sell and distribute slaves throughout the New World. It was a new world full of folly and grandiose beliefs about its own goodness, devoid of the vision to see the way. The rivers and streams would soon be filled with waste from the greedy thoughts of the men who came with the ships. The Natives of the land would also suffer badly, and be enslaved or die in battle. The lucky ones retreated to the inland tribes to get away from all the madness.

Chapter 3: the underworld of the chain gang

Wibari woke to shouting and sudden lurching sensations in the ship, then a thump and a loud cheer from the humans. She realized they had landed, but had no idea where they were. All she knew was that it was time to face her destiny. She looked across at Tellam, whose face had suddenly gone blank. It was as though her spirit was no longer in her body. Wibari then

72 The trade in body parts

knew evil was at their cage door. It wasn't long before Zedd came to their cage and opened the door. Wibari turned to look at Tellam.

Zedd pushed Wibari up to the top deck. There was a lot of noise and a lot of movement coming from the humans. The noise was deafening to a little hyrax. She soon fell in line with all the other hyraxes that were being pushed along to a hole in the ship's side where the anchor hung. It was early morning, and the sun was barely visible.

Idi called out orders as they were moved through the hole and down a thick rope that tied the ship to the shore. They pushed Wibari and others along the rope. Wibari was tempted for a moment to throw herself into the water at the thought of what may lie ahead, but then she heard Kinni scream. She looked over to the gangplank on which the humans were descending and saw her friend trying to regain her balance. Kinni had lost her balance when she was pushed by the greedy slave traders eager to get their money.

'Oh my poor friend!' cried Wibari as she stopped for a moment to watch her Kinni. 'At least she is alive and well, just as my dream showed.'

But that was the last time for many days that Wibari would think of Kinni. Wibari was herded with the others through the noisy stinking streets of Richmond. It was dark down at their level, with only glimpses of sunlight here and there. The noise was deafening after the rhythmic lurching of the ship and the splashes of the waves. The horses and carriages were terrifying as they came speeding past. These were things Wibari had never seen. All she knew of humans was village life – barefoot people and unshod animals. Now the force of the vibrations from the sound of these beings was deafening, and there was death all around. Hyrax and rats alike were crushed under wheels as they tried to weave through the night traffic. Wibari was terrified she would be caught up in one of the great spinning wheels. Finally they were pushed down a hole, which went down into darkness and an even worse smell. When her eyes adjusted, she could see they were moving along the side of the banks of a dirty river. A stinking great body of water, stagnant and full of things floating! They hopped quickly past the river. Wibari's mind flashed back to the clear blue sea of the Siinegana coast. A wave of despair rippled through her.

Finally, they stopped at a hole in the wall of an old building. The hole led into the basement. There they were confronted by a group of large, ugly rats. They were the biggest rats Wibari had ever seen. She couldn't believe their size. One particularly strong-looking rat stepped forward and gruffly ordered Idi and the Ocean Boys to follow him with the slaves. They all moved slowly to the back of the room where an imposing-looking rat stood on a box. He scanned the slaves and then glared at Idi.

'Well, this is them', announced Idi proudly to King Rat. 'And I have got a special golden one. She is worth all of them put together, so I expect extra grain for her', demanded Idi as he shouted up at the King.

Wind Watchers' tale: Wibari and the Rogue Protectors 73

'Golden one? What rot! Show me this so called golden one!' scoffed King Rat.

Zedd quickly pushed Wibari forward. Wibari was resisting as much as she could, as she didn't want any attention brought to herself in this evil place.

'Hmm, so she is golden, fancy that! So what, Idi? All I want is workers, you dumb fool. I don't care what colour she is. You have been hanging around those humans too long. They care about colour and all that other fancy stuff, but all I want are workers. You get no more for her', yelled King Rat as he moved as though he was about to come down to Idi and bite his head off.

'So pick up your grain and piss off', screamed King Rat, who was quite capable of snapping Idi's neck. Idi resented his size, but knew if he ever got King Rat off guard he would kill him instantly.

'Piss off yourself', yelled Idi as he indicated to Zedd and the others to pick up the grain. In a flash, they were gone.

King Rat turned his gaze to the hyrax slaves. As he scanned their faces, a ripple of fear ran through the soft-natured creatures, for they had no idea whether this large rodent would bite off their heads or skin them alive. King Rat could feel their fear, and laughed out loud.

'Move the idiots along. There are no troublemakers amongst them. There is too much fear for a brave one to survive. They would stamp the poor devil to death if he tried anything brave.' Again King Rat and his fellow rats roared with laughter.

But just as Wibari came hopping past King Rat, he stopped laughing and looked more closely at her.

'She really is a beauty – look at that coat! It's a shame she is not a rat; I would have made her my mate', thought King Rat admiringly. 'Bet she has never been near a sewer nor missed a meal.' But they were thoughts King could not afford to have. He was into the business, and female rats were there for his pleasure and nothing else. He had to stay on top of his game if he was to survive – especially when the likes of Idi were after his head.

The hyraxes were then herded along the side of the inside wall until they came to an old chimney that went up through the building. On all sides of the chimney Wibari could see dozens of the little creatures, sleeping on jutting-out bricks right up to the underside of the floorboards above.

The group stopped and the hyraxes were told to join a group of others that were huddled into a corner.

'Sussi, get this lot organized', gruffed King Rat as he walked past a weather-beaten female rat. Sussi was plump but strong looking. As the hyraxes passed her, she handed them each a piece of cloth, which was their bedding, and a few grains of rice. Wibari was starving and gobbled down her grain immediately.

'Don't worry about food, Missy', said Sussi as she waddled through the group. 'There is plenty of grain for you to eat.'

'Now move along and up to the top row of bricks, just below the floorboards', shouted Sussi as she directed the new slaves to their precarious sleeping quarters. The little creatures peered up to the great height of the floorboards.

'Get moving and get to sleep as you have work to do tonight.' And so they cautiously made their way up the precarious heights. The other hyraxes looked down from their beds as they watched the new recruits moving up the bricks. Their look was glazed rather than curious.

Wibari found it was rather scary moving up and over other bodies and crumbling bricks. But eventually she made it to the top and found a suitable brick, laid down her piece of cloth and settled down for the long-awaited motionless sleep. No more motion sickness, no more waves crashing on the walls and, surprisingly, no more stench. Wibari drifted off to sleep on her piece of cloth, which had a familiar smell about it that made her feel comforted. She slept deeply, but kept waking from horrible dreams in which she saw Kinni's body floating down the river and her calling desperately out to her.

Chapter 4: sold to the good doctor

The ship berthed at the Manchester Dock on the James River, which flowed through Richmond. It was a formerly beautiful river turned putrid with all the waste from the greed and cruelty inflicted on the millions of African and American Indian slaves who would be shipped up and down the shores of the New World. This was one of the main hubs of the slave trade in the 1760s.

As the ship docked, the sailors came down below and began to unlock the slaves ready to move them up onto the deck. Once Kinni and Khmet were on deck and waiting, Khmet quickly pulled Kinni to one side and told her to sit down on the deck. Kinni did as she was told. Immediately, Khmet put her hands around Kinni's painful ankles. She could feel a warm sensation, which was also pulsating through her body. She looked to her ankles as Khmet released her hands. To her complete surprise, her ankles were healed. She looked at Khmet's ankles and realized they too were healed. But before she could say anything, a sailor shouted at both of them and pushed Kinni down the plank.

She stepped down onto the dock and followed the other slaves to the yards where the slaves were being put up for auction. Kinni had no idea what was happening, nor had she ever seen such large buildings and so many horses and people. And the smell from all the horse manure in the street kept making her gag.

'Don't worry, Kinni. We will be alright. Just remember all that I told you and keep your wits about you and stay near me', said Khmet as she followed behind.

Wind Watchers' tale: Wibari and the Rogue Protectors   75

Kinni soon found herself in the yard with the other captives and Khmet. She was pushed to the side of the yard and up against the fence. This brought her face to face with a strange-looking woman. She was smaller and had brown skin and straight hair in plaits. The woman looked straight back at Kinni with the same curious look. Kinni had never seen an American Indian, nor did she know they were slaves in their own country and were sent out to work with the Africans on the plantations.

Kinni was suddenly grabbed by the auctioneer, an ugly fat man who pushed her up onto the auction stage.

'How much for this pretty one? She's healthy and worth a good pound or two or twenty – nothing less than twenty', shouted a man who Kinni thought stunk like a dead hyena.

Kinni's mind was spinning at the thought of one of the ugly white men touching her. All that strange pale hair and their pale faces made them look like a sea of noisy ghosts. But before she could focus on what was going on, she heard the auctioneers say, 'Yes, the gent in the brown hat, sold to that gent!' Kinni looked at the face of her new master. He was a tall and slender ghost of a man with a kindly but sad face. Kinni immediately thought she had been bought by an evil one the Dogon talked about. She was then pushed off the stage and pushed down the stairs.

'I represent Dr Valentine Thomas Hart', said a regal looking African who stepped forward to catch Kinni as she was about to fall from the force of the auctioneer's push. The greedy man wanted to move things along as quickly as possible before his customers got bored standing around.

'Where's the money, nigger?' said the smelly auctioneer.

'Here, Sir', a bag of money was exchanged and Kinni left with the elegant and, to Kinni's great relief, very pleasant-smelling man.

'My name is Saliou', said the man in Kinni's language. 'I am from your homeland. I am from the Joola tribe.'

'Yes, you are right!' cried Kinni, who nearly jumped out of her skin with joy.

Saliou was not only from Kinni's homeland, but had also been a king. He had been sold into slavery by a jealous brother. And even though he was now a slave and coachman, he had never lost his regal bearing.

'Saliou, you must forgive me, but can you tell me if the Master is one of the creatures the Dogon speak of? The Master is tall and pale like the creatures.'

Saliou laughed. 'Not all tall and pale humans are evil creatures, Kinni. You will have to learn to tell the difference yourself. You will find the Master will protect you from any creatures if they come into the house.'

He further assured Kinni that she would be alright, and that the Master, Dr Hart, was a kindly man. He then led her away to a waiting wagon. As she sat down on the seat of the wagon, she felt dizzy, as it seemed so high and there was nothing in front of her except the team of horses. As the horses pulled the wagon through a maze of carts and market stores, Kinni put her hands up to her ears, as the noise was deafening. She had never heard so much clamour. Her mind was racing, as was her pulse, and she was sure she would faint. But Saliou began to sing as he could see she was frightened out of her wits. Eventually they came to Shockoe Street, one of the most prestigious streets in the town. The street was lined with large townhouses. Halfway down the street, they stopped at a house with a beautiful little garden full of brightly coloured flowers in the front and fenced by an ornate iron gate and fence.

'This is your new home, Kinni. You are a lucky girl to be bought by the Master. Now be good and your life will be as best it can when you have been stolen from your home. I am just going to take us down the lane to the back entrance. Slaves always have to come in through the lane. Only white folks are allowed in the front door.'

Kinni looked at Saliou with surprise. 'What's so special about white people, Saliou?'

'Oh, they just own everything – including you, I am sorry to say.'

'Someone owns me?' whispered Kinni as she looked up at Saliou in disbelief.

'Yes, Dr Hart now owns you, little Missy. You just come in and have a good meal.'

Kinni walked into the back door and stopped as she took in the sight before her. She could not believe how big the kitchen was. There was a big table and lots of chairs. Kinni had never seen so many things in her life. The ceilings were so high and the walls were a pretty yellow colour. Once again it was the strange smells that affected Kinni the most. There was so much to see and take in that Kinni fainted.

The next day, Kinni awoke in a pretty bedroom. It was very unusual for a slave to have a bedroom. In Kinni's mind, however, it was all strange. As she took in her surroundings, she suddenly remembered Khmet, and sat up and called out her name.

To her surprise, Khmet opened the door. She had come over that morning to see how Kinni was coping. Khmet had been auctioned shortly after Kinni and had been bought by Dr Hart's neighbour and fellow surgeon, Dr James Malloy. And so Khmet's prophecy had come true. Dr Malloy was a jolly personality and, just like Dr Hart, thought of slaves as fellow human beings. Kinni soon realized that she was very safe, and that the power of her ancestors to protect was indeed strong.

Little did they know that evil lurked at the very doorstep of this fine house. Dr Hart was being courted by the sinister Dr Venture and his African accomplice, Ayi. Ayi was a freed slave who was part Arab. He was from the Turgar tribe from Mali. It was hard enough for Hart to put up with

Venture, let alone Ayi. He could only tolerate Venture because he said he supported the abolition of the slave trade. Venture had freed Ayi as proof of his beliefs. But Hart was suspicious of this act of generosity, as Ayi did not seem to move far from the side of Venture other than to carry out what he called his traditional healing practices and other gifts for the patients. So every time Hart was invited to dinner at Dr Venture's home to speak about abolition, Ayi would invariably be there.

As for Dr Venture, well Hart was not sure what his game was. He appeared to fancy himself as a pioneer in understanding the human body, a man destined for fame and wealth. But Hart's good friend Malloy had other ideas about Dr Venture. Malloy had warned Hart, 'You be careful of him, old man. I tell you there is something fishy about Venture. I have an awful feeling he has blood on his hands, and not patients' blood either. But blood ill gotten.'

'Oh you exaggerate, Patrick Malloy. You're just letting that Irish leprechaun in you get carried away', laughed Hart.

'Mark my words, Valentine, you will learn that this leprechaun knows a bit more about human nature than your kindly soul will give due credit to', sulked Malloy.

Chapter 5: Manchester Docks on the James River

Deep in the night, Wibari and the others were awoken by the loud screech of Sussi's voice.

'Get up you lazy lot! Time to work!' she ordered as the hyraxes began to make their way down to her. Sussi stood in front of a large bag from which she scooped grain and passed it to each hyrax as they filed past. Sussi had very large paws, so the hyraxes had to be careful that the grain did not drop through their own tiny paws. Wibari was surprised at how much grain they were each given. However, there was not much time to eat before they were being herded outside into the darkness and along the side of the old derelict house in which they lived. As they came out, the putrid smell of the river entered Wibari's little button nose. The smell sent a shiver through her body.

She and the others were then herded down an alley towards the river by several large rats. Wibari had never seen such large, ugly rats. They moved with military precision. This made them even more frightening. They were efficient and knew just how to keep the hyraxes hopping along past the old buildings along the rotting dock. They would nip the heels of any wayward hyrax. There were dangers all around in this rotting setting, for the dock had gaping holes in some places.

'Ahh!!'

The line slowed down to see what had happened. A hyrax had hopped too far to one side and had slipped through a hole in the dock, and was now drowning before their very eyes.

78　The trade in body parts

'Get on with it!' yelled the rat next to Wibari. This shocked all the hyraxes, who now hopped even more cautiously as they made their way towards the edge of the dock.

Wibari could just make out several lines of hyraxes pulling something in the distance. She could hear them humming the Great Song. Before she knew it, she was being dragged and chained up with a group of hyraxes. They were all being forced to file along beside a great chain that was coming out of the water. Due to all the effort being made by the other gangs, she realized some huge load lay under the filthy waters of the river. She watched as the other gangs heaved and heaved. 'Whatever it is, it must be heavy', she thought. Then she was nudged and pulled instantly into place, and found herself heaving and heaving – pulling something that was indeed very heavy. Even though there were 10 hyraxes pulling the load, she could sense its great weight.

She and the others were straining under the weight, but even under such strain she still had time to notice the next chain gang, whose burden was finally coming to the edge of the river. To her utter shock, she saw a human arm, grey and washed out. She vomited at the sight of it. Her mind had gone wild; for a moment she thought it might have been Kinni's arm. But before she could steady herself, she was being screamed at by the hyraxes in front of and behind her.

'Errr, watch your mess!!! It's hard enough for us as it is without you spewing on us!!!' yelled the hyrax in front of her.

The body part was pulled closer and closer to her as they heaved it further and further up onto the dock. The hyrax behind her said, 'You're lucky that your first body is only an arm! Wait to see a half-eaten head, then you are really going to spew!' Wibari let out a cry of fright and turned to the hyrax behind her. It was a male with a very blank look on his face. She could see he meant no malice by his statement; it was simply a matter of horrible reality. She now felt her life would become one gruesome event after another, a never-ending stream of human body parts!

How could her ancestors be helping her? Why had her grandmother let this happen?

Chapter 6: the encounter

The nights blurred one into another until they became weeks. Finally she began to focus again, and began to dream and call out to her grandmother. Her grandmother soon appeared.

'You are now part of a "chain gang" and there is no individualism of thought or action on a chain gang, Wibari', she counselled. 'As you have realized, you either move with the gang or else die underfoot.'

The Great Song, her Grandmother explained, gave the hyraxes strength and bonded them together as one to survive just like on the ship.

Wind Watchers' tale: Wibari and the Rogue Protectors   79

'There is a great power in the oneness', she said.

'Grandmother, I realize the hyraxes use the Great Song to stay sane, but why haven't the hyraxes used the strength the song gives them to escape?'

'You are wrong, my little one. Some have used the power and have escaped but most can't get past just surviving.'

'Some have escaped?' this made Wibari's ears prick up.

'Yes, they are called maroons. They are clever and cunning and live by their wits. But you are different from all of them. You have something the others do not have.'

Her grandmother then told her to smell the cloth on which she was lying. As she did this, she realized it was the cloth from the dress of her human friend. She was so excited to think this was her beloved friend's clothing, but then her body seized into a spasm.

'Grandmother, tell me that this cloth does not come from Kinni's dead body?'

Her grandmother told her not to worry, as the cloth had been stolen by the rats after Kinni had been stripped of her old clothes and given a new set as she was put up for sale. The huge rats had taken advantage of the discarded clothes, which were thrown under the auction stage.

'Kinni has been sold to a rich slave owner. She is now living in the grand home of a wealthy doctor. Kinni's life will be good. So do not worry about your friend. There is something special about her, just like you. The good doctor will come to realize that as well', smiled her grandmother.

'But for now, you must stay on the chain gang until you can truly "feel" this powerful Song that binds the hyraxes together as one force. And then you will use the force to set yourself free.' Wibari was about to ask her grandmother how that would happen, but sleep overtook her and she found herself curling up and falling off to sleep.

So Wibari endured the chain gang. She began to truly become one with the other hyraxes. She did not see herself outside of them; she began to listen to their stories of their long-lost homelands and how their stories of home soon became part of the Great Song. She stopped thinking of how hopeless they all looked and began tapping into the Great Song. She lost her sense of difference, which in turn broke down her resistance to the Great Song. And so she learnt to walk in her mind the Great Song lines that were sung about in the songs. These lines were the tracks on which people had walked across their homelands for centuries and as she sang the songs, she was transported back to her home. Eventually, after many weeks, Wibari found herself travelling back home in her sleep. She was once again a happy hyrax bounding around the rocky outcrops of home.

But just as she was beginning to accept her life, Wibari was woken by something dropping on her face. She opened her eyes slowly and saw soot trickling down from the floorboards above. Wibari's brick was the closest to the underside of the floorboards. She could just faintly hear movement above. 'Other rodents?' she thought, 'Who could they be?' Most likely it was more evil rats, chasing some poor hyrax that had escaped. Wibari sat up with a start. 'Could it be a maroon on the run? No! There is no way out from this huge place', she moaned to herself and slumped back down on the hard brick.

But Wibari was wrong: these were not evil rats, but hyraxes that had long ago been enslaved, but had escaped. They were maroons on the run. They had escaped through their cunning and bravery. These were truly brave little hyraxes, who were not intimidated by the brutality of the rats, nor the humans who helped them.

As Wibari lay on her brick, worrying about who these horrible new violators could be, a strange sensation took over her heart; she could hear a new song. She didn't know why she could hear the song, but she knew it made her feel safe. She then changed her mind and thought, 'These are not evil rats but helpers. They are maroons.' She quietly got up and moved over to where she had heard them stop. She softly tapped on the boards and listened intently for a reply. The next minute she noticed an eye peering through a gap in the floorboards. She gave a little signal with her paw, which in her hyrax sign language indicated she wanted help. The eye quickly disappeared.

A few seconds later, a floorboard began to shift and a rather beaten-up looking hyrax with one eye covered peered down at her. Her heart immediately went out to him and his to her. This shocked them both, and actually nearly unbalanced the male, whose name was Hyad. Hyad was not used to falling in love in the middle of a heist. He put his paw down and helped her up through the space. Both immediately came together, which only made both of them even more unbalanced. Their eyes locked, and their bodies almost did so too, until Hyad quickly pulled back and signalled her to follow him.

'What about the others?' Wibari whispered to Hyad. He signalled back that they would help them later. She then looked up at the band of hyraxes running ahead of her. She had a sense of foreboding at what she saw.

Chapter 7: the Amigos

Wibari did well to be wary of this group of maroons, as they were edgy and fierce and did not like newcomers. One had lost an ear; another hopped with a limp. One had lost most of his paws and another had a burn mark on her fur. Among them were the Three Amigos – Hyad and Dassy, two daring males, and Nyin, a clever quick-witted female hyrax. They were siblings and had been called the Three Amigos by a chinchilla they had helped to escape back to South America. The rats had mistaken the chinchilla for a baby hyrax.

Wind Watchers' tale: Wibari and the Rogue Protectors   81

That very night, they were helping a group of hyraxes to escape from the Skin Boys, who were the security guards for King Rat. The Amigos were experts at starting fights, especially on the unsuspecting. Their own sibling rivalry gave them plenty of training. Through their own fighting, they had learnt just about every trick in the book, including how to start a fight between the guards. It was during these fights that the Amigos were able to slip through and free the slaves. They often found the simplest tricks worked on the most evil of the rats. The Skin Boys were indeed evil, and always expected something more sinister and complex. It was therefore easy for the Amigos to set one guard against the other just by throwing a stone at one, who would instantly blame the other rather than looking for an intruder.

As she travelled with them through the soot and dirt and rat droppings, Wibari felt as if she were walking on air. Was it the escape or was it her one-eyed saviour, she wondered, as she hurried along behind them.

It wasn't long before they arrived at what looked like their hideout. There was food cooking and a pile of grain in a small makeshift basket. As she sat down and let the smell enter her nose, she realized there was meat in the soup. At first she wondered what kind of meat, then the smell registered: she had smelt that ghastly smell before. It was human meat. The rats lapped it up all the time.

'Ahhh', she thought, 'they are no better than the rats. They are murderers.' She jumped to try and escape. But Nyin was already beside her, and she was trapped. Nyin could see the fear in her eyes and so she pushed Wibari over near the soup pot.

'Well, my new friend, won't you have a bowl of luscious soup?'

'No, it has human meat in it. I will eat grain, thank you!' Wibari said indignantly.

Nyin laughed and said, 'Sorry Sis. We thought we would never have to eat human meat, but we had no choice as all our other food has gone; the grain is a luxury. This is the first time we have had it', said Nyin as she looked at the sack of grain over in the corner with hungry eyes.

'It is a luxury and not a choice for you to make. We give it out sparingly, knowing how good it is for us. You cannot have the grain; you must eat the meat or nothing at all. This is an ugly place and you are in ugly circumstances, which gives you no choice', Nyin shouted as she stared down at Wibari, who had begun to crouch away from her.

'The rats gave you the precious grain because they needed you to be strong and bulky so that you could haul the human body parts, not because they were keeping the meat for themselves. Human meat is easy to get; it is the grain that is precious. Why do you think the rats are in the slave trade? Certainly not for human meat!'

'You can't afford to be stupid anymore, my friend. Your life and our lives are now one. Your mistake is our risk. We don't take unnecessary risks

82 The trade in body parts

with the lives of others or our own. So anyone who is an unreasonable risk is a threat. Think again before you reject the soup.' Nyin moved away in disgust and went over to Hyad to report on his hapless new friend.

Wibari settled back and tried to sleep; she had to come to terms with the knowledge that it was not a luxury to eat meat, and the fact she may never taste grain again – that is, if she wanted to stay alive. This was all too much for her and she passed out.

Nyin saw her fall; she glared at Hyad and told him of Wibari's naivety and likely threat to the safety of the group. Hyad sat solemnly, considering the news.

'Leave me to think about this', said Hyad, as he moved away from the group and up to a window sill. The room they were in was empty – as was the whole building, except for the basement in which the hyraxes were enslaved. It was a derelict house that had been left to rot for many years. His heart felt heavy as it had already been caught by the 'song of love' and now it was being turned into a 'drum of doom'. The beat of the drum of duty drowned out this new-found love.

He then hopped over to Wibari and looked down on her sleeping body as he twirled one of his whiskers. 'Is she of use, can she be used as a decoy or is she the risk my sister suggests?' he thought. 'I'll watch her more carefully tomorrow and make my decision. If she is a risk, I will just arrange an accident.' As he moved away, Wibari's body shuddered. Hyad turned and was stunned by Wibari's ability to detect a threat even when she was asleep.

Chapter 8: protectors

Wibari woke up out of habit and thought she must prepare for the evening's work. As she rose, she realized she was no longer sleeping on a brick high up in the air, but rather was flat on the floor and in a room full of unfriendly hyraxes that looked like they wanted to murder her. She therefore moved slowly so as not to draw attention to herself. She gazed around the room and regarded the group more carefully. As she looked at them, she could feel their deep need to protect themselves. It was as though they thought there was a snake in the room, and it was slithering around them, unable to make up its mind who it would strike first. That snake, of course, was death itself. Death was out to get them. This thinking made them ugly and wanting, she thought.

'Who are you, anyway?' she asked as she moved over to Dassy, who was sharpening a piece of wood with his teeth.

'We are the ones who stayed behind after the great escape that happened a few years ago. We stayed behind to help others escape. Hyad, Nyin and I are known as the Three Amigos because we are siblings. It is easier for us to stay as we have each other, but as for the others – well, they come and go. Sometimes one of them will escape with the others but then

Wind Watchers' tale: Wibari and the Rogue Protectors   83

another stays behind. It's funny how it kind of works out. There is constant balance in our numbers. Of course, your arrival puts the numbers out, so you must move on soon or disappear', he said nonchalantly, which made Wibari feel even more insecure.

'What does it mean to disappear?' asked Wibari cautiously as she began to back away from him.

'Work it out yourself', grinned Dassy, as he maintained eye contact with her.

Wibari turned her face away quickly so that Dassy would not detect the fear in her eyes. She moved back to the corner. Wibari didn't want to work anything out; she just wanted to 'feel' exactly how she was supposed to 'feel' her way out of this mess! This dark, filthy place was no better than the rat's hole! They frightened her and made her feel dispensable to her very core. Her hero was no better than the rest, she thought, as she looked at his face from a distance. Even though he had a kinder face, she could see in him a susceptibility to the opinions of others.

As she sat watching them, they began to gather in a group and appeared to be planning their next move. After a while, she thought, 'No point watching them any longer. I have no power over their decisions.' She began to settle down and tried to 'feel' her next move.

She closed her eyes, and as soon as she did she could see Hyad's face, kind and strong. Her heart went out to him again. Then she saw an image of him calling her to follow him. So she followed him to what looked like a window and found him pointing to something on the horizon. As she looked, she could see the white sails of a ship. She then turned to him and asked him what the importance of the ship was. As she looked at him for an answer, she could see that he was looking at her with tender eyes that revealed nobility and love. She then realized he was indeed in love with her. She immediately opened her eyes and looked for him in the group.

Their eyes met and they both knew what she had seen. He turned his eyes away immediately, then screamed at his sister. Nyin stepped back in shock then swung around and glared at Wibari. Wibari dropped her eyes and began to eat her soup, but just as her tongue reached the side of the bowl, she vomited from the smell of human body parts. Regaining her composure, she moved away from the soup and over towards the grain. This made Nyin move quickly towards her to stop her.

'Don't worry, Nyin. I am not going to eat your precious grain. I just wanted to check the quality', she said.

'Check the quality – Miss High and Mighty? Since when did you know the difference?' demanded Nyin.

'In my home country of Siinegana, I lived with humans, so I learnt a lot about the grain that the humans grew and harvested', said Wibari arrogantly. 'But of course it was nowhere near as tasty and filling as the grass seeds of the wild.'

84   The trade in body parts

'That kind of knowledge is of no use here, Miss Smart', spat Nyin.

'You never know, Nyin; my knowledge might just come in handy one day. Actually, my knowledge of humans might be very handy one day', said Wibari in a sassy voice, as she fluttered her eyelids at Nyin.

'What do you mean by that? We don't have anything to do with humans; they are a hindrance to us – not useful at all! They only help rats', retorted Nyin, who looked as though she was about to hit Wibari.

'Oh yeah?' said Wibari, as she hopped slowly around the grain. 'You might take some time out and consider whether having a hyrax that can communicate with a human could just come in handy, especially if that human can bring about our freedom', said Wibari, winking at Nyin – which further infuriated her. Actually, Wibari couldn't believe how smug she was being – exactly what was she trying to do? But she was winning this argument, and that was all that mattered. After all, they intended to make her disappear, so why not play with their minds?

'What good are humans?' snorted Nyin, as she pushed Wibari away from the grain. 'They work with those accursed rats!'

'Not every human loves a rat – actually, most hate them. And it's very handy to know a human when you want to take out the rats', purred Wibari as she moved back again to the grain sack. 'Humans think hyraxes are just cute dumb animals. They think rats are smart and cunning, and need to be exterminated. So if we tell the humans where the rats are, they will do the rest and exterminate them.' Wibari put her paw into the grain.

Nyin was about to stop her until she made her last comment. 'Exterminate the rats? Okay, clever, but just exactly how do we talk to humans?'

'If you help me find a human called Kinni, that's the beginning of the extermination of the rats', she continued, as she ran her paw through the grain. She then turned to Nyin and said, 'It's like this, Nyin. What I learnt from hanging around humans is that they love acquiring things. They think rats will destroy those things. Therefore they want to exterminate them at any cost.'

Nyin sat there looking at Wibari as she tried to come to terms with this shift in power. She was not used to being outdone by a slave hyrax – especially one that wouldn't eat the meat.

Chapter 9: the revelation

As the two female hyraxes eyed each other off, Hyad was looking out the window. Even though it was night, he could see the chain gang of young hyraxes dragging a body part. This was the most important part of the body run. The young could be terrified into silence and doing anything the rats wanted. They would chain them up into a gang and make them drag the hessian bag of body parts up to the yard, where Sarat would collect it. If one faltered in any way a rat would bite the little hyrax's head off and spit it out in front of the other hyraxes and frighten the living daylights out of them.

Hyad had one great weakness. He was not in any way able to contain himself when he saw the little hyraxes being exploited by the rats. Hyad's paws dug into the windowsill. He raged inside himself. Then he saw it: the murder of a little hyrax. It was the moment that sent him off his head. Hyad convulsed and, as he did, his spirit left his body. It flew down to the murderer and his hands wrapped around the rat's neck. The rat fell to the ground and struggled with this unseen force. The rat was unable to call out. His fellow rats just left him to struggle on the ground, suffocating from this unknown, unseen force. They all secretly believed it was an avenging angel rebalancing the death of a young hyrax. The experienced rats knew very well why the killer was being executed. They had seen the payback in action enough times to stay well clear of killing young hyraxes. But there was always one among the new rats who couldn't help but be seduced by the power to dominate and exploit the young and vulnerable. That power of domination was an aphrodisiac to those worthless rats who found themselves drawn into this world of death.

Once the payback was inflicted, Hyad's spirit returned to his body. But Hyad had no idea what his spirit had been doing. All he knew was that he felt incredibly depressed after his moment of rage. Of course he should have felt great satisfaction at seeing these deaths, but it bothered him that he did not really know how or why the rats died. He felt somehow the answer was inside him, but he did not know how to find the answer. For many moons, he had watched this event and thought about it, but no answer came – only the depression, and of course the revulsion, which led him to vomit after each encounter.

Wibari noticed the change in his behaviour.

'What's wrong with Hyad?' she asked, as she watched Hyad hopping around in circles.

'He's going crazy. He must have the little ones in sight', said Nyin thoughtfully. 'Come over and watch – that's if you can stomach what you will see.'

As they came up beside Hyad, they could feel the anger in him and the stench of his vomit.

'You see there, Wibari, see that big bag? It's full of grain as payment for the body part', sniffed Nyin.

As they looked down, they could see the gruesome scene.

'Killers, that's all they are – born killers; they are all killers – the humans and the rats', grunted Nyin.

They then turned to Hyad who by now had moved away from the window and was resting.

'Wibari thinks she has a way of exterminating the rats! Well, so she brags!' said Nyin in a singsong tone. This immediately focused Hyad's deep-brown eyes on Wibari. She became nervous. But then a thought came into her mind – or was it a feeling?

'Actually', said Wibari flippantly. 'I can't think on an empty stomach. Give me a bowl of grain and I'll set out the plan.'

'Rubbish', said Nyin indignantly. 'No way!'

'Shut up, Nyin! Give her a bowl of grain. All I care about is those little ones, not your ego!' Hyad shouted, then hopped over to a corner where he settled down.

Nyin hopped slowly over to the grain sack, scooped out a paw full of grain and pushed it into Wibari's paws. Wibari gave her a thankful smile and moved back over to the corner and began to eat the grain. Hyad collected some grain and went into his corner and watched her.

As he sat looking at her, he began to feel the strength from across the room. He could feel it coming into him and calming him down. As a trance-like sensation took over his body, his eyes closed on the image of Wibari slowly nibbling on the grain. It was the slowness that was affecting him – her slow, measured movements were hypnotic. Somehow, she – or whatever it was that protected her – was hypnotizing him from a distance. Slowly he began to feel his spirit loosening from his body. It drifted above his body, up and outside the building. He was amazed at this experience, this freedom from the weight of his turbulent body, a body disturbed by so many traumatic scenes. He felt wonderfully light and loving. It was amazing. He felt so clean, as though the dirt of fighting with the rats had been washed from his soul. It was like a deep grime of hatred had also left his soul. As he floated, he could see back into the room where his two siblings and the others lay. He could now see the hardness on their faces, the hardness of their lives. He looked across to Wibari and saw the difference. There was no hardness. What he saw was firmness – firmness in the knowledge of being protected. And then he saw what protected her. Up above Wibari floated many older hyraxes.

'It must be her ancestors', thought Hyad. 'She has so many of them around her! How is it that her ancestors are protecting her and my siblings and I have none? They were fighting for the lives of others. Why weren't they protected?'

Just as he was thinking this, he noticed to one side an ethereal shape moving towards him. At first it looked like a mist, but soon took a form he recognized. It was his grandfather. He had spent many a fun time with this grandfather back in Siinegana. He was full of funny tricks, and often pulled his little ear when he was small and running around wildly through the bush. He pulled it whenever something was about to go wrong. This was his way of watching over him.

Just as that thought came into his mind, he remembered that when he was on the run from the rats he would sometimes feel a sensation like someone pulling his ear. 'How could I be so stupid to forget this kindly act? This was my grandfather warning me of impending danger!'

'Yes', said his grandfather. 'We are also there. But you and your brother and sister won't let us help you. Wibari is always looking for help from her ancestors while you young warriors are too full of confidence. You do not need us. You have been very successful at keeping ahead of the rats, but it wears you down carrying all the weight by yourself. Always having to watch your back instead of leaving that to us. If you let us help you, Hyad, you would think up better and easier ways of outwitting those stupid rats.'

Hyad thought about how stupid he had been. His grandfather moved closer and pulled his ear. This made Hyad look up at his grandfather again and smile. 'Hyad, you're a silly hyrax. You have great ability. You are meant to be a Protector.'

'What?' said Hyad 'A Protector – me?'

'Have you not wondered how the rats are killed after they murder the young ones?'

'Yes', said Hyad cautiously.

'We did not have time to tell you about your heritage before the slave ships came and stole you away. Therefore you have come to this knowledge the same way an orphan does. When the descendant of a Protector is orphaned, their dead ancestors find them and pass the knowledge down to them. They do this by causing coincidences that lead the orphan hyrax into experiences and situations that will allow the ancestor to work through the orphan until that orphan is conscious enough to see the misty spirit of their ancestor. You are one of those orphans, Hyad. We have been using you, and finally – because of Wibari – you can see me.'

'What – you used me?' Hyad moved uncomfortably at the thought that he was not in total control of his actions.

'You think you are depressed when you are actually just being a Protector.' Hyad's ears pricked up when his grandfather said this.

'When you finally accept that your depression is us pushing you out of your body so that we can work through you, the depression will go away. When you work with us, we can be a great team. The depression is just a fight for control.'

Suddenly Hyad could feel a surge of love shooting through his soul. Tears began to trickle down his little furry face.

Chapter 10: the plan

Wibari was ravenous, so she gobbled the first couple of mouthfuls of grain. But then she realized she would never think of anything if she kept gobbling her food. So she slowed down and began to eat more deliberately so that she could chew over her ideas. Sure enough, as she did this, the Great Song began to surface in her mind and she knew she had to 'feel' the solution, not think up an answer. 'Don't force it, just let it come to the surface', her grandmother had taught her.

88 The trade in body parts

So she ate slowly and felt the song in her body, and soon enough a solution began to materialize in her mind. Her thoughts then turned to Kinni.

'I wonder where my friend is? Could she help me?'

She would have to take the time to 'see' her and travel to her in her dreams. As dawn was about to break and all the rats would have scurried home, and as the maroons settled down, Wibari began to drift off into a trance-like sleep.

'You had better come up with something smart tonight, Miss Smart, or you are going to be one dead hyrax', shouted Nyin as she passed Wibari. This jolted Wibari out of her trance.

'Don't worry, Nyin. There is more to this situation than the eye can see', she said philosophically.

'Rubbish!' declared Nyin, hopping off to her corner.

Chapter 11: the raven

So Wibari lay down and began to relax and move into the trance through the humming of the Song. It wasn't long before she changed from the body of a hyrax into that of a raven flying through the air above the houses. She was amazed at the sensation and shocked to be looking down on the world rather than up into the sky. She tried not to think about how she was flying, for fear of falling out of the sky, so instead concentrated on finding Kinni. It was pre-dawn, so there were not many people about. But Wibari knew Kinni always said her prayers to the rising sun so she hoped she would be somewhere in the open air where she could find her.

She could see a yard where a young woman was carrying out some kind of ceremony. The sun was just beginning to rise. Wibari carefully glided down, as she was sure it was Kinni. She landed on a pole and looked, and sure enough it was her beloved Kinni – safe and well! Kinni had just finished praying when she noticed the raven. Curious, she called out to the raven.

'Well, hello Mrs Raven. What brings you here on this fine day? I don't have any bread for you, if that's what you are looking for!' Kinni laughed to herself and then noticed the raven had begun to dance around. 'How strange', she thought. 'Tell me, clever raven, as you can dance so well, do you know where my friend Wibari is? She is a lovely hyrax with a shiny coat and beautiful black eyes. Have you seen her?' Kinni was shocked as she was sure the raven actually nodded its head as though to say yes. So Kinni got up and walked slowly over to the raven.

'Do you know my friend Wibari?' she asked timidly. The raven again nodded.

'Where is she?' cried Kinni in a joyful voice. The raven flew to the gate and indicated she wanted Kinni to follow. Kinni began following the raven as it slowly jumped from fence to fence alongside the back alley behind the town houses, so that Kinni could keep up.

Chapter 12: the undertakers

Finally the raven stopped and landed on a gate in front of a derelict house with a cart parked in front of it. Kinni called up to the bird and paused in front of the gate of the two-storey ramshackle house. As she observed the house, she thought, 'A house only fit for rats and dirty deeds. My poor Wibari must be trapped inside this monstrous place. I wonder who owns the cart and whether they are inside?'

So she crept past the gate and down the path leading to the front steps. She listened very carefully for noises as she climbed the stairs. As she came to the door she could not hear any sound. Her heart was thumping loudly, but she had to save her friend. She then noticed a window with most of the glass missing. Slowly she made her way over to it, through the thick weeds. It was not easy, but she was able to climb through the window. She cut herself as she went through, but not badly enough to stop her. As she got down on the other side and stood up, she could not but help but recoil from the smell as she glanced around at the walls covered with stains and peeling wallpaper. The house smelt putrid and she nearly threw up. Suddenly an image of dead bodies came to mind, but she pushed these images away as she was barely containing herself as it was. Little did she know that this house was the drop-off point for the Body Run – the trade in body parts. Nor did she know that on the second floor Hyad and his gang were hiding.

She moved quietly from room to room when suddenly she could hear voices. She froze and then quickly moved back into the shadows. Around the corner came a large man, wearing scruffy, grimy-looking clothes. He was accompanied by a thin, dishevelled man. He was a hungry-looking soul, thought Kinni, and actually reminded her of a rat, while the other man looked more like a bulldog. As they passed her, she nearly fainted from the dreadful smell. The lean looking man was dragging a sack with something very wet inside it.

'Dawk, you know I am sick of this filthy job', said the rat-faced man. 'Doctors make me puke! I don't let my family near them since starting this racket. Why, you never know whether they would cure your kid or cut them up for their body part', spat Sarat.

'Now, now, Sarat,' said the bulldog-faced man, 'Not all doctors are killers, just our friend, Dr Venture.'

At the mention of Venture's name, Kinni froze.

'Khmet was right. He is wicked!' she thought, alarmed.

The men then passed Kinni in the shadows without noticing her.

'You just keep in good with your friends, the rats, and all will be well.'

Kinni's mind was spinning. 'What does he mean – keep in good with the rats? Is this man a witchdoctor who can speak to the rats?' she wondered. She knew of people in her home country who could talk to some animals, but these men did not bear the dignity of such people – if anything, they looked like the rats themselves. Perhaps they were shape-shifters and were indeed rats!

Sarat certainly could speak to the rats, though not in the way she imagined.

Sarat was a ratman. He looked like a rat, with his brown, limp hair and large hook nose. The nose of a mongrel – too many cultural mixes in his blood – made him look mean. He didn't know who he was, just that he felt an affinity with the rats. He had been left in the streets as a young boy when his mother had been mugged to death by a group of female bandits who roamed the back streets in search of human prey. These were mean times and one's gender meant nothing when it came to survival in the prosperous streets of Richmond at the height of the slave trade. The trade in human flesh indulged its ugly taste for the exploitation of one and all. Woman, child or man – everyone was for sale as the New World began to take its place on the world stage, so its residents became part of the great global market in human flesh.

Life was cheap and Sarat's mother was one of those cheap buys, used and discarded. Sarat had seen too much from the sewer and hated humans, especially those who could afford to buy other humans. He hated the whole business, but he had to feed his family and his friends the rats. And worst of all, it was his and King Rat's idea to profit from the Body Run.

'Ah, shut up. You forget it was your idea in the first place', said Dawk. Rodney Dawkins – or Dawk, as his acquaintances called him – was a large man, well fed on vice and pottage. Dawkins was an undertaker and ran a respectable undertaker's business, which was a front for this more ghastly enterprise, which he could not resist when Sarat had told him about the approach from Dr Venture, and his need for body parts. Venture was a wealthy man and could pay good money for the traffic in body parts.

Dawk stopped and turned to Sarat, slapping him on the back. 'We get paid good money for this, and just as long as we cough up the grain for the rats, all is fine. So stop carrying on like a cry baby!'

Then Dawk stopped and looked closely at Sarat.

'Now look here, Sarat. You aren't having second thoughts, are you?'

'No, I'm in too deep and anyway, King Rat loves the game. You should see the size of his gang now', said Sarat, shaking his head.

'Even if I wanted out, I reckon he'd rip my feet off if I tried to walk out on the deal.'

'Well, that's two of us – let alone what Venture would do. Probably set that witchdoctor Ayi onto you', warned Dawk.

'He gives me the creeps, Sarat. I'd rather spend a night in the morgue than spend five minutes with him.'

Wind Watchers' tale: Wibari and the Rogue Protectors 91

They continued to walk down the hallway. Meanwhile, Kinni was panicking at the thought that she might not get out to warn Dr Hart. But then what would she say?

'I heard two men talking about Dr Venture and how they and a pack of rats were doing some kind of business with body parts.' How ludicrous it would sound. Oh, this was horrible! And where was Wibari? 'Why did the raven bring me to this terrifying place?' she moaned to herself.

The two men were now loading the bag into the back of their cart.

'Now come on, Sarat. I can see you are feeling low, so tell me the story again about how you came up with this deal.'

'Well, as I told you, when I was a kid living in the street I learnt a lot from watching the rats. They are born opportunists, as my Aunty Mary would say. She was the only human I had time for. She wasn't me real aunty, just a friendly old bag lady I'd see in the streets. Cunning woman – always looked kind of forsaken, but was hard as steel at heart. Amazing the people you meet in the streets', reminisced Sarat.

'As I told you, I would watch those rats and see how they grabbed opportunities to take up anything that fell their way, so I began to copy them. And as with any two people working in the same territory, you soon run across each other and you either work together or kill each other. I decided I was going to work with them and figured out how to help them. Before I knew it, we were all partners in crime. They wanted food; I wanted money. They would fetch, I would sell. All went well until we found we were doing so well we needed more rats, but there weren't enough, until the day one of those African slaves brought with them a big rabbit – well, we thought it was a rabbit.'

The two men sat down on the stairs while Sarat prepared to finish his story. This gave Kinni time to catch up and get close enough to overhear the rest of the horrid tale.

'Now, where was I? Oh yeah, me and King Rat were sitting down on the dock when we see this fine-looking animal arrive with a slave. We thought at first it was hare or a black rabbit. They look very similar you know', he said in an authoritative voice. 'We, of course, didn't know what it was – just what it looked like. But hey, that didn't stop us. We both knew an opportunity when we saw it. So I trips over the slave, and this little creature drops, and King Rat grabs it by the ear and pulls it down under the stairs and – Bob's your Uncle!'

'King Rat found that this creature was a timid animal and easily pushed around. He got it working morning, noon and night. It was a good worker, you just had to keep it scared. So once we realized the value of these animals, we paid a visit to the ship's rats, those Ocean Boys and their boss, Idi. We found out they weren't rabbits but were called hyraxes. King Rat sorted out the deal and, lo and behold, the next ship arrives a few months later and down the rope come a chain gang of hyraxes. And so we fix our labour problem.'

92 The trade in body parts

'And then with our own labour force we could "expand our operations", as they say in the big city hall. Yes, me and King Rat began to look for new opportunities and we spied a beauty the day we saw the first body part floating down the river. There it was, plump, grey and horrible. King Rat jumped to his feet and ran down to the river, and of course I followed. At first it made me a bit sick but then I stood there with King Rat just watching it float by. I knew we both were thinking about how to get it out of the river and how we could make money out of it.' Sarat laughed and slapped his thigh – he was so pleased with himself.

'Like all opportunists, we knew that as soon as we thought about it, an opportunity would present itself. Life's just like that. It's like there are these Big Ears of Life, just listening out for any chance to show off', he said philosophically.

'So the next time, I was pretending to be a drunk', he said quietly, leaning towards Dawk. 'You know, pays to act like that – especially in toffs' areas, late at night. Those toffs are like cats sniffing around at night looking for a bit of excitement', winked Sarat. 'I was leaning up against the wall of the fine chambers where the big knob doctors work when I heard these two toffs talking about the need for body parts to try out their experiments. One doctor was all for it, while the other was outraged.'

'Of course, the doctor who wanted the body parts was our benefactor, Dr Venture. Most appropriate name, don't you think! While his mate said it wasn't ethical. That made Venture laugh and say, "Ethics is for the uncivilized. We are professionals and we must make breakthroughs at any price, so that we can save more lives".'

'Yeah, I laughed to myself, and thought just whose lives are going to be saved – the rich first and then us poor bastards if we are lucky!'

'Dr Venture's mate, who I think is named Hart, then left in a huff', said Sarat. 'Can you believe that, among those toffs, some of them actually do have a conscience? But then those toffs are just as greedy as the rest of us, so he might have changed his mind later.'

Sarat moved his leg and scratched his head. 'So after they left, I got up and start thinking about how to contact Dr Venture, as I headed off to tell King Rat. Well, as soon as I hit the drain where he holds court, he came rushing out and led me to an old building on the wharf and around the back to a basement window. Well, I tell you Dawk, it nearly made me sick to see what I saw. I saw this witchdoctor – you know, one of those Africans that are supposed to be a healer. Healer all right! There in his entire glory making what looked like a sacrifice of a little kid? Just cutting him up there on an altar and, can you believe, there were white people there, as well as Africans, watching on. I tell you mate, I just had to spew. After all, I got kids. Just as well it was the dead of the night. I mean, I may come from the sewer, where life is cheap and death your neighbour, but I don't revel in it, like these people, if you can call them people. No, Dawk, it taught me there are human beings and then beings pretending they are human.' Both Sarat and Dawk fell silent for a moment, taking in the scene Sarat had described.

Kinni was barely keeping herself upright at the thought of what she had heard. She leaned against the wall and put her hand to her mouth to stop herself from screaming at the horror of it all.

Sarat gave a sigh and went on, 'But King Rat wasn't havin' any of my spewing. It didn't take King long to find out who this witchdoctor was and what his game was. Turns out his name is Ayi and he does all this hoodoo voodoo to make his customers lucky or something.'

'I tell you, I do this job, but I still don't like it. I'm always worried my kid is going to end up in a bag one day. Like somehow I did a deal with the devil and it will come back on me.'

'Yeah', said Dawk as he squirmed uncomfortably at the thought. 'I hate to say this, but it's us stupid bastards who are being done over by those toffs. We are the ones who do the worst things to our own kids.'

'It's like those toffs have a way of making us do all the dirty work and they stay all clean, when in fact it is them who are "guiding" it all, their filthy system – the rich get rich and the poor get poor. Rich kids are safe and poor kids are rubbish. Poor kids do all the dirty work for the rich and we just keep on doing it like mindless sheep.'

'We are no better than those hyraxes. The only difference is that we think we are free because we don't get locked up like the hyraxes each night', Dawk said sadly as he rubbed his nose.

'But that's the way it is and there's no point complaining, as we can't get out of this filthy mess, so we have to survive. So tell us, Sarat, what happened then?' He was enjoying this macabre story.

'You mean after I learnt to stomach the scene? Well, King Rat and I thought we would take in the neighbourhood to see whether there were any opportunities, you see. We found that the place backed onto the river. We saw them all come out of the back door. Seems when they finished their dirty work they dragged the bits out to the river bank and threw them in. Well, King Rat and I were beside ourselves seeing this easy gain, going down the river, right our way', smiled Sarat with a smirk.

'That's an amazing story', Dawk said shaking his head. 'But how did you get Dr Venture on side?'

'Ohh, he was unbelievably easy. You see, me and the King learnt a long time ago that when there is evil in the heart, you just have to basically dangle the dead meat in the air and the bastard can smell it and before you know it they are on your doorstep. So we pulled out a nice juicy torso and put it in a bag and left it outside the good doctor's outhouse, with a little note saying there was more where that came from. Soon enough a note was left asking for the deal. And Bob's your Uncle', chuckled Sarat.

94 The trade in body parts

'Of course, we had to make it all look very innocent and so we worked out that the hyraxes could pull the bodies out of the river in the cover of night and then the rats would deliver the parts to the old house. Seems they get young hyraxes to do that for some reason. Then when you, as the respectable undertaker, comes along to collect the body parts for our Dr Venture, you pass me a little bag of gold and leave a bag of grain for our friends the rats. No names, no contact, just keeping to the deal and all goes well', smirked Sarat with a self-satisfied look on his face.

Dawk slapped Sarat on the back, 'If I didn't see it with me own eyes I wouldn't have believed it.'

Sarat leaned back and said sadly, 'Yeah, kind of unbelievable if you live in a big house and eat three times a day, but when you have to live in the streets by your wits, there is nothing strange about human–animal relationships. And I suppose nothing strange about rich bastards wanting us to do their dirty work', he said and turned to Dawk with a knowing look.

As Kinni stood silently listening, she had an image of Dr Venture bringing her sweets and pinching her arm, and saying what strong stock she came from. 'Yuck – he was thinking of me like a horse or a cow. And that horrible Ayi – Khmet warned me about him!'

Khmet had warned Kinni that within the slave world, there were many very bad people and some very good people all mixed in together. This made you work things out, instead of just relying on the skin colour to tell who was good and who was bad. But how would she react the next time she saw Dr Venture? She sneaked along behind the men, who had begun to move towards the cart. She realized that she had to find another avenue to get out of the building.

She moved slowly back down the hall and out through a battered side door then, slipping through a decaying back fence, made her way home to tell Khmet.

Hyad and the others were already up watching the humans from the second floor. There were many gaps in the floorboards so they could see the humans below. Wibari could just make out a human.

'A human being!' thought Wibari. 'Could it be Kinni? Had she been dreaming of being a raven or was she really a raven and had brought Kinni to the house?' It was all too confusing at first.

She quickly sniffed the air to pick up the scent. 'Would it be a familiar scent of my beloved human friend, Kinni? Yes, yes!' she squealed as she lunged towards the large being, but just as she began to hop excitedly towards Kinni, Hyad grabbed her hind legs and yanked her back and placed his paw over her mouth. She struggled, but Hyad was powerful and held her firmly. The large figure continued to move quietly out of the room.

Dassy whispered, 'That human was hiding from the other humans. The Body Run humans', The Amigos were used to hearing the humans stomping through the building, but this was a stranger, an intruder – someone spying on the Body Runners.

'Who do you think that human was, Hyad?' quizzed Nyin as she moved closer to Hyad, who had let go of Wibari. Just as Hyad was feeling satisfied that he had saved Wibari from sure doom, she screamed at him before he could answer Nyin.

'You idiot, that was my human friend Kinni! I led her here in my dreams. Why did you stop me from talking to her? Now we are lost, you stupid, stupid hyrax', she shouted.

Hyad moved slowly away from her with a hurt and confused look on his face. What did she mean she had brought her here, and through her dreams? Surely Wibari was not a *Saltigue*? he thought, as he moved over to the others. They all looked at her in amazement. They then began to whisper amongst themselves.

Was she really a *Saltigue*? Could she really have brought this intruder into our world? Could she really talk to humans?

Wibari took no notice of their whispering, and just paced around and around in circles yelling and complaining that all her hard work had gone to waste and saying how stupid these creatures were.

'No wonder the rats are able to treat you with such disdain. You can't cope with anyone or anything different. It all has to be drudgery, filth and disappointment. You live for the desire for despondency just like humans. You are addicted to disappointment. You just can't cope with anything different; it would mean you were out of control. I am so mad', screamed Wibari, who was actually starting to over-react, as she desperately tried to think of what to do next.

Chapter 13: the adventure

Just as Kinni was telling Khmet about the evil she had discovered, Malloy came down the stairs and told Kinni to tell Dr Hart to visit him that night, as he had noticed something rather strange going on in the neighbourhood. Kinni looked at him with disbelief.

Could he also know what had been going on? Had he seen the terrible things as well? She didn't dare ask him, but simply nodded and said she would inform her master on his return.

After dinner, Hart ventured over to his friend's townhouse to listen to the latest mystery. He imagined he would have a fine night of storytelling. Malloy's fiancée Elizabeth had often told him he was lucky to have a friend like Hart who brought balance into his life, for she had found it quite useless to try to distract him from his more fanciful pursuits. Malloy was athletic and excitable, and therefore very good with young patients, while Hart – who tended the elderly – was more reflective. Hart was a deep thinker due to his Scottish ancestry, which made him very cautious about the words he uttered. He knew words had power. Malloy was sure he was a Druid and had magical powers.

Malloy, on the other hand, had no magical powers; instead, he liked to think of himself as a modern man equipped with all the latest inventions, his favourite being the telescope. He had the latest version imported from Italy, which then gave him the right to call himself an astronomer – an amateur astronomer, of course, but a very competent one in his own mind. On most nights, he had his head tilted towards the stars. However, he did have one little 'bent'. On so-called cloudy nights, he tended to use his telescope to spy on the neighbours. Also, he particularly liked to watch what was going on down at the docks as the two physicians lived on a hill, with a fine view of the James River as well as the Manchester docks. He found the traffic around the warehouses fascinating, especially at night when most black-market goods were unloaded from ships by sea captains trying to avoid taxes.

However, there was another view, and that was of a few old grain warehouses and derelict houses that had been abandoned after a strange plague went through the area. For some reason, it was just in that one area – the rest of the Manchester docks were clean of any plague. Some said it was due to rats that had taken over the area. Malloy, however, had other ideas, as he had noticed that Ayi was using one of the old places for some reason, which Malloy was sure was for some ghastly deeds that Malloy was determined to uncover. He may not have been a Druid, but he had a nose that could smell a rat, and in his mind Ayi and Venture were the two biggest rats in all of Richmond.

Dr Hart liked to think he was above this kind of voyeurism, but unfortunately when he visited Malloy and came into the room, viewing time on the neighbours became an intriguing game. Malloy knew where everyone lived and was full of gossip about all sorts of goings on.

Malloy poured their brandies and began telling his story. He pointed out to Hart that after a solid night of viewing over the last month, something strange was afoot amongst the rodents. He recounted how he had noticed the strangest goings on in the derelict house at the back of one of the old grain warehouses – the very warehouse he had seen Ayi entering. The warehouse backed onto the river.

Hart knew from experience that when Malloy was onto something there was something feral about him. His face changed slightly as he spoke and he tilted his head upwards as though to pick up the scent in the air. Deep down, Hart respected this animal instinct as he knew from his Scottish training that the animal in all persons had something to say to humans in times of danger.

'You may find this hard to believe, Hart, but the other morning I woke well before sunrise as I had been dealing with a very difficult case and couldn't sleep. So I got up and did some viewing. I turned the telescope towards the backyard of a series of old derelict houses along Barlow Street near the older end of the dock. I saw the strangest sight. In the backyard were all these rats, I think, or some sort of animal, and I swear they were dragging a bag across the backyard. As I watched the scene, two men appeared on the back porch and went over and picked up the bag. I tell you Hart, I wasn't sure whether I was hallucinating or not. But not long after the men disappeared in to the house, I saw them on a horse and cart making their way down Jamestown Street. Hart, I want to go down and investigate – will you come back at about 3 a.m. and go down with me?'

'Steady on man, that's a bit late!'

'Yes, but it is Sunday tomorrow, so you don't have any patients. Come on, Hart, don't be a stick in the mud!'

'Very well, but I must say Malloy, I do think you have been overdoing it', said Hart as he reluctantly agreed.

'Good, go. Hart, I'll tell Khmet you'll be returning later tonight.' The two men then rose and Hart left, not quite sure of what he'd just agreed to.

Chapter 14: the investigation

At the designated time, Hart rose and went over to join Malloy. As soon as Hart arrived, Malloy quickly went to a cupboard and pulled out a sack and gave it to Hart.

'What's this?' queried Hart, as he took the sack and began to open it.

'All we need for a perfect break-in. You can't just go tiptoeing around the outside of the building; we will have to go right in and see what is up. So I have put a few handy items into a sack. A torch, a small crowbar and, of course, a weapon or two. You never know who you are going to meet on a dark night, old boy!' laughed Malloy as he threw his sack over his shoulder and began to walk out of the room. Malloy was jumping out of his skin in excitement; he just loved this kind of investigative stuff. He adored poking his highly sensitive nose into places he knew very well he should not be investigating. He felt quite macho when he did this.

Hart was dumbstruck by Malloy's cavalier behaviour. He could see that any sensible conversation would be lost on the man. Malloy was in his element, and there was no stopping him. So he thought it best just to follow the intrepid investigator as he opened a doorway hidden behind a curtain. Upon sighting the doorway, Hart knew he was not only on an adventure but perhaps a journey to other possibilities of reality.

They quickly made their way down a set of stairs and then into the cloudy night. They then headed along the back streets that Malloy constantly surveyed at night through his telescope. 'Be careful, Hart, or you will go rolling down the slippery cobblestones. It's a grimy place down here', said Malloy.

They finally reached the old house. Malloy gave the signal and they silently made their way down the path and up to the front steps. As they did this, they could hear voices at the other end of the house. So they crept up to a window. Malloy was now in his element as the leader of this dangerous expedition. He signalled for Hart to follow him through the same broken window that Kinni had climbed through. As they snuck down the hallway, they were overpowered by the stench. Malloy signalled once again for Hart to follow him into the kitchen, where they could look out the window and view what was happening in the backyard. This was the same view that Malloy had from his high perch on the hill.

Chapter 15: the capture of evil

'There's the sacks', said Dawk, as he pointed to two large sacks in the back-yard. 'Can always rely on those rats. They're born traders – or, as you say, Sarat, born opportunists!' They both laughed as they picked up the sacks.

'Let's get these body parts to Dr Venture. He will be pleased with this fat lot. Ayi must have been working overtime on the altar sacrificing these little fellas. God, this Ayi and Venture are evil bastards!' complained Dawk.

'Yeah, and the rats must have had to whip those little hyraxes extra hard this time. Will you look at the size of this sack?' Sarat lifted his sack up.

'Hey Dawk, just check that mound over there, I bet below that are a lot of little hyrax bodies', cried Sarat as he pointed to the corner of the yard.

'You know, Dawk, that's what I like about rats; they have enough nous to cover their tracks. The longer they hang around humans, the smarter they get. They probably lost a lot of hyraxes hauling this load. I will leave them extra for this bounty as they will have to buy more from the next ship', Sarat said, as he walked to the back porch and picked up a large sack of grain.

The two men then began to come into the house. This made Hart and Malloy jump quickly behind the door before they could be seen. The two undertakers then made their way to the front of the house and with them went the awful, overpowering stench of death.

Hart and Malloy stood up and, wide-eyed, looked at each other in disbelief. They both slowly moved down the hallway, listening to the horse-whip and the movement of the cart in the distance. The two men then moved quickly to the front door.

Hart turned to Malloy and said, 'If I hadn't seen it with my own eyes I would never have believed such a story.'

'It is beyond belief', said Malloy in a daze.

'Man and animals and, in this case rodents, have a way of communicating when it is to their combined interest. It is a fact of Nature if you bother to look and listen', counselled Hart.

'Well, what next, Hart. Do we stand here or take action?'

Wind Watchers' tale: Wibari and the Rogue Protectors   99

'What do you mean, Malloy?' queried Hart, wrinkling his brow.

'This is our opportunity to catch Venture and those killers in the act – to follow them and then call the police', said Malloy.

Hart was not sure about this act of bravery.

'On what grounds do we confront Venture? He is hardly going to admit to dealing with rats, and we are going to look quite deranged if we try to sell that story.'

'No, my man. We just catch him receiving the bag. Doesn't matter where it came from – the fact is that it contains body parts, and that's enough.'

'You are so right, Malloy!'

'Right!' said Malloy. 'I know a quicker way to get to Venture's home.' He then led Hart up the back alleys until they came to the lane that ran parallel with Hamilton Street, where Dr Venture lived in an ornate sandstone terrace house. When they came to a stop, Malloy pointed to Venture's house. Hart looked along the architectural sweep of courtly houses. Their facade of purity hid pure evil, he thought.

'How easily these grand houses make us believe that the owners can only be good citizens. How easily we are fooled by appearances – appearances created from bricks and mortar', he said, appalled at the irony of it all. Hart then turned his mind back to the job at hand.

'They will be along shortly to make the delivery', whispered Malloy. 'Let's find a hiding place and wait.' Malloy then signalled to Hart to climb over the fence into the backyard of a neighbouring terrace house.

'What's our plan, Malloy?' asked Hart, whose face had gone ashen grey. Not only had he never run so fast, but also he had never been in such a territory of terror.

'We'll let them make the delivery and then wait until we see Venture come and collect the goods, then we can jump him, tie him up and call the constable. After all, it's not the suppliers we want; it's the buyers. They are the true murderers', whispered Malloy snidely as they peeked through the gaps in the fence.

The early-morning breeze began to fan their sweat-drenched faces. Both men began to breathe more easily, until their breathing became silent and in that silence the sound of horses snorting and the squeak of a loaded cart could be heard in the crisp air. The clunk of the cart's steel-rimmed wheels against the uneven cobblestones sent shivers down Malloy's back. He began to wonder whether he was so brave after all.

There was no other sound, for the two undertakers knew better than to draw attention to themselves. As the sound of shod hooves shuffling on the cobblestones came closer, Hart was sure his nerves would fail him.

'Swak Swak!' Suddenly a crow came screeching towards the back of the cart. The scent of meat had drawn the predator. Sarat spun round with lightning speed and knocked the bird to the ground. 'I hate those mongrels', he spat.

Both Malloy and Hart nearly wet themselves when they heard the screech, as neither was really a hero, but merely a physician playing at being one. In unison, they sank to the ground and looked at each other.

The horses came to a standstill and the noise of the back gate opening could be heard by the two heroes, who now rose to their feet and once again looked over the other side of the fence. They could then see the undertakers heaving and dumping the sacks on the ground. The two large, bloodied, smelly bags were then put down the coal chute. Dawk gave a whistle like an early morning songbird. Within seconds, a light came on at the upstairs window. The window opened and down from the window dropped a small bag of money. 'Gotcha' whispered Dawk, and shook the bag so that Sarat could hear the jingle of gold paid for their grisly deeds. The two men then hopped back up into the cart and went on their merry way.

The clip-clop of the horses faded as the two doctors slowly rose to their feet. As they looked over the fence, they could see a light come on in Dr Venture's basement. They quickly jumped the fence and ran over to the basement window. As they crouched to take in the view, they saw Venture open the sacks and inspect the contents. He seemed unperturbed by the smell. 'An indication of his own deep stinking self', thought Hart. Venture then went over to his bench, took off his jacket and put on a work apron. He put on a pair of gloves and opened the first bag. He looked inside at the pitiful contents and smiled. He then turned to the second bag, and also glanced at the grisly contents. Satisfied, he went to his bench and pulled out some instruments from a drawer. He then returned to the first bag and drew out a torso. Both heroes covered their mouths in horror, watching the macabre scene as he began to cut pieces off the body.

Malloy and Hart having regained their composure, Malloy indicated they move to the back door, as he was sure Venture would be too self-absorbed to hear anything. He then leant down to the bag he was carrying, pulled out a piece of wire and began to fiddle with the lock. Hart wondered how this respectable doctor knew how to pick a lock. Once inside, they tiptoed to the doorway that led down to the basement. Once again, Malloy reached into his bag and this time pulled out a small plank. Gently, Malloy opened the door and crept down the stairs.

Venture was enmeshed in his work, but just as Malloy raised his arm to hit him with the plank, Hart accidently knocked a book off a table. Venture swung around instantly and grabbed Malloy's arm, and the two men struggled. Instruments went flying through the air and glass crashed. Hart tried to intervene but the two men kept swinging around and he couldn't get a grip on Venture, let alone hit him with his plank. Malloy eventually wrestled Venture to the ground and sat on him; this allowed Hart to grab Venture's jacket and throw it over Venture's face. This disorientated the man and allowed Malloy and Hart to tie him up.

Wind Watchers' tale: Wibari and the Rogue Protectors 101

It did not take Hart long to find further evidence of Venture's part in the body trade. Slices of human skin and bones were kept in containers or had dried out and been stored in neat piles and tagged. There were specimens still under the microscope. Hart gagged when he realized all the specimens were of children; Dr Venture had noted their ages on the tags. Hart immediately had murderous thoughts as he turned and looked at Venture lying on the ground, looking defiant. He felt like reaching for a machete, which reflected the light from a nearby candle. It lay on the table beside the cutting board. It was obviously used to hack through bone. Venture knew where the machete was, and therefore what Hart was looking at. He began to sweat as he wasn't sure what these two vigilantes would do to him.

Just as he was entertaining that thought, Malloy began hitting him across the face and telling him to admit to his crimes.

'We have enough evidence to incriminate him, Malloy. And don't worry, Venture will soon have a noose around his neck so you don't have to beat him up', Hart said as he grabbed a piece of cloth to gag Venture.

'There is enough violence in this hell-hole to last a lifetime, and no need to add to it, Malloy', Hart said sternly, which made Malloy feel quite guilty. Malloy took the cloth from Hart's hand and proceeded to tie it around Venture's head.

'All we need to do now is call the sheriff. I will go upstairs as the staff know who I am', said Hart quietly as he began to leave the room. Malloy then moved Venture over into a corner, while he examined the evidence on the laboratory table. He did not want to look at the face of this murderer and instead took out a small notebook he had in his waistcoat pocket and started making notes for the police.

Chapter 16: to catch a witchdoctor

It wasn't long before the sheriff arrived and bundled Venture off to the local watch-house. The sheriff also requested that the two heroes accompany them. It was therefore well into Sunday afternoon by the time they returned home. Khmet and Kinni were beside themselves with worry.

Exhausted but relieved, Malloy and Hart found themselves once again sitting in Malloy's lounge sipping brandy. This time, however, there was no light banter but rather brooding contemplation about how to deal with Venture's accomplice, Ayi. As they sat there, suddenly Kinni came running into the room in a distressed state.

'What is the matter, Kinni?' asked Hart as he stood up and moved towards her.

'Come quickly down to the kitchen, a little boy is bleeding badly', cried Kinni desperately, as she turned to go back down the stairs. Hart ran downstairs after her.

102 The trade in body parts

There, lying on the kitchen table, was a little boy bleeding badly from a great gash in his side. Khmet was trying frantically to stop the bleeding.

'What happened?' shouted Hart as he quickly moved to the boy and took over from Khmet.

'Quickly, Kinni, go and get my medical bag!'

'What happened, Khmet?' asked Malloy as he took in the scene.

'I found him down the alleyway screaming; he was running for his life. Then I saw that evil Ayi coming after him, but when he saw me, he turned and fled', she explained as she turned and walked over to him.

'Look at what he has done to this little boy', cried Khmet as she covered her mouth in distress. 'They are evil people. They kill children so they can gain power. You must stop them, Dr Malloy!' she pleaded as she looked into Malloy's face. 'You must stop this evil. Ayi is not a healer – he is a murderer!'

'Don't worry, Khmet. We think we have already stopped one half of this evil and now we will finish it', Malloy declared as he watched Hart working hard to stop the flow of the boy's blood.

Hart soon had the bleeding under control, and gave the child, whose name was Joshua, a potion to help him rest. He lifted the fragile boy and placed him in a bed near the kitchen stove. He told Khmet and Kinni to watch him, and said that if he was in pain when he woke up they should give him more of the potion. As he said this, Khmet met his eyes. Both knew it was not the pain that would kill the boy but the trauma of nearly being hacked to death.

Chapter 17: the capture

The two men dashed down the alley and made for Ayi's hideout in the basement of the old warehouse. As they approached the building, they slowed their pace and began to tiptoe towards a ground-level window. There was Ayi frantically packing up his potions and instruments into a carpet bag. He was also taking some of the objects and throwing them in the fireplace. The two men looked at each other and smiled, for they knew they had him trapped. Malloy noticed a broken window to the next room and indicated to Hart that he would climb through. Hart pointed to the back door and signalled his intention. Malloy gently lowered himself into the room and then made his way to the door. But before he could turn the handle, Ayi slammed the door into his face. This knocked Malloy over, which gave Ayi the chance to jump on Malloy.

Luck was with Hart, for the back door was already open as Ayi had intended to leave through that exit. He heard the fighting, and ran down the steps to the room, grabbing Ayi from behind just as he was beginning to choke Malloy. Hart wrenched the writhing Ayi off Malloy, which gave Malloy time to jump up and pounce on Ayi. However, Ayi was tall and strong, and it took all the might of both men to contain him.

Unfortunately, Hart had to let Malloy use all his might to punch Ayi out; otherwise they would never have been able to hold him. After Malloy finally succeeded in knocking Ayi unconscious, he got back up.

'Well Hart, I am amazed you allowed me have my way with the man', said Malloy half-jokingly.

Chapter 18: the rescue

The two heroes again returned to Hart's home to report to Khmet and Kinni. Khmet had a meal ready for them, as she had been told by the Jinn that the two men were returning safely.

'Well, all is well', boasted Malloy as he walked in to the kitchen. The two women beamed with pleasure. Hart was taken aback that a hot meal was waiting on the table.

'How did you know we would be coming, Khmet?'

They all just laughed as they all knew exactly how Khmet knew.

As they sat and discussed the capture, Kinni suddenly blurted out, 'But what about Wibari?'

'Oh dear, yes I wonder where your little Wibari might be now the trade has ended.'

'Oh Master, they won't throw her into the river, will they? Now they don't need the hyraxes?' cried Kinni who now had tears in her eyes.

'Don't worry, Kinni, we will find her', assured Hart, who was not quite sure how he would achieve this.

'No Master, if you will forgive', interrupted Khmet, 'but I think it is Kinni who must find Wibari. She has a love for Wibari which will lead her to Wibari. We call it *ubuntu* – no amount of distance or even death can separate two beings when they are linked by *ubuntu*.'

Kinni rushed out the kitchen door before anyone could say anything further. She ran like lightening to the house of horrors, which had now been eradicated of its human vermin, if not the rodents. This time she could go through the door and ran immediately to the old clock that stood in the hallway. She searched madly for the signs of a hole as she pushed the clock to one side. While she did this, she kept calling out to Wibari.

Hyad and the others froze at the loud sound of the human voice.

'Kinni has come to save us!' called out Wibari.

Frightened, Hyad and the others looked at her with bewildered eyes. They could not believe any human could bring good fortune.

'Wait here, Hyad, while I go to my friend. Just wait and don't stop me this time.' She hopped up to the entrance and gave out a loud grunt.

Kinni's warm arms immediately greeted her. She snuggled close to her friend and they both cried, as they were so happy to see each other. To the surprise of both, they found themselves talking to each other. They could understand each other at last – not by words, but by feelings.

104 The trade in body parts

Then Wibari came rushing through the door calling out, 'We are free! We are free! Come on, let's go and get the others!'

Hyad, Dassy and Nyin and the others did not quite know what to do other than just follow Wibari. They came out and found a human staring down at them with a smile on her face. Wibari hopped ahead and led Kinni and the others down the stairs to the basement where Sussi, the matronly rat who was guarding the hyraxes, was handing out the grain. She squealed in horror to see this unknown human. She ran for her life, as she was sure the human would want to kill her.

Sussi ran as fast as she could, but not to tell the other rats. Instead, she ran in a different direction, for Sussi hated seeing the hyraxes abused – she had not had a choice. This sighting of the human had given her something she didn't expect: the courage to run! So she fled so she could get as far away from this foul place as possible.

All Kinni was interested in was rescuing the hyraxes. She didn't care where Sussi went. It was at that point that she realized she had not made a proper plan for the transportation of the hyraxes out of this basement. Both Wibari and Hyad also realized that the lack of planning could endanger all of them.

'I had no idea there were so many of you', she said to Wibari. 'I will need some sort of cart to get you all away at one time. I shall ask the master and Saliou for help.'

'Let me run and get one. Just wait here – I know Saliou will help me with the wagon', Kinni said as she began to move towards the lane.

'Then I can take you down to the port and...' Suddenly she stopped in mid-sentence.

'Well, I suppose you could get on a ship? Oh dear, what are we going to do?' said Kinni with a bewildered look on her face.

Wibari was not going to let a little detail like having nowhere to go get in her way, so she told Kinni to get the wagon before they decided what to do next. Kinni ran off, and Wibari noticed the Three Amigos watching. Their faces dropped in horror.

'Don't worry, she is just going to get the wagon to take us away', she smiled.

'Away – away where?' asked Dassy suspiciously.

'To the ship', said Wibari confidently.

'So have you booked passage for us as well?' asked Dassy sarcastically.

Wibari knew she was cornered, and called on her grandmother for help. It then came into her mind that they didn't have any other solution either.

'Well, have you got a better plan?' asked Wibari defiantly.

They all fell silent, and watched Wibari climb up onto the windowsill to watch for Kinni's return.

As Kinni entered the kitchen, she ran straight into Dr Hart.

Wind Watchers' tale: Wibari and the Rogue Protectors   105

'What is the matter? Are you being chased by a Jinn?' he said jovially.

'No, Master; it is my friends the hyraxes, I must save them, Master, before the rats come back to get them. Master, can I ask Saliou to take the wagon and take them to the dock or some place of safety?'

'Don't worry about that, Kinni, just go and get them. Malloy and I will work on a plan. We seem to have become quite a team of late. We might be able to get them on a ship yet', he said to Malloy.

Kinni dashed out the door and saw that Saliou was already up in the wagon and ready to go. She quickly climbed up, Saliou cracked the whip and they were away.

'Here she comes!' called out Wibari excitedly.

'What?' said Dassy in disbelief.

'Don't worry, I will check', said Hyad as he jumped to the windowsill and sat beside Wibari.

'She's telling the truth. The human is taking the wagon around to the side of the building. Start moving everyone over that way', he commanded.

At that moment, Wibari swung around and found her face close to Hyad's – so close that they could touch noses. Hyad knew deep in his heart that this actually was the worst time, but also the only time, he would have to get close to the hyrax he loved. His instincts were telling him this would be his chance to reveal his feelings. So he put his paw on hers and she stopped and looked into his big black eyes – well, the good one anyway! She smiled and leant forward, letting her nose touch his. Both could feel the electrical charge pulse through them as it had the first day they met.

The door swung open and Kinni quickly guided the hyraxes up into the wagon. It wasn't long before they were all in the wagon and Saliou was back up at the reins. Wibari sat up in the front with Kinni. She then turned to look for Hyad, who was way down the back keeping guard for any signs of the arrival of the rats. And sure enough he saw the rats looking at them from the windowsill. There was King Rat, standing defiantly watching them escape, a defiance that indicated the game was not over yet. He could feel fear and death in the pit of his stomach as he looked at the figure framed in the window.

The wagon bumped and bounced along at a great speed and some of the little hyraxes nearly bumped straight out over the side. Luckily they had big paws and so the older ones were able to hold them down. Hyad laughed at this sight as he looked up at Wibari, who was also smiling.

It wasn't long before they reached the dock. Kinni called out to the hyraxes that they had reached safety, but of course only Wibari could understand her. She therefore turned to the group and told them they were now safe. The wagon came to a stop and two men and a woman came over and looked into the wagon. The hyraxes looked up in fear. Kinni indicated that perhaps the humans should step back a bit in case the

106 The trade in body parts

hyraxes were scared of humans, or until they felt safe with the humans around them.

Chapter 19: the ship

'Well, Kinni, you are in luck', said Dr Hart as he moved away from the side of the wagon. 'There is a ship leaving tonight and it is headed for Siinegana. I told them I have an important shipload of special animals I want to cross-breed back in Siinegana. I told them it was an experiment that was funded by the government and that the hyraxes could be bred to help rid us of the rat problem. After all, the hyraxes are larger animals and are carnivorous – well, maybe not carnivorous, but who's to know they only eat twigs and plants?' laughed Hart. Kinni thought it best not to tell Wibari what Dr Hart was saying.

'Also, Kinni, I have told them that I am sending three of my best slaves to accompany them back to Siinegana. Those slaves are you, Khmet and Saliou. I will miss you all very much and I will especially miss you, Kinni', he said with a tender look in his eyes that shocked Kinni. 'I would send the little boy, but he is far too sick to return. Instead, I will care for him and when he is well enough I shall travel with him to Siinegana to check on my new species', laughed Hart.

'I will count the days, Master', said Kinni humbly.

'By the time we meet again, I will no longer be your Master, but I hope your friend', said Hart in a low voice. Kinni smiled and nodded her head as her heart skipped a beat.

Kinni then turned to Wibari and yelled 'Wibari, there is a ship, yes a ship to take us all back home!'

Wibari explained what was happening and all the hyraxes began hopping around, including Hyad who had jumped up to be with Wibari. They both looked into each other's eyes and thought of a happy future back in the rocks and hills of Siinegana.

'But you must hurry!' said Hart. 'The ship leaves on the evening tide. I will give you money to pay for your passage. Also, Malloy has put food and supplies in a trunk for you. He has also bought many bags of grain for the hyraxes. Khmet is gathering your things and will be here shortly with Saliou.'

The time flashed past in an instant for both the lovers and the slaves. They were all moving along the road to the port before they knew it. Wibari was now in the back huddled next to Hyad. She loved being pushed up against him: he was so strong and his body so firm. She felt so secure and loved. Hyad couldn't think of anything else than the beautiful furry bundle beside him. His heart was thumping so loud he was sure everyone could hear it. They were free at last!

Chapter 20: the final battle

As the wagon came to a halt, suddenly all the love drained out of Wibari's and Hyad's hearts and instead they could feel death running through their veins. They both looked at each other. The look was that of a last long look into the eyes of the beloved.

'No!' cried Wibari, but before Hyad could answer, out of nowhere hundreds of rats invaded the port. Their snarling teeth – sharp as swords, ready to rip all and sundry apart. They were everywhere! The older hyrax jumped to the challenge and locked together as a shield around the younger ones who were being shepherded onto the gangplank by Wibari, Kinni, and Khmet, while Saliou, Hart, and Malloy helped the hyraxes fight off the rats.

The fight was a bloody mess with heads and body parts flying through the air. Heads rolled as the rats attacked. Humans bled as the rats bit at their hands but their long leather boots saved most of their legs. The screeching and yelling sent many of the sailors back up onto the ship from where they watched the battle unfold.

They knew the lore of the sea and that the rats are part of that lore. They had to live with rats as they sailed the high seas and they were not going to do anything that would incur the wrath of the rats. And so, outnumbered, the good doctor and his stoic friends suffered the torment of the rats as they bit into them and likewise the humans smashed the rats with every weapon they could muster.

Kinni made an attempt to go back and help the men, but Khmet pulled her back and said, 'We have to look after the future, Kinni. That's what women are about, the future. It is the men who must protect the present. Women protect the future generations.' Kinni then turned to find Wibari.

As soon as Wibari hit the deck she raced to the upper deck so she could watch the battle. She could just make out Hyad in the filthy melee. Wibari could not take her eyes off the battle even when Kinni came running over to her to watch the horror before them.

The slaughter was devastating as the hyraxes reclaimed their strength – a strength born of slavery. They took to the rats with every fibre of their tough little bodies. Gnawing teeth ripped into any part of an opponent's body, claws scratched, hind legs kicked the rats with their larger bodies. There were more rats than hyraxes, but the hyraxes were bigger. And now the hyraxes were free, they no longer had any fear and so became a formidable force against the rats. The casualties were great on both sides.

Hart, Saliou and Malloy were doing their best by swinging planks at the rats, crushing them under their boots and picking them up by their tails and dashing them to pieces on anything hard nearby. It was not easy, as with all the blood it was hard sometimes to tell who was a rat and who was a hyrax.

Just as Kinni reached her, Wibari saw King Rat had wrestled Hyad to the ground. His great teeth wrenched into Hyad's throat and ripped until he tore Hyad's head off. Then King Rat flicked Hyad's severed head up into the air. It spun with the force over the side of the dock and down towards the water. Wibari screamed a deathly scream and collapsed into Kinni's arms. Her spirit immediately left her body. Kinni was stunned at the sudden limpness of her little friend.

'Is she dead?' screamed Kinni. At that very moment, the body that lay in her hands shape-shifted into a raven and flew up into the air. The raven flew directly to the rolling head of Hyad, which by now had hit the water. The raven dived into the water and caught hold of the head just as it was about to sink. It then flew high into the air and turned and flew back to the ship and settled on a lookout on top of the mast.

King Rat had already returned to the battle with vigour and the taste of Hyad's blood in his mouth. He now felt he could kill even a human. He therefore did not see the rescue of Hyad's head by the raven. Had he seen it, he would have known that Hyad was not dead but transformed into something even more powerful.

Instead, as King Rat licked the blood off his lips, he was viciously attacked by his arch enemy, Idi. Idi was on top of one of the wagon wheels, and had spotted King Rat standing below. He pounced on King Rat and grabbed him around the neck. Idi killed King Rat in the very same way that the King had killed Hyad. But this time there was no raven to salvage his head. It just sank to the bottom of the filthy river. Nor was there anyone to care if Idi died, for just as he was licking his lips, Malloy slammed him up against the side of the wagon. Malloy was swinging his plank at every rat that moved. He had no idea that he had just killed one of the major players in the hyrax slave trade. The battle continued until all were exhausted. The few rats that were left ran for their lives once they could see the hyraxes were winning.

'All aboard!' called out the captain of the ship. This sent a panic through everyone. Kinni called out to Hart, who was now leaning against the wagon and trying to steady himself as he knew he would soon collapse from the pain.

'Saliou, come quickly', yelled Khmet as she desperately waved her hand at him. Saliou looked up from his bleeding legs and tried to run. Khmet could see he would not make it, so she ran down the gangplank to him. He then put his arm around her shoulders and staggered to the gang-plank and then safely up onto the deck. The gangplank was drawn up and slammed shut. The ship then began to drift slowly out into the river and onto the great ocean. Kinni watched from the ship as the constables reached the doctors and helped them to a waiting wagon.

The two doctors were never the same again. Hart became more active in the emancipation of slaves, and eventually travelled to Siinegana and, to everyone's surprise, he stayed and married Kinni. Malloy married his fiancée, Elizabeth, who to his surprise wanted to bring little Joshua up as their adopted son – especially after the great battle, for she saw an enormous change in Malloy. No longer was he the aspiring shallow young man she had first met, but had become a man of substance. Malloy no longer needed society's approval; he now knew where respectability came from – the soul.

The remains of Dassy, Nyin and the others would never be found, for they became part of the mash of broken bones and streaming blood that seeped into the river below. The river of death eventually claimed all the lost souls of the rats. And so ended the slave trade, as both the King's and the would-be King's carcasses floated down the river and out into the sea, untouched and repellent to any scavenger of the sea – crab, prawn or fish.

Kinni watched day and night as the silent raven kept guard over the head. Seagulls and sea eagles tried to peck at it, but the raven fiercely fought off any intruders. The raven stayed on guard until the end of the voyage back to Siinegana. Hyad's soul was now safe, safe in the protection of his beloved – for this was a sacred head, a head of a Protector who would be remembered by the Wind Watchers for centuries to come. And the raven, well it went down in the storylines as the totem of the shape-shifter, the supreme Wind Watcher.

Chapter 21: home at last

Kinni's ship made shore in record time, for the winds were with them all the way to Siinegana, and not a moment went by that the wind did not fill the sails. As Kinni lay back watching the raven, she slowly died in her own way: she shape-shifted from a slave to a formidable Wind Watcher. She did not need any training, for the battle and the death of Wibari had opened a portal in her mind and allowed all the knowledge she needed to flow through. However, the loss of her brave friend left a hole in her heart that only the Great Song could fill. And to the Great Song was added a new song: the song of the raven and the brave hyraxes. And so this story comes to an end, until it is time to begin again.

Chapter 13

A poem

An ode to the children of Guatemala

They came in search of blood,
those vampires of the night,
dressed in uniforms which sparkled in the light,
covering their dirty deeds full of ghastly intent.
Children their target,
full of flesh and blood.
Ready for the profit margins of the West,
these little ones born in worlds of so much less.
Drained of life, blood and human rights.
Open to the market of the biotech,
Making governments rich in sales
of their blood and body parts.
Military aid said to protect,
but in reality only there to ensure the protection
of the countries that invest.
For it is not only the children who suffer
but the nations that cannot hold up their heads,
unless with the support of a gun up their arse.
For the children die but come again
and again and again.
And as their numbers increase they spill into the lands
that invest and search out their blood
and body parts long lost.
For no matter how many lifetimes it takes,
they will return and take back what is their right
from birth.

Chapter 14

Modern cannibalism
The trade in human body parts

(Dear Reader: remember that the following is purely to stimulate your own thoughts, not to win you over.)

Body parts afloat

Five human feet have washed up on the island coastline around Vancouver since August last year, including two in the last four weeks. All but the one on Westham Island have been right feet; all but one appear to have been male and all have been wearing trainers – Reeboks, Nikes and Adidas. The first four were all size 12.[1]

Since 2007 [until 2012], nine disembodied feet, most still inside sneakers, have washed up off the coasts of British Columbia and Washington state, sparking an international guessing game over their ghoulish origins.[2]

Sixteen of these detached human feet have been found since 2007 (–2016) in British Columbia, Canada, and Washington state. Most of these have been right feet. All of them have worn running shoes or hiking boots.[3]

But what is this that floats so insidiously into the glorious Salish Sea and beyond? Disembodied feet afloat, ready to run in their famous sprints; Nike and other such splendid names branded on their soggy shoes. Still surfacing in 2016. Suspicious in their number and size to boot! Flotsam expert Curtis Ebbesmeyer scratches his head as he dismisses the cluster myth:

'The big picture is that there are body parts washing up all over the place all the time', said Curtis Ebbesmeyer, a retired oceanographer-turned-beachcomber who is writing a book about flotsam and jetsam to be published next year titled *The Floating World*. But this, he admits, is different. 'I've never come across a time when we've had five of one kind at one time. It's highly unusual.'

The police see it as a mere coincidence, but former Toronto police detective Mark Mendelson says there are just too many for it to be a coincidence. He said:

> You have to ask yourself: why is this only happening on the West Coast? Why aren't these body parts floating up in Nova Scotia, or St John's or off the coast of New Jersey? Something is very, very strange here.[4]

What is it that makes for human body-part news that culminates in the land of Lotus-eaters, an affectionate name used by the Nation to describe Vancouverites?[5] Is there a larger story of body parts afloat? Is it a story of lawful behaviour of the ritual of death with all parts intact? And what does this story tell us about the predatory behaviour of the North upon the South? Finally, who will be the heroes and heroines in this chapter?

A killer on the loose

The Canadian newspapers tell us that the arrival of these runaway runners began in 2007 and has continued ever since: a foot here, a foot there. And, as though enthralled with all the missing parts, killer Magnotta of Montreal engages in a copycat act at the height of the foot-inspired hysteria in 2012 by sending body parts of hands and feet in the mail to the Canadian Conservative Party and later to two schools in Vancouver.[6]

Perhaps Magnotta saw no ill in his bizarre deeds – after all, school children were being bussed into the city to languish in the Body World's exhibition of the recently dead and enact a voyeuristic delight in seeing bodies flayed of their skins and plasticized to keep them fresh. All in the name of education.

And can this be the clue to the arrival of the feet? Were they aware that other parts were on display and lost also from both their bodies and their dignity? Did they float down in solidarity?

Body worlds

Just like our forebears of the past, who enjoyed the freak shows that displayed biological rarities, the German Body World company has been capitalizing on the inherent curiosity of society, and has been exhibiting in cities such as Toronto, Montreal, Vancouver and Edmonton for years – all thanks to the 'generosity of body donors' who have insisted upon their cadavers being included in such displays.[7]

A winning exhibition by all accounts, Body World advertises a close-up look at 200 skeletal, muscular, nervous, respiratory and digestive systems – all for the price of just $17.00.[8] Knowing that such exhibitions were delighting the young and old, might we then ask whether the floating body parts might be arriving to warn the local Lotus-eaters that it is time they opened their eyes and questioned displays of human bodies devoid of skin?

Do they really need a skinned cadaver to show them the workings of the human body? Having taken on the role of the surgeon, can the viewer – and especially the young – now say they are informed about the workings of the human body, and so the world around them is enriched by their newly acquired knowledge?

Or does it encourage a Magnotta-like disregard for the human body and the sacrality of its parts, and encourage in our youth an expectation that some bodies are meant for sacrifice to satisfy the needs of others? After all, if you want to exploit something in the market, isn't it the trick to turn it into entertainment for the children and so normalize the questionable in the future?

The Lotus-eaters

Let us now move from entertainment to mythology for a deeper understanding of what is afoot in the land of the Lotus-eaters. We find mention of the Lotus-eaters in the ancient Greek classic *The Odyssey* – Homer's tale of the adventures of the Greek hero *Ulysses* and his men upon their ship, afloat in a distant time and place. As they venture around the world unknown, and meet strange creatures, they are struck down by a storm. Men fall overboard and are lost to the sea, their surviving comrades heartbroken until they come upon the land of the Lotus-eaters. It is a welcoming land for the men to ease their minds of their distress – that is, until Ulysses realizes that this state of bliss can permanently disable men of brave intent. And so they quickly depart before the men succumb to an opium-like state.

However, for our modern day Lotus-eaters, the luxury of doing nothing, or just dismissing the floating feet as a coincidence – even though the feet continue to float down the coast – is strong in the Canadian psyche, as we saw in the earlier example of the plight of Native women – murdered and missing, with people not willing to be fully conscious of what goes on in the deep, dark woods. However, this discourse is not a continuation of that former chapter on Canada; rather, it is a starting point, for Canada – like many Western countries – finds itself unintentionally caught up in the illegal trade in human organs, which includes skin, teeth and eyeballs. It is a trade that also encompasses the legal trade in organs, which if legal academic Michelle Goodwin has her way in relation to inheritance rights (which will be dealt with later in the chapter), will see the whole human body kept on ice, ready to be sliced into saleable parts on the open market and put up for auction by the children of the dearly departed, happily claiming their dues from their inheritance. The following, therefore, covers these issues, which will make some uncomfortable and others angry; yet we must all have a say and show our biases, as this is a story of our future – a story with lessons that have not been learnt from a slave past that has just shape-shifted into Afro-American poverty and high incarceration rates as African-American neuroscientist Carl Hart argues so passionately in his book *High Price*.[9]

Neo-cannibalism

So let's get down to some of the facts – particularly the grizzly reality of our poor brothers and sisters in the nations that have become the killing fields of Eastern Europe,[10] from which these body parts are swept up – including the soft tissue used to plump up the faces of the citizens who hunger after such offerings. University of California anthropologist Nancy Scheper-Hughes, illegal organ trade sleuth par excellence, rightly calls it neo-cannibalism of the wealthy feeding off the poor – a transnational violence of self-righteousness that is bio-ethically endorsed by those who profit from such inequalities in the medical markets.[11] Pharmaceutical companies have found a nice little earner from the anti-rejection drugs used for a lifetime that go with any kind of transplant, which the body vehemently rejects, as though trying to tell us, 'Just because you can do it, it doesn't make it right!'[12]

The folk heroine title of 'Organ Detective'[13] was coined by journalist Ethan Watters when he interviewed Scheper-Hughes about her career spent uncovering the trade in human flesh:

> When she first heard about the organ thieves, the anthropologist Nancy Scheper-Hughes was doing fieldwork in north-eastern Brazil. It was 1987, and a rumor circulating around the shantytown of Alto do Cruzeiro, overlooking the town of Timbaúba, in a sugarcane farming region of Pernambuco, told of foreigners who travelled the dirt roads in yellow vans, looking for unattended children to snatch up and kill for their transplantable organs. Later, it was said, the children's bodies would turn up in roadside ditches or in hospital dumpsters.[14]

Post-modern human sacrifice

As Scheper-Hughes points out, 'Global capitalism and advanced biotechnology have together released new medically incited "tastes" for human bodies, living and dead, for the skin and bones, flesh and blood, tissue, marrow, and genetic material of "the other".' She calls organ and tissue transplants a 'post-modern form of human sacrifice', and accuses transplant surgeons of conspiring to invent an 'artificially created need ... for an ever-expanding sick, aging, and dying population'.[15]

Just as abolitionists fought hard to convince their slave-trading and slave-owning compatriots that human beings existed within those dark skins, so too Scheper-Hughes reminds us that the shameful trade in human body parts brings us a repetition of the horrendous past of slavery – but this time the bodies are divided into saleable parts. This, then, is the essential element of this argument, for the 'business as usual' in the slavery trade now known as human body part or organ trafficking is every bit as lucrative as it was in the past. This moral delinquency is still in plain sight, with the public as complicit as ever. In the past, the trade in slaves was for essential economic reasons to build nations; now the trade in body parts is to keep the citizens alive – but of course the rich first and the poor last.

Death dismissed

Unwilling in their ignorance (or is it immaturity?) to accept that impending death is a natural part of being a human being, wealthy patients from the global North are turning surgeons into demi-gods, aided or forced by technology and a proudly amoral law to do as the profiteers see fit. For indeed there are large sums of money to be made in this lucrative industry – just as long as there is healthy supply of body parts from the global South. How ironic it is that, in the global South in general, the dead are honoured in great festivals, such as Mexico's Dia de los Muertos (Day of the Dead), intended to honour the dead and to remind the living that they too are mere mortals, while in the global North death is something that is avoided at all costs. Those costs begin with products and technologies to keep the body young and beautiful, to avoid facing the truth of ageing as the beginning of the journey towards the ultimate rite of passage: death. The acceptance of death is an important lesson, and mark of maturity.

Children of the South

But why is it that I care about and write such a gruesome tale of rats and body parts? This trade found its way into my life many years ago when I was approached by a group of Guatemalan musicians who thought that, as I was interviewing them for an Australian Radio National programme on the Mayan people and their music, I might also be able to speak about the theft of the organs of young children by those pretending to be the US Army Blood Bank sent to help the children.

Unfortunately, I was no Charles Bowden – the author of *Murder City: Ciudad Juarez and the Global Economy's New Killing Fields*.[16] Bowden was an investigative reporter who wrote so eloquently about the manifest evil in Ciudad Juarez brought on by the exploitive nature of the American corporations in northern Mexico. He was hailed a hero for even going over the

116 The trade in body parts

border into this 'Murder City' and reporting on the uselessness of the 'War on Drugs' funded by US citizens' tax dollars, when drugs were in fact one of the commodities that kept the Mexican economy afloat. Bowden writes:

> There is no serious War on Drugs ... Rather, there is violence, nourished by the money to be made from drugs. And there are US industries whose primary lifeblood comes from fighting a war on drugs.[17]

Bowden ventured down into the pits of despair to report on the drug trade and its impact on the locals, with all the bodies sacrificed to keep the American drug runners in cocaine and champagne. But, as Bowden states in *Democracy Now*,[18] he was a coward compared with the bravery of his fellow Mexican journalists who reported on the slain, left to rot in the streets of the US industrial town of Cidual Juaraz. Bowden was seen by his fellow Americans as incredibly brave to report on the drug lords and the trade, let alone walk the streets strewn with murdered bodies. Not surprisingly, Bowden dressed like a cowboy, as though it were the old Wild West revisited. You would need to have imbued some kind of mythological essence to be able to report such atrocities caused by your own society, let alone know that you could depart on the next plane while your fellow Mexican journalists had no escape and so knew that one day soon their number would be up.

This predatory world, is powerfully portrayed in the film *Inhale*,[19] set in Ciudad Juarez, in which a young Mexican urchin is kept 'on tap' as his body is a genetic match for a whiskey-drinking drug lord. And, just as Bowden wishes his fellow American citizens to take account of the plight of their neighbours over the border, so too the film brings to the forefront the way some Americans cannot believe that they must face the same fate that they expect the lesser nations of the world to endure on a daily basis. It is alright for the inhabitants of the global South to die an untimely death, but not a wealthy American child for whom money should be able to buy life.

The main protagonist in the film, who is the father of the dying child, must come to terms with his right to claim the bodies of other nations and therefore, like the abolitionists, question his rights over other human beings' bodies. In the end, he takes the morally mature road and realizes he must not take another life to save that of his own child. His wife rejects his moral stance and indulges in bitter resentment. But this wife is not the exception, for a blind eye is turned towards many a trade worldwide – for example, the trade in Chinese prisoners executed and then skinned like beasts:

> A Chinese cosmetics company is using skin harvested from the corpses of executed convicts to develop beauty products for sale in Europe, an investigation by *The Guardian* has discovered.[20]

The skins are sent into the lucrative trade of beauty products, for which wealthy women and men pay unbelievable prices in the hope of avoiding the signs of ageing and approaching death. Is this not cannibalism in another form?

Cannibalizing the law

My hypothesis is, therefore, that if a society indulges in unlawful behaviour and tries to avoid death, rather than following lawful behaviour and preparing and embracing the rites of passage of death, it will – as Scheper-Hughes quite rightly terms it – turn cannibal and go in search of bodies, both dead and alive, to sustain its avoidance of death. For in these cannibalistic societies, youthfulness is aligned with wealth and power. Many an ancient sorcerer and priest were well acquainted with this human weakness.

Muti killings

The African *muti* killings are also the domain of the devilish hunters who pursue young children for their body parts, all in the name of keeping their elders alive. The following was reported in 2011 after a 10-year search for the killers.

> Will O'Reilly, a former detective inspector who led the original Scotland Yard investigation, told the programme that police had searched Osiagede's flat in Scotland and found clothing from the same company and the same size as worn by the boy.
> The boy's headless, limbless body was found in the river near Tower Bridge on 21 September, 2001.[21]

My close association with my friends in Senegal and other African nations brought to me the heart-wrenching stories of *muti* killings, a practice of taking the body parts of young children to bring about 'powers' to enrich the buyer of the particular part. This practice reached right up into the United Kingdom, where it was reported that the torso of a young child was found floating down the Thames. Reporter Christopher Szabo goes on to make the following assessment:

> Simon Fellows, author of the survey results report, titled *Trafficking Body Parts in Mozambique and South Africa*, said: 'There is a clear link between *muti* and business. With the World Cup approaching, people we surveyed believe more people will be killed and their body parts used in *muti* that is bought to ensure business's prosperity.'[22]

This practice has the side effect of defaming traditional healers and the benefits they bring to many a poverty-stricken person across the African continent.

But let me add another group of people who I would call into question, and who I am sure would be seen by traditional healers as nothing less than witchdoctors: the researchers who mix embryos of both humans and animals. These scientists who see themselves at the forefront of science lack the maturity to understand the long-term effects of their actions on the standing of the human body.

> Embryos containing human and animal material have been created in Britain for the first time, a month before the House of Commons votes on new laws to regulate the research.
>
> A team at Newcastle University announced yesterday that it had successfully generated 'admixed embryos' by adding human DNA to empty cow eggs in the first experiment of its kind in Britain.[23]

The Robin Hoods

It is therefore no wonder the reporting of organ theft by an Israeli doctor caused an uproar:

> In August Sweden's largest newspaper published an article suggesting that Israel had been taking Palestinian internal organs. The article, by veteran photojournalist Donald Bostrom, called for an international investigation.
>
> Israel and its partisans immediately cried 'anti-Semitism', and *Commentary*'s Jonathan Tobin asserted that the story was 'the tip of the iceberg in terms of European funded and promoted anti-Israel hate'.
>
> The fact is, however, that Israeli organ harvesting – sometimes with Israeli governmental funding and the participation of high Israeli officials, prominent Israeli physicians, and Israeli government ministries – has been documented for many years. Among the victims have been Palestinians.[24]

Scheper-Hughes, co-founder of Organs Watch at the University of California, Berkeley, found in her research that the Israeli doctor Hiss saw himself and his colleague, Dr Kugel, as 'above the law, as representing the law at a much higher law, his law, supremely cool, rational, and scientifically and technically correct'.[25] The country was at war, blood was being spilled every day, soldiers were being burned, yet Israelis refused to provide the tissues and organs needed. So he decided to take matters into his own hands and sought bodies of 'the other'.[26] He saw himself as a saviour, stealing body parts to heal the wounds of Israeli soldiers.

There are two frightening aspects to this story. The first is the lack of citizen response to calls for the donations of organs and skin; the second is the use of the bodies of the enemy. Why bother vilifying 'the other' if you are going to incorporate them into your own bodies? But instead what we find is that questioning such activities leads to anti-Semitic debate rather than focusing on the issue. The anti-Semitism debate assumes that every Jew on the planet is the same, rather than that one Israeli citizen must be made accountable for his actions and that it is no reflection on the rest of his nation, let alone his heritage.

'Organ-importing countries'

In her ground-breaking book *Commodifying Bodies* (2003),[27] Nancy Scheper-Hughes says:

> Increasingly the body is a possession that does not belong to us. It is bought and sold, bartered and stolen, marketed wholesale or in parts. The professions – especially reproductive medicine, transplant surgery, and bioethics but also journalism and other cultural specialists – have been compliant partners in this accelerating commodification of live and dead human organisms. Under the guise of healing or research, they have contributed to a new 'ethic of parts' for which the divisible body is severed from the self, torn from the social fabric, and thrust into commercial transactions – as organs, secretions, reproductive capacities, and tissues – responding to the dictates of an incipiently global marketplace.

Scheper-Hughes is passionate about the wrongs of such vanities, willing to investigate and trail the ungodly, as her work reveals. She is hot on the trail of the 'organ-importing countries' – Australia, Canada, Israel, Japan, Oman, Saudi Arabia and the United States.[28] Those great nations flaunt their human rights regimes as signs of their civilized superiority, but at the same time are complicit in keeping their Native peoples and minorities in poverty-stricken enclaves, trying desperately to disconnect them from their land in an attempt to turn all and sundry into property, as Ed Cohen argues in his book *A Body Worth Defending*.[29] Our deep connection to the environment manifests as the disconnection of the body as sacred. It has become a game of words, sanitized by what basically is body snatching of the highest order in pursuit of the vanities; they are viewed as greater than their god, whom they all so constitutionally acknowledge. My book review of his work was an honour to undertake, as it supported many of my own observations of this trade:

> *A Body Worth Defending* has much to offer the diligent reader, who is interested in tracing modernity's genealogy and its shape-shifting over

time in its understanding of the nature of the human and its present manifestation as a biological phenomenon separated and distinct from the environment. A separation which has come to dictate not only how we care for the ill and our system of healing but more insidiously our entire political and economic relations. Ed Cohen offers a provocative and demanding account of what he calls the 'back story' of the apotheosis of the modern body through the thought-provoking trajectory of immunity as an unquestioned metaphor which unreflectively incorporates juridico-political assumptions. This unquestioning, he argues, has led to a disconnect between the body and its environment and the de-legitimizing of other ways of seeing humanness and the models of care and treatment. This argument is tantalizing for those who may wonder why the 'individual' has become inordinately central to the thinking of the West. As though the individual is a bundle of rights floating 'discretely' above the planet neither connected to nor responsible for that which pours forth from such thinking. Furthermore, it empowers advocates in poverty stricken domains with a substantive argument as to why the 'drugs into the body' type campaigns appear to suffer from the blindness of the poverty and conditions which bring about the disease in the first place. Cohen's book therefore can be recommended to be of use beyond the Anglo first world borders of the predominant neoliberal world, to that of those who depend on aid from wealthy nations.[30]

Organ transplant tourism

Let us return to Nigeria, a nation perhaps seen to be trying to civilize the witchdoctor and make their practice respectable in the new form of medical tourism. As Babatunde Salako, Professor of Medicine at the University of Ibadan, pointed out when speaking on the subject of 'Ethics and Legal Issues in Organ Procurement and Sale of Human parts' at his university:

> Transplantation tourism has the potential of leading to abuse of human rights or in fact exploiting the poor. It may lead to unintended health consequences, provide unequal access to services and may ultimately cause harm either to the donor or the recipient.[31]

And so it becomes tourism – in other words, normalized into a kind of lifestyle choice for the citizens of the 1 per cent of countries wealthy enough to prey on the rest.

Does this not remind us of the heady days of slavery when it was normal to own slaves? When the ownership of another's body was normal? The desire to do as you wish with that body was also a God-given right to the point where medical science in America depended on the use of the bodies of the slave, the Native and the Irish – all devoid of rights before the law.

In his book *Ebony & Ivy: Race, Slavery, and the Troubled History of America's Universities*,[32] MIT African-American academic Craig S. Wilder tells us the gruesome tale of how the bodies of slaves were boiled down to be used in the burgeoning medical sciences, a practice that Wilder suggests began around 1760. Medical science, he informs us, was finding its feet in the university curriculum thanks to the fact that those not protected by the law represented a steady stream of bodies.

The making of a folk heroine

But there is more to contemplate, for this issue did not knock upon my door to tell me of such inequality between nations; rather, it conveyed something more about empathy and the rise of a folk hero. For it would seem that even the academic can become a folk hero once they challenge their disciplinary constraints. Scheper-Hughes found that she had to cross the boundaries of her anthropologic pledge and get down and dirty to turn into an Organ Detective:

> She subscribed to an academic school of thought that swore off imposing Western notions of absolute or objective truth. As much as she wanted to show solidarity with the beliefs of her sources, she struggled with how to present the rumors in her 1992 book, *Death Without Weeping: The Violence of Everyday Life in Brazil*.
>
> In the end, she argued that the organ stealing stories could only be understood in light of all the bodily threats faced by this impoverished population. In addition to pervasive hunger and thirst, the locals also faced mistreatment at the hands of employers, the military, and law enforcement. The medical care available, she suggested, often did more harm than good. Local health care workers and pharmacists gave the malnourished and chronically ill locals the catchall diagnosis of *nervos* and prescribed tranquilizers, sleeping pills, vitamins, and elixirs. The locals were well aware that wealthier people in their country and abroad had access to better medical care – including exotic procedures like tissue and organ transplants.[33]

This behaviour brought scorn down upon her from her colleagues in the 'study of the practices of the illegal organ trade'. They lamented that she had become too involved and should have viewed the whole trade from a distance.[34] But Scheper-Hughes had that essential human characteristic: empathy – an empathy that saw her determined to rid society of the racketeering from which some were profiteering. She also had another essential

122 The trade in body parts

characteristic that, as history shows, drives the empathetic: a tendency to become 'compulsive'. A comparison can be found in the character of Robert F. Kennedy, in his pursuit of the great racketeers of the 1950s – an era that made the gangsters of the Roaring Twenties appear tame. The 1950s and 1960s, which harked back to an era known for its conservatism and the burgeoning of liberalism, were full of unbelievable treachery, and it took a special type of man to make a dent in that level of corruption.

Just like Scheper-Hughes and her relentless drive to 'surgically remove' the organ trade, Kennedy had to carry out surgery on the American legal system, and particularly the powerful Workers Unions. His story is worth revisiting to give the reader a sense of Scheper-Hughes' task in dealing with a sacrosanct body of citizens – in Kennedy's case, Teamster union boss, Jimmy Hoffa:

> On January 31, 1957, the Senate Select Committee on Improper Activities in the Labor or Management Field, better known as the Rackets Committee, was born. Its driving force was chief counsel Robert Kennedy, who led the investigation and a series of public hearings into corruption in the trade union movement. While the Rackets investigations generated more heat than light, they did open the eyes of many Americans to the disturbing relationship between some labor bosses and the Mafia.[35]

What was most amazing was that the regulators who had come before Kennedy in an attempt to clean up their society had failed, while once Kennedy – who Allen Roberts called 'a compulsive politician'[36] – took the reins, in just three short years 1,525 people were brought before the Rackets Committee and over 500 sessions were held.[37]

Bobby Kennedy specialized in outing the racketeering in his beloved America, but of course was eventually gunned down like a character in a 1920s gangster movie:

> The cast of characters Kennedy encountered or brought to the witness stand were straight out of an Edward G. Robinson or James Cagney gangster movie ... There was evil abroad in the land, and it had to be surgically removed. No other course was possible, he felt. 'When there is corruption at the top and a close association with the underworld this kind of power is a threat to every decent person.'[38]

A man of his times in strong relief, this folk hero was murdered. But this audacity is what I see in Scheper-Hughes and Charles Bowden – larger-than-life characters with a strong sense of empathy for the poor and suffering, but knowing that their lives could be wiped out at any moment by a well-aimed bullet. This tells us that cleaning up racketeering requires compulsive personalities who are a match for the racketeers themselves. Now let's listen to the other side of the argument: a tale of cowboy shoot-outs in respectable surgeries and the dirty backstreets of former American boomtowns.

The argument for the sale

I met African-American ethics professor Michelle Goodwin when she was giving a lecture at Griffith University in Brisbane, Australia in 2001. Her work was focused on campaigning on behalf of the homeless people of Chicago, who were being subjected to what I could see in my mind's eye as a scene from the futuristic film *Bladerunner*.[39] I could not but help think Chicago had become a kind of *Bladerunner* world, in which paramedics waited like bio-tech wolves to snatch body parts from the recently dead drug addicts who happened to fall to their deaths on the back streets of Chicago. Goodwin told us that their eyes would be snatched and quickly put on ice for sale on the European market.

Over the years since I first heard this horror story, Goodwin has thought long and hard about the issue. In her article, 'Empires of Flesh: Tissue and Organ Taboo',[40] she introduces us to celebrated dental surgeon Michael Mastromarino, arrested for his part in pillaging 1,800 corpses from a series of funeral homes:

> Mastromarino pleaded guilty to pillaging 1,800 bodies for bones, ligaments, heart valves, organs, and other valuable tissues. After excavating the bodies, the defendants stuffed the corpses with plastic tubing and plumbing piping to deceive the decedents' relatives ... His scheme is believed to have generated more than four million dollars.

Perhaps his mistake was pillaging from a well-known identity, Alistair Cooke of the famed *Letters from America* and the Masterpiece Theatre. As I had spent many a pleasant Saturday afternoon listening to his gossip from the opera and the fine music, I was quite shocked that someone of that calibre could end up in what Goodwin calls 'a human chop-shop'.[41] However, even more galling is the fact that legitimate tissue banks can sell human bodies for up to $250,000 profit.[42]

But what of the legal trade?

It appears that when carried out by legitimate institutions, this trade is still susceptible to tissue being obtained through surreptitious means – that is, through brokers who solicit from dental offices, hospitals, medical schools and coroners' offices as well as funeral homes and morgues. This makes 1.3 million Americans annually susceptible to the effects of diseased body parts, which are then used for everything from dental surgery to knee replacements and, of course, the booming plastic surgery industry, which includes genital enhancements and thickening of lips.[43]

This last category is the most insidious, for it is the cult of the consumer culture that will dictate in the future how this industry will be legislated. As Goodwin points out, with the advancements occurring in technology, we have seen an industry that has developed from primarily serving burns victims to now enjoying a burgeoning growth in plastic and other allograft surgeries, including reproductive resurfacing surgeries.[44]

Goodwin's solution to this trade is to open it up to the individual to either sell their body parts or allow their dependants to sell their deceased bodies. She feels this will have the side benefit of people being more inclined to keep their bodies healthy for their saleability. As she argues:

> Third, incentives will likely promote health outcomes for potential sharers and recipients. Those interested in receiving a payment for sharing tissue and organs will have an incentive to stay healthy during their lives so that their organs will be 'picked' for transnational sale.

Goodwin justifies this argument by saying:

> To the extent that what scholars indicate is a loss of personhood or human dignity, we should acknowledge the difficulty in quantifying that possible result. We would, however, be able to balance the perception of lost dignity against the restoration of health and the restoration of families made whole again through T&O transplantation. Organ and tissue transplantations produce third-party benefits, including restoring family relationships, allowing parents to re-engage in their children's lives, returning dialysis patients to the workforce, and bringing people who were once sick back in full health to their communities.[45]

Milton Friedman would commend Goodwin for her balanced approach. The wonders of technology are remarkable – as long as you can afford them.

Goodwin, however, sees this more in legal activist terms and declares that the rights of the individual should be taken into account, and they should be able to enter the marketplace and sell their own organs and tissue. She argues:

> Incentives are the best solution for increasing the supply of human tissues and organs and decreasing black markets and exploitation. By allowing a market, we remove the incentive to exploit because tissues can be obtained legally for a fee. The suggestion here is not to do

away with altruism but rather to advocate for a new brand of legal realism, one that acknowledges that with a million allograft surgeries taking place each year in the United States, Mastromarino is not a big fish, but rather a small one in an ocean.[46]

Indeed, her argument goes on to address the long waiting lists, and particularly the discrimination experienced by the African Americans on those lists. There does not appear to be any mention of Native Americans, when in fact they are the least healthy group in the country. But perhaps I am biased in thinking that the original inhabitants of the country should have a special place on the list.

And so I end this flow of thoughts and ask whether it is really a matter of supply and demand; instead, should there be deeper thinking as to where this will lead in light of technological advancements that will one day make the trade in illegal body parts a thing of the past – just as some believe slavery is a thing of the past? It does not take away the essential problem – that is, the avoidance of the honouring of death as an important rite of passage not only for the deceased, but also the family.

So let me now turn to a lawful account of a jurisprudence that might lead to a more lawful approach, one that calls for lawful relations. Shaun McVeigh, rather than taking the surgical approach of Kennedy and Scheper-Hughes, takes a slow, lawful approach to dealing with the thorny issue of the repatriation of the Indigenous dead.[47] He carefully crafts an article that reveals the importance of the meeting of laws to carry out lawful relations for the return of the Indigenous dead: 'The narrative of this essay runs from the concern with repatriation, to the conduct of the meeting of laws and on to the forms of responsibility for the conduct of lawful relations.'[48] His thesis, therefore, relates to the lawful passing of the dead from one jurisdiction to another.

This is what bothers me so much about the accounts I have given of my two heroines. There is an awful habit in the Rule of Law of treating even the body as either dead or alive, as though it were property. There is a total lack of 'care or feeling' in those conversations. In turn, this reinforces to me why the land as the source of the law, which patterns us into its ecosystem, also shows us how the land heals us so that we can in the end allow … earth to earth, ashes to ashes, dust to dust…

Notes

1 Glaister, D., 'Whodunnit: Community Baffled by Severed Feet Washed up on Shore', *Guardian*, 21 June 2008. www.guardian.co.uk/world/2008/jun/21/canada, accessed 15 November 2015.

2 Callahan, M., 'Agony of the Feet', *New York Post*, 4 March 2012. http://nypost.com/2012/03/04/agony-of-the-feet, accessed 15 November 2015.

3 Wang, Y., 'Severed Feet – Still Inside Shoes – Keep Mysteriously Washing Up on

Pacific Northwest Shores', *Washington Post*, 11 February 2016. https://www. washingtonpost.com/news/morning-mix/wp/2016/02/11/severed-feet-still-inside-shoes-keep-mysteriously-washing-up-on-pacific-northwest-shores/?tid=pm_national_pop_b, accessed 13 February 2016.

4 CTV News, 'Ex-cop Baffled by Severed Feet Mystery in BC', *CTV News*, 1 September 2011. www.ctvnews.ca/ex-cop-baffled-by-severed-feet-mystery-in-b-c-1. 691469, accessed 10 November 2011.

5 Thomas, A., 'Summer in Vancouver: Land of the Lotus Eaters', *Lonely Planet*, June 2012. https://www.lonelyplanet.com/canada/vancouver/travel-tips-and-articles/70211, accessed 4 April 2016.

6 MacCharles, T., 'Second Body Part Discovered in Ottawa After Severed Foot Sent to Conservative Party Headquarters', *The Star*, 29 May 2012. www.thestar.com/article/1202364–package-sent-to-conservative-party-headquarters-contains-human-foot-report-says, accessed 1 June 2012.

7 Perkel, C., 'Activists Warn *Bodies Revealed* Show May be Using Executed Chinese Inmates', *The Star*, 6 September 2014. www.thestar.com/news/canada/2014/09/06/group_decries_possible_use_of_executed_chinese_prisoners_in_bodies_display.html, accessed 15 November 2015.

8 'Niagara Area Activity Deals', *TravelZoo*, www.travelzoo.com/ca/local-deals/niagara-area/Other/138465, accessed 15 November 2015.

9 Hart, C., *High Price: A Neuroscientist's Journey of Self-Discovery That Challenges Everything You Know About Drugs and Society*, Deckle Edge/Simon and Schuster: New York, 2015.

10 Lundin, S., 'The Valuable Body Organ Trafficking in Eastern Europe', *Baltic Worlds*, 1(1) 2008: 6–9. http://balticworlds.com/the-valuable-body-organ-trafficking-in-eastern-europe, accessed 4 April 2016.

11 Scheper-Hughes, N., 'Parts Unknown: Undercover Ethnography of the Organs-Trafficking Underworld', *Ethnography*, 5(1) (2004): 29–73.

12 'Side Effects of Anti-Rejection Medications for Kidney Transplant', Sutter Health, www.cpmc.org/advanced/kidney/news/newsletter/kidneytransplant_medication_sideeffects.html, accessed 15 November 2015.

13 Watters, E., 'The Organ Detective: A Career Spent Uncovering the Trade in Human Flesh', *Pacific Standard*, 7 July 2014. www.psmag.com/navigation/business-economics/nancy-scheper-hughes-black-market-trade-organ-detective-84351, accessed 15 September 2014.

14 Ibid.

15 Ibid.

16 Bowden, C., *Murder City: Ciudad Juarez and the Global Economy's New Killing Fields*, Nation Books: New York, 2010.

17 Bowden, C., 'The War Next Door', *Democracy Now*, 16 March 2010. www.democracynow.org/2010/3/16/charles_bowden_on_the_war_next, accessed 15 November 2015.

18 Bowden, C. 'Murder City: Ciudad Juárez and the Global Economy's New Killing Fields', *Democracy Now*, 14 April 2010. www.democracynow.org/2010/4/14/charles_bowden_murder_city_ciudad_jurez, accessed 15 November 2015.

19 *Inhale*, dir. Baltasar Kormákur, 2010.

20 Cobain, I. and Luck, I., 'The Beauty Products from the Skin of Executed Chinese Prisoners', *Guardian*, 13 September 2005. www.theguardian.com/science/2005/sep/13/medicineandhealth.china, accessed 4 April 2016.

21 Quinn, B., 'Police Fly to Nigeria Following New Lead in Thames Torso Case', *Guardian*, 29 March 2011. www.theguardian.com/uk/2011/mar/29/police-nigeria-thames-torso-link, accessed 15 November 2015.

22 Szabo, C., 'Human Body Parts Trade Could Increase Before Soccer World Cup', *Digital Journal*, 9 February 2010. www.digitaljournal.com/article/287296#ixzz1Cs6iv7OC, accessed 15 November 2015.

23 Slade, A., *Where to from Here*, Xlibris Corporation, 2011: 54.

24 Weir, A., 'Israeli Organ Harvesting: From Moldova to Palestine', *Washington Report on Middle East Affairs*, November 2009. www.wrmea.org/2009-november/israeli-organ-harvesting-from-moldova-to-palestine.html, accessed 15 November 2015.

25 Scheper-Hughes, N., 'Body Parts and Bio-Piracy', *CounterPunch*, 25 October 2010. www.counterpunch.org/2010/10/25/body-parts-and-bio-piracy, accessed 4 April 2016.

26 Ibid.

27 Scheper-Hughes, N., *Commodifying Bodies*, Sage: Thousand Oaks, CA, 2003.

28 American Transplant Foundation, Vail Symposium Forum on Transplant Tourism, 11 March 2008, www.americantransplantfoundation.org/wp-content/uploads/2010/04/VailSymposiumForumonTransplantTourism-Handout_000.pdf, accessed 15 November 2015.

29 Cohen, E., *A Body Worth Defending: Immunity, Biopolitics, and the Apotheosis of the Modern Body*, Rutgers University Press: New York, 2009: 281.

30 Black, C. F., 'Book Review of E. Cohen, *A Body Worth Defending*', *Leonardo*, 44(1) (2011).

31 'Organ Donation Transplants Need Urgent Attention', *The Tribune*, n.d., www.tribune.com.ng/health-news/item/4318-organ-donation-transplant-need-urgent-attention-fg, accessed 20 August 2011.

32 Wilder, C. S., *Ebony & Ivy: Race, Slavery, and the Troubled History of America's Universities*, Bloomsbury: New York, 2013.

33 Watters, 'The Organ Detective'.

34 Ibid.

35 'People & Events: James R. ("Jimmy") Hoffa (1913–?)', www.pbs.org/wgbh/amex/rfk/peopleevents/p_hoffa.html, accessed 1 February 2015.

36 Roberts, A., *Robert F. Kennedy: Biography of a Compulsive Politician*, Branden Press: Boston, 1984.

37 Roberts, *Robert F. Kennedy*, p. 83.

38 David, L. and David, I., *Bobby Kennedy: The Making of a Folk Hero*, Dodd, Mead and Co: New York, 1986: 83–84.

39 *Blade Runner*, dir. R. Scott, 1982.

40 Goodwin, M., 'Empires of Flesh: Tissue and Organ Taboo', *Alabama Law Review*, 60(5) (2006): 1220.

41 Ibid.

42 Ibid.

43 Ibid.: 1223.

44 Ibid.

45 Ibid.: 1219.

46 Ibid.: 1220–1221.

47 McVeigh, S., 'Law as (More or Less) Itself: On Some Not Very Reflective Elements of Law', *UC Irvine Law Review*, 4 (2014): 473.

48 Ibid.

Part IV

Bioinsecurity

Chapter 15

Some words

This final tale comes from my own homeland of the Yugumbeh language speakers. I reference the language as it covers my many ancestors who have lived for over 50,000 years in the area of South-East Queensland, Australia. Part of that land includes the protected area of Guanaba, a peaceful piece of hilly, hidden bush landscape. Very few people have access to this land, so it has proved to be a place where little potoroos could breed – one of the last colonies in South-East Queensland at the time of writing this book. And just as this tract of wilderness is known to very few people, so too are some of the animals in this story. I wanted to let people from afar be aware of the small animals of Australia that hardly ever get a mention. Little potoroos, hopping mice, numbats, bandicoots and quolls are introduced in the hope that readers will venture to look them up and become acquainted with them. For it is their light touch upon the vast landscape that reminds us of lawful behaviour and how to step upon this land. The issue of biosecurity and the subsequent securitization came to my attention during the time I was writing stories for my grandchildren about these little creatures, due to the outbreak of the Hendra virus in our traditional homelands.

The subsequent chapters give a tale from my homelands but also a jurisprudential reading. I felt more drawn to give a lawful reading as this issue affects the very homelands of my grandfather's country – Munaljahlai country.

Chapter 16

The Wind Watchers' tale
Bringers of the Red Dust

The story of old

The old Clever People had kept watch over the doorway since ancient times. They say that when the Earth was still yawning and making up its mind as to how it wanted to feel, there were two brave dogs that lived in the land now known as Beaudesert. They ran and hunted with the great hunter from the south, then came the day when the old hunter was not paying attention and those dogs got eaten by those lazy boys, and that's when all the bad things began to happen. Little did they know that through their selfish acts they had brought into being the Great Hounds. The gateway had been opened by the wilful act of killing the hunting dogs. The people did not know that the dogs were Law dogs, magic dogs that guarded the gateway. But now it was laid to waste, and through the gateway came the Hounds.

So quiet they were! No one heard the Hounds come through. Nor did they see them slip into that cave. There they waited for the evening dew to refresh the nocturnal brothers and sisters of the land, as they scurried and hopped across the starlit terrain. Unbeknown to them, the Great Hounds were watching them and planning. And as time stretched out and the land settled into its present pattern, the Hounds grew mightier. And as they grew, they gathered the red dust around them until they became so large that their dust storms were a mile high and miles wide. To all the little beings of the land, they became known as the dreaded Bringers of the Red Dust.

A koala's tale

'Big as ponies!' said Colly the koala, as she sat high in the gum tree. 'The red dust is so thick you can barely see. They are known as the Bringers of the Red Dust!' Colly's eyes widened when she said those words. For such words were full of power – destructive power that sent shivers down the spines of all the koalas listening to the genteel Colly.

Up in the high branches of tall gum trees that forested the highlands of Guanaba sat the koalas, listening to Colly recount her tale about the Great Hounds. She and her family had seen them on the outer reaches of the dense scrub where the Aboriginal Dreaming paths crossed. Colly didn't believe her eyes at first, but after Captain Koala saw them and little Pengana took fright and turned into a sparrowhawk to get away, Colly knew they were real.

'Real as you and me', she whispered, as she wasn't sure whether the Hounds could hear her, even way up in the tall gum tree. Colly snuggled down into her little branch, even though her rather large backside hung over the edges. This in turn made the koalas who were listening crane their necks to hear the rest of the tale.

'But Burbi knows better than me where they came from. I've only seen them – and that was enough for me!' she said, as she shivered once more, which made the whole group shiver. The group then turned their heads up to Burbi, Colly's older sister, who was sitting on a high branch.

Burbi then spoke: 'They roamed the lands with no natural predator, but instead they fought amongst themselves and eventually formed two large packs: the Hounds of the North and the Hounds of the West. "The Bringing of the Red Dust" was the ancient way of speaking about them. These Hounds devastated all the land on which they fought, bringing with them disease and destruction, all carried in the great dust clouds. Like tsunami waves of dust surging from an inland sea of ancient times, these ancient beings would drown anyone who got in their way', said Burbi sadly, as her eyes glazed over in horror at what she had seen. For this scene was the future that was coming towards the little community of nocturnal animals that lived in the beautiful valley of Guanaba.

Over the generations, the koalas – and especially those known as the Wind Watchers, like Burbi – kept up a surveillance of the Hounds and their ongoing fights. They telepathically transmitted to other koalas across the land the movements of the Hounds, and so had given everyone time to burrow down, or get out of the way, or disappear in other ways that suited their constitutions. It was actually the larger marsupials like the kangaroos and wombats that suffered the most. Size was against them. The smaller marsupials were most likely to survive. And one of those little tribes was the potoroos of Guanaba – little bundles of grey fluff with long snouts and little paws, which they held out in front of them as they hopped around the undergrowth.

The last of the tribe

Deep in the dense undergrowth of the bushlands of Guanaba, the last potoroo tribe was hiding out for fear of being run down by the Great Hounds of the North. The potoroos had originally been in many places across Australia, but as time went by and the Hounds roamed the land, the little group had been whittled down to just a few dozen potoroos hiding out in Guanaba. Their small numbers had made them susceptible to the koalas' stories, and the thought of their pending death at the whim of the Great Hounds had nearly driven the community mad. They therefore gladly welcomed a small pack of quolls, which were much larger than potoroos and more attractive with their honey-and-white spotted coats and long tails. Their tribe had died of asphyxiation, when the Hounds of the West had run them down.

The chant of Charlie Numbat

But that was just one story that was crossing the land; there was another that was making its mark on the landscape. The bearer of the story was Charlie Numbat. He was an excitable character, especially when he had news. His rich brown eyes would flash and his perky little ears would twitch. His long tail would swish back and forth over his furry back, which had the most striking black and white bands across it. The numbat was a great traveller, and had come far across the land from the ancient west and home of the westerly winds. He travelled the land and gathered news of the humans, bringing it back to the little marsupial communities that dotted the land in silence. Charlie Numbat felt it was his moral duty to snoop out the news and spread it to one and all.

And so Charlie hopped into the little community of marsupials who were living at the base of the great gum trees of Guanaba. Charlie hopped onto a log and called to everyone to listen. The first to come forward were the little fat, grey, furry potoroos with their large snouts. They hurried out of their burrows, rubbing their little front paws in anticipation of the news from Charlie. Then came the larger spotted quolls from behind the ridges. They kept their distance, as they were a suspicious lot.

Charlie began to tell his tale in his quick, lively voice. Everyone listened carefully because the little marsupials admired Charlie's cleverness and ability to understand humans. The general consensus among them was that humans were not of any great interest, other than when one of them came smashing through the bush and destroyed their habitat with their large, clumsy feet.

Charlie held forth, telling the little group as it gathered around him that the humans were warning of the coming of a pandemic spread by the bats. But the numbat was sure that more was involved, and that the bats were innocent. The bats had come down out of their lofty hiding places and down to the level of the humans. This had then made them targets for all that human stupidity. The bats had been caught on many an electricity line and other such silliness. Numbat warned the potoroos to be ready for a pandemic, and said that humans, bats and birds may begin to die,

Wind Watchers' tale: Bringers of the Red Dust

and so spread disease. Worst of all, the dead could actually fall into their little hiding place in Guanaba! The little inhabitants of Guanaba gasped in horror at the thought of birds and bats falling from the sky, let alone having some enormous human falling into their homelands.

Having successfully frightened the living daylights out of his audience, Charlie further puffed up his chest and deepened his voice so he sounded very authoritative.

'Of course, if you ask me I believe the source of the pandemic was the horse stud down in the lowlands.' All the marsupials were aghast to think such a thing was so near. 'So those koalas had better be careful', said Charlie as he looked up into the trees to see whether any koalas had come to hear him speak. To his disappointment, none could be seen.

'Hmm, as I was saying', he said in an even louder voice, 'those koalas that live in the trees around the horse stable need to be careful.'

'Well, I must be off to warn others!' cried Charlie as he jumped down from the log and quickly disappeared into the undergrowth, leaving his audience stunned.

Bring it on!

A sickening, deep fear pervaded the very souls of the potoroos and quolls. Souls were about that would pack their bags and vacate the animal form for the spirit world at the slightest hint that the Bringers of the Red Dust were nigh. But three valiant potoroos were not to be deterred as they stood on a small log and called out to the moon as though it could hear their every word and would dutifully send their challenge to the Bringers of the Red Dust.

'Bring it on! Bring it on!' shouted Motty, Potty and Roosevelt as they stood up on the log and called out into the night air, for they were sick of living in fear of the Great Hounds. And Charlie Numbat's news of a pandemic was just too much for them to bear. They had already been living with the never-ending whispers coming from the koalas that the Hounds were about to descend on them. And most annoying were the times when some overly excitable koala with bad eyesight would say it could see the Hounds and instead the sighting turned out to be a big red kangaroo or an emu. These reports had caused a wave of frantic behaviour among all the animals, not just the potoroos. The air was full of the electricity of fear, which seemed to call out, 'Get ready! Get ready! Run and hide! Run or you will die!'

However, Potty, Motty and Roosevelt were sick of the whispering, and were impatient to see these Great Hounds and fight them to the death. Of course, they hadn't quite thought all this blustering through or they would have remembered that they were tiny, grey, furry hopping marsupials with long snouts – hardly a challenge for a Great Hound! Actually, the Hounds had never seen the potoroos they had trampled to death. They were merely collateral damage in the bigger game.

After venting their fears at the moon, Potty sat with Motty and pondered the great danger that could be visited upon the tribe by the Hounds of the North. They had no idea at what moment these wild Hounds might come charging through their bushland and rip them apart. All they knew was that if the Hounds arrived, it would be the end for the potoroos. This tension was almost unbearable and Roosevelt had truly lost it, manically digging a bunker to hide everyone. No one would stop him, as they knew it was good therapy and a coping mechanism for the uncertainty. Male potoroos had to feel they were doing something when danger lurked, while females felt they had to think about all the ways they could help the community to cope – not only with the possible arrival of the Hounds, but with the aftermath: the destruction, the deaths and the wounded, let alone the famine that always came in the wake of any battle.

Captain Koala

It had been a bad night for the potoroos, as not only did they receive the devastating news from Charlie Numbat, but earlier in the night Captain Koala, Colly's partner, brought news back from the pond. He was a great one for visiting the waterhole. He called himself the Captain because he believed that if he had a boat, he could sail right around the waterhole. All sorts of birds and beasts came there to drink and tell their tales. Captain Koala was a regular and so, after an evening of drinking and stories, he would make his way back up to Guanaba and spread the latest news. That evening he had been conversing with the pelicans that had just flown back from Lake Eyre and had seen the Western Hounds at their worst. They said the Hounds had raised a great dust storm to cover their misdeeds. The poor pelicans had nearly lost their way due to the dust as they had flown low in the sky to observe a tribe of bandicoots that had been ordered by the Hounds to go out and kill a tribe of the delicate hopping mice.

The tiny hopping mice had large brown eyes and pretty pink paws. Their tawny brown fur and white underbelly gave them an air of being the most genteel of mice. They lived among the sharp Spinifex of the desert to protect themselves, but once the bandicoots were given their orders there was no way they were going to survive the genocide. As with all genocides, it was only the few chosen by fate who ever survived. It was neither skill nor brawn that was the determinant, but rather plain, straight out luck. The tiny hopping mice were of little relevance to the Hounds, but the Hounds needed to keep the tough little bandicoots in line, as they were becoming a touch too clever and were beginning to rally other marsupials to stand up to the Hounds. The Hounds were having none of this, and wanted to make sure all the marsupials knew who was boss.

Roosevelt the Potoroo

For a koala, looking down on the vista below, it would be hard not to discern the tracks of the potoroos, which were reminiscent of the great Dreaming tracks that crossed the whole of Australia. One set of tracks was trodden much more deeply than the others. They were the tracks of Roosevelt. He was a large potoroo and very sturdy, but unfortunately had a very straggly coat. He just would not attend to his looks. He thought his scruffy coat made him look more rugged. And, like all good heroes, he had come up with a grand plan. He was digging a bunker-like warren for the tribe so that they could hide as soon as they got the signal. He had gone to a lot of trouble to work out just the right size for the bunker and was willing to put in the effort to dig it out. And indeed it was going to take a lot of effort for him, as he would not hear of anyone helping him. He was a true alpha male, and only he knew best. But there was a problem, which stemmed from generosity and a sense of community. His sister, Motty, had felt compelled to invite all and sundry to hide in the bunker, including Kozy the Quoll and his family. This had sent Roosevelt into a tizz, as the quolls were larger; this meant Roosevelt had to dig even deeper to fit the quolls in. And as he had no idea when the Hounds would arrive, Roosevelt had begun his manic digging, believing fervently in every whisper of impending doom that Kozy the Quoll delighted in spreading.

Kozy the Quoll

Kozy the Quoll was a dapper-looking quoll, with his fancy white spots and lovely black coat. He thought himself quite the dandy, even though he had a large nose on the end of his pointy face. He had long whiskers that made him look quite continental. And his eyes were intense, as was his appetite for potoroo stew. Kozy had a rather seductive way of swinging his tail and licking his lips, especially when a potoroo was close by. He was forever trying to scare the living daylights out of Roosevelt with his stories of doom in the hope Roosevelt would keel over in fright and then he could pop Roosevelt into his pot, which was forever on the boil.

However, Kozy's preferred scenario was to seduce Motty and Potty – who were two of the chubbiest potoroos – right into his pot, especially as Motty was particularly taken by Kozy's stylish looks and his cooking. Motty fancied herself as quite a culinary expert, but didn't quite ever get around to cooking anything other than insects on toast, and therefore went to great lengths to try to get Potty to accompany her to Kozy's pot for a tasting session.

Kozy was really a strange and dangerous character, with his large teeth and taste for potoroos, but unfortunately the potoroos were a kindly lot and didn't notice the unusual looks he would give Motty as she hopped past his pot. However, Kozy had one alarming weakness; he could not abide fruit bats, and went ballistic when he saw them, accusing them of all sorts of evil deeds, shouting up at them as they flew overhead. He had been beside himself with joy when Numbat stood up and declared that the humans were about to annihilate their numbers because he believed all bats should be killed. Actually, he was downright racist and wanted all fruit bats tagged with identity tags. He had heard that humans were doing this when he was last down drinking at the pond. He liked that idea, as he was convinced quolls were superior marsupials and potoroos were only really good for eating, but bats had to be exterminated. He hated bats not because of the colour of their wings, though, but because they could fly and were free to go wherever they wanted. This is why Kozy was always climbing the trees: he wanted to kill all things of flight that made him feel so – well – grounded. He felt that being on the ground was somehow demeaning for a species so highly evolved as his own.

Furthermore, he had pontificated to his partner Doll after hearing the Numbat's news, 'they're not as pretty as birds and therefore should be despised for their ugliness'. This remark made Doll retort, 'Have you looked at your reflection in the pond lately?' But Kozy was having nothing of this foolishness from a mere female; he knew best, so he went on ranting: 'And the worst thing about them is their population size – it's getting bigger and bigger each year.'

'You've never seen a flock of them block out the sun, have you Doll?' Kozy questioned with an accusing eye. 'Just look at the birds up there in the sky, they fly in nice little flocks and all in line. I like that', he said smugly as he promptly stepped in a large pile of bird poo. 'Eek!' he yelled as he slipped and lost his balance, and ended up face down in the poo. His snout and whiskers were covered in a white, sticky mess.

This was most upsetting, as Kozy's snout was his pride and joy. You see he actually felt that his snout said everything about what he really was: suave, debonair and continental! But as Doll looked down at him, spread-eagled on the ground with his nose firmly stuck in a pile of bird poo, all she saw was a little quoll who was frightened by the great black masses that filled the sky at sunset. It was this black mass that disturbed him to the very end of his spotted tail, for he had been brought up on old stories about bats and how dangerous they were – stories of bats that befriended the humans who did terrible things to animals and even other humans. As the bats had a terrible habit of always fighting and squealing when they landed in the treetops en masse, all Kozy's beliefs were confirmed. Poor Kozy, he was a product of his upbringing, thought Doll, and just couldn't work it out as an adult. You see, Doll was a bit of an intellectual and Kozy hated that, as he wanted to be the smartest quoll in the community. There was no end to Kozy's vanity. Kozy was sure Doll thought that he was a few spots short of a full coat, but he wasn't really. He just had a hearing problem

Wind Watchers' tale: Bringers of the Red Dust   139

and didn't always catch what she was saying. She talked too fast; it was all Doll's fault that he looked a bit stupid sometimes.

Doll moved over to Kozy and dragged him out of the mess, then took him down to a little stream she had found the day before on one of her ventures. She cleaned him off and straightened his whiskers, while thinking what a racist old coot he was. Doll had become increasingly concerned about Kozy's behaviour because she knew it spelt trouble if they were all going to be squashed into a bunker. The infusion of fear would cause havoc with the minds of the feeble-minded, like Kozy. His relatives were no better – especially Mutface, who thought the sun shone out of Kozy's proverbial back end. She had seen them all sitting up in the trees laughing and making unsavoury comments about poor little Roosevelt, who was basically saving their gluttonous lives.

She had no one to talk to because the quolls were also the last of their tribe; they had been pushed out of their habitat, first by humans and then, as they roamed, the Hounds. This unfortunate state of affairs had actually made her quite sympathetic to the fruit bats, and therefore it was not surprising that Doll had formed a friendship with one of the female leaders of the bats, Mrs Fruit-Tingle.

Their friendship had made her more sensitive to Kozy's racist comments, and his boasting among his fellow racists had begun to speak of surveillance – she could feel that a dangerous line of thinking was beginning to take shape in their chatter. For it was foolish types like this, whose egos ran away with their common sense, that were inherently dangerous to the whole population. For they moved into a space in which they became obsessed with boundaries, yet saw no need for any limits to be put on their own behaviour or thinking. They were in charge of everyone else. And what better way to start such dangerous thinking than through the act of surveillance and spreading tales of terror.

The joys of the surveillance team

Kozy licked his lips and whet his whiskers, and began to preen himself as he chatted to his fellow racists.

'I think there should be surveillance of these potoroos and especially those lazy fat koalas. They are a threat to our safety when the Hounds come. We need to make sure they don't invite any koalas into the bunker and definitely no bats', declared Kozy.

At first his little clan just looked stupidly at him, as none of them had any idea of what the word surveillance meant.

Kozy soon detected the dumb silence.

'Ah yes, surveillance. It means to watch, and when the animals realize you are watching them they get real nervy and do stupid things and become real easy to control.'

140   Bioinsecurity

'For example, I could see that stupid Motty inviting them in. We therefore must form a crack surveillance team considering we are more nimble and intelligent than the rest of them. Actually, if I had my way, just before the arrival of the Hounds I would throw all the potoroos into the pot and cook them for food to hold us over until the hounds have gone', laughed Kozy, as his mates cheered with glee.

'Yeah Koz, I like that idea', said Mutface, a white-faced quoll with surprisingly few spots. This was the reason he admired Kozy so much, as his spots appeared to be perfectly positioned all over his body and down to the tip of his strong tail. What Mutface wouldn't give to have a spotted tail like Kozy.

'We are the boss animals. This is our country! We are the predators and they are the prey. If they get out of line – it's into the pot as far as I am concerned', cried Mutface triumphantly. Kozy came over to Mutface and flicked his tail in approval.

Kozy and the beggar bats

The fruit bats had become so ragged from being chased by the humans they could no longer hunt. This gave Kozy his chance to be even meaner to the fruit bats. 'Poor things!' said Doll, 'they have now come to the ground in the hope we will feed them'.

'No!' said Kozy jumping to attention and assuming the role of a dictator. 'No feeding bats! We should ban this kind of begging; it will allow them to spread their disease.'

'But there is no proof they have a disease, Kozy', said Doll, as she walked around behind him while he strutted about giving out orders to begin the surveillance.

'Yes they have – just look at them and their dark strange looks. No, we have to ban them from begging for food. I will tell Roosevelt – he will do something about them.'

'But Kozy, they are so poor and harassed. In these hard times, they are the most vulnerable of all of us, and we have to do something for them. After all, Kozy, if we think we are so superior why are we so scared of such a vulnerable species as the little fruit bat? Haven't we got bigger problems with the Hounds of the North?' she asked as she looked deep into his eyes.

The fear returned to his eyes, but only momentarily. 'No, Doll, we have to be vigilant and make ourselves stronger to fight the Hounds. First we kill all the bats, then the potoroos, and then the Hounds!' shouted Kozy, which in turn brought about a cheer from his fellow quolls.

'First the bats, then the potoroos, and then the Hounds?' shrilled Doll. 'Exactly who is going to do all this killing? Because it sure won't be you stupid lot!' She sneered as she came right up to Kozy's snout. 'Just look at you! Has it ever struck you that you might be too fat to fit into the bunker?

And that you had better let up harassing Roosevelt or he might not dig the hole deep enough. Have you thought about that, my mighty bat killers? Kill the Hounds? How can you be so delusional?' Doll shouted back at the rather overweight lot as she stomped off.

Mutface turned to Kozy and said under his breath, 'What does "delusional" mean, boss?'

'Beats me, Mutface' shrugged Kozy, 'but knowing my wife it's something real mean. She just doesn't appreciate how lucky she is to have such brave quolls as us to protect her.' He growled as he moved gingerly over the ridge. Mutface and the others trailed along after him. However, they could not help noticing just how fat Kozy's backside was. They had all understood Doll very clearly when she said they were too fat for the bunker. That came as a terrible shock to all of them – including Kozy!

The lowlands of Beaudesert

And so that was life on the hill, but down in the lowlands where the tall, graceful eucalypts grew among the savannah where most of the koalas resided was the infamous waterhole. This was the drinking hole where all the wayward males would go to drink. Little did the furry and feathered friends know that evil lurked in their very midst.

There were ghastly plans afoot – for deeds intent upon spreading disease and making profits from the despair of human and animals alike. For here in this picturesque setting were not only the happy sounds of animals and birds drinking at the pond, but also a laboratory hidden within the confines of an exclusive horse stud – an exclusivity that saw more horses go out in the knacker's cart than in private pony trailers.

The two detectives

Captain Koala was a nosy koala, who could neither shut his mouth nor keep his nose out of other animals' business. So he just salivated at the idea that the horse stud could be a cover for something more sinister. He had a partner in crime when it came to snooping out a story, and who better than a Yank. The Yank was a horse that hailed from Kentucky. The only problem was that during the trip from America to Australia, the horse had bumped his head on a steel pole and promptly forgotten his name. So when he met Captain Koala, the Captain – who liked to call a spade a spade – decided to name him 'Horse with No Name'. The Yankee horse liked this, as it reminded him of a song he thought he had once heard. But of course he couldn't remember the name of the song.

Horse, as Captain Koala called him for short, was one handsome thoroughbred stallion. His black silky coat was magnificent and made him stand out from the rest, but at the same time gave him a lot of leeway to

142   Bioinsecurity

roam wherever he pleased around the horse stud, as he had been bought as a breeder. This privilege made him the perfect sidekick for the koala sleuth. A regular Sherlock and Holmes! Koala, of course, was Sherlock in his own mind.

The pandemic

After getting over the sulks because Numbat had one-upped him, Captain Koala made his way down to visit his friend to get the truth from 'the horse's mouth', as he would later tell his friends at the pond. He was determined to find out whether Numbat was right and, if so, he was going to find even more sensational news for the Guanaba clan regarding whether there was a pandemic disease being developed by the humans. As he cautiously made his way down a tree near the edge of the horse stud boundary, he could see his friend Horse with No Name standing near the building. 'Perfect!' thought the Captain, 'We can look through the window and see what these stupid humans are up to.' He then waddled over to Horse, who was watching the body of a young Asian human being carried out the door of the laboratory.

'Hey Horse, it's me! What's going on? What happened to the human?' he yelled up at Horse as he reached his side. You see there is quite a bit of distance between a little fat koala and a thoroughbred stallion, even if the koala's ego is as big as an elephant. Koala resented having to look up to Horse; after all, he was the brains of the outfit.

Horse with No Name may have been a mighty steed, but at heart he was a real softie. His leanings were more towards making music than mounting mares – not that he minded doing that, it was just that he had a poetic side to his nature that no one seemed to appreciate, other than Burbi the Koala. But then again, he wasn't 100 per cent sure she wasn't patronizing him. If only he could remember his name, he would be feeling more confident about himself.

He looked down at Captain Koala and said, 'Hey there bro! What's up?'

'Is that young man dead?' whispered Captain Koala, which in turn made Horse drop his head down to the Captain's level.

'Sure is. Dead as a doornail! I saw him keel over at the laboratory bench when I was taking a peek through the window. It's exactly what happened to the mare I mounted just yesterday. She was a great breeder and such a fun horse to be around, and now she is dead', said Horse, shaking his head in dismay.

Just then, two humans came out of the building and lit up a cigarette as they leaned against a wall. The authoritative-looking, tall, blond-haired male said to the shorter male with thick grey hair, 'Well, we got at least one out of the three, those other two … and excuse the pun, must be as healthy as horses!' They both laughed a menacing laugh.

Wind Watchers' tale: Bringers of the Red Dust   143

'Yeah', said the grey haired man as he puffed out smoke. 'I think we are just going to have to develop a stronger strain of the virus to do them in. Looks like young Asians aren't as susceptible as we thought. I mean, it is the young ones we want to take out.'

'Those other two had better succumb to the disease by next week or Colonel Rumbolt will cut our funding', said the tall blond in a Swedish accent.

'I can't wait to see what happens when they drop the virus into the prevailing winds and just let it rip', laughed the grey-haired man.

'I don't know how many other horses we can kill before the neighbours start becoming suspicious', said the Swede. 'You checked on those bats you caught the other night, didn't you? I want their bodies to be found around the barn so it looks like they are spreading the disease.'

Horse and Captain Koala looked at each other in horror as they listened from outside the window. They had positioned themselves so it looked like they just happened to be grazing near the building. The humans appeared not to take any notice of them; after all, there was nothing suspicious about a horse grazing with a friendly little koala at his side. After the two men went inside, the two amigos pondered the human activity and the removal of the body.

'I tell you, Horse, something is rotten in the state of Denmark!' said Captain Koala, as he rubbed his furry chin.

'Was there a horse from Denmark here?' asked Horse quizzically.

'No stupid, but any bat with half a brain ought to get flapping and head for Denmark while they still can. You bet the next thing those humans are going to do is put a bounty on their heads and every bat will become a criminal to be shot at on sight', said the Captain, shaking his head.

'Of course they will bung it on – they just want to catch them to tag them, just to be sure they are not infected. It will be bat genocide!' said Captain Koala in disgust as he turned to head back to the pond.

Horse walked along slowly beside him, listening carefully to every word. Horse thought the Captain was the smartest animal he had ever met.

'The problem is that they just don't understand how the world works', pontificated the Captain. 'If they take one species out it causes a ripple effect all the way through Nature. They never learn, even when they do it to other humans. They exterminate one or two ethnic groups and think it won't make a difference. But humans are like wildlife. They are all interconnected. If you take one ethnic group out, it has a subtle ripple effect. It weakens the whole human race. But then humans are the dumbest creatures on the planet, so what can we expect?'

As they arrived at the fence, the Captain turned and said to Horse, 'I had better get back and warn the bats, before the humans send out the word to catch them.' The Captain then scampered back up to his tree.

Colly and Captain Koala

Colly the Koala was a gatherer. She was always gathering little seeds and other things. Captain Koala wholeheartedly supported her in collecting seeds and other food, but it was the other junk she picked up on the way that disturbed him. He just couldn't abide all the rubbish she stored in the bow of the branches, let alone how hard it was to negotiate the way over all the junk to get up to her. This justified the fact he preferred to spend his time at the pond, rather than sitting up in the tree with Colly.

'She would give a bower bird a run for its money', said Captain Koala to his mates at the pond.

Little did Captain Koala know that Colly had a plan! For many years, she had been stocking up on seeds and hiding them in the trees, because she had noticed the bees were disappearing and she knew that somewhere at the other end of the westerly winds were the Hounds and their touch of death. Colly's Great-Granny had been through a famine, and she had told Colly the terrible stories of how famine always came hand in hand with the Hounds. It had not always been like that, for once the winds had brought beneficial red dust, but now the Hounds had infected the red dust with their diseased thinking.

Colly had also noticed how, slowly but surely, it was getting colder – she was not sure whether it was the fear of the Hounds or that the climate was actually changing. It was a dry, cold Antarctic chill, not a wind full of moisture.

Colly was an encyclopaedia of medicinal uses of all things in the bush. Captain Koala was very proud of Colly's knowledge, and made sure every newcomer to the pond was given an ear-bashing on the wondrous bush wisdom of his wife, Colly. Little did they know that, when Colly and Captain Koala were alone, this fame became quite a strain on Captain Koala's ego.

'You female koalas think you know everything', snapped Captain Koala one night.

Colly looked over her large button nose and retorted with a bit of slur in her voice, just to antagonize the Captain even more, 'We don't think – we know!' She turned her large, fluffy backside towards the Captain and climbed further up the tree until the Captain got over his attack of the sulks.

Burbi the Wind Watcher

Burbi was Colly's main source of information, as Colly was a touch too busy to give the Eucalyptus Dreaming the focus that was needed to be able to hear the messages from the other marsupials, and particularly the Wind Watchers. For Burbi was a Wind Watcher. Burbi had been trained by her

Granny to watch the winds and listen to its calls and the messages it sent around at the height of the wet season. It was during the times when the monsoons of the north were on the move that messages came down on the winds from the north. Then there were other times when the westerly winds brought whispers, messages and bad spirits that caused illnesses and other calamities.

Burbi was forever trying to get Colly to cover her face in honey when the westerlies came, because the honey would protect her. But Colly was too busy and then wondered why she got sick. As for Captain Koala, he just thought it was madness from his crazy sister-in-law.

Colly had to repeatedly remind Captain Koala that Burbi was communicating telepathically with the other koalas, who were strategically placed throughout Guanaba and were keeping an eye on the movements of anything or anyone who could endanger the animals, including self-deluded busy-bodies like him!

Horse with No Name

It was Captain Koala who had told Horse with No Name about Burbi, and the fact that he felt she needed help. Horse, who sometimes jumped the fence at night, came from a Native American ranch in Kentucky, so he knew all about healing. For some reason, he didn't forget this fact. Captain Koala told him the reason he didn't forget was because healing powers don't come from individuals but from the ancestors, and they just used him as a conduit. Horse therefore felt he could heal Burbi of her strange behaviour by singing to her. He couldn't play a drum, which was part of the healing ceremony, but he thought if he trotted around it would sound just like the sound of a drum. So he would circle around Burbi's tree stomping heavily with his feet and singing a song he had heard. He had no idea what the song was about, but thought it might help. Burbi liked the song, but she thought the horse quite crazy, albeit rather cute – she thought him delightfully eccentric. Of course, Horse didn't know this and would have been mortified to think he wasn't being taken seriously. Burbi imagined she could see herself riding on Horse's back, telling him all sorts of Dreaming stories about the land and he would take her on delightful rides. This was, of course, far from Horse's mind!

The fight

Charlie Numbat had brought the first news about the bats, which later was confirmed by Horse and Captain Koala. The dear, naughty little bats who squabbled all the time had been branded by the scientists and the likes of Kozy the Quoll as 'wandering, disease-carrying vermin'. Alas, the bats' bickering nature, which had nothing to do with humans, was misunderstood and unfortunately made them an easy target for discrimination. They just couldn't control their yelling and fighting when they were settling into the trees.

Kozy exploited this foible of the bats and tried his hardest to spread lies about them. Mutface and his mates loved listening to Kozy's lies, which made them feel superior. But that was only half of it; their game of surveillance had proved to be far more enjoyable. Kozy had worked out a system of undermining the confidence of the potoroos, and especially Roosevelt. Kozy and the others would constantly bail up one of the potoroos and tell them they had seen either Motty or Potty hiding food off in the bush and that there was a secret bunker no one knew about except Motty, Potty and Roosevelt. They said the one Roosevelt was digging wouldn't be big enough for all of them. Kozy convinced them that it was the duty of the quolls, on behalf of the other potoroos, to watch the movements of the three culprits. But it was also important to watch the movements of everyone just to make sure Roosevelt wasn't trying to recruit others. Yes, the Quolls were on their side and were there to help! Kozy had even come up with the clever slogan, 'We have spots because we can spot the crim.'

Actually, Mutface got so carried away with it all that every time he bailed someone up he repeated the slogan. You see Mutface was short of a few spots, so liked to make out that he was totally spotted. The potoroos were in such a state of fear that they believed Kozy and put up with the constant harassment over their movements and the annoying repetition by Mutface. As for the three amigos, Motty, Potty and Roosevelt, they were allowed to go about their normal business. This became evident to the other potoroos, who started to resent their apparent freedom of movement.

Kozy may have been dumb about some things, but when it came to other things he was a downright genius. He knew that surveillance has a way of making the watched into watchers. The potoroos became so neurotic from this behaviour that they finally lashed out at Roosevelt. One group of nervy potoroos, who had just had a heady going over by Mutface and his mates, were incensed and went after Roosevelt. They bailed poor Roosevelt up in the bunker, rammed him against the wall and demanded he show them his other bunker. He was dumbstruck, but fortunately – due to the fact he was the only one in the community doing any real work – he could easily push them back due to the strength he had developed from all the digging. He called them on their accusations and demanded that they look around and tell him if the bunker wasn't big enough for all of them. The silly potoroos soon realized they had been tricked by Kozy.

They apologized to Roosevelt and went off to find Kozy and his mean-faced friends. It was not a pretty sight, as the potoroos – who were already in a frenzy from all the fear the quolls had spread – had called in the bats for help, so when 15 potoroos jumped on five lazy, overweight quolls, the bats screeched so loud that it was the noise, more than the scratching by

Wind Watchers' tale: Bringers of the Red Dust

the potoroos, that nearly killed the quolls. Kozy was particularly trauma-tized due to his fear of bats. It was only thanks to the arrival of Doll, Potty and Mrs Fruit-Tingle that the aggressive behaviour stopped.

The revelation of the plague

Captain Koala and Colly watched in horror from the tree tops. Captain Koala instantly knew he had to report this riot to the pond dwellers. So he quickly climbed down the tree and scampered off to the lowlands. He was sure he would now out-do that smart-aleck Numbat and regain his title as the king of sensational news. First, however, he must tell his friend Horse. To his utter disappointment, though, Horse did not seem to hear him, nor was he interested. So he immediately turned around and scurried off to the pond, where he knew everyone would listen to his every word.

Horse, on the other hand, had begun to think about Burbi. As soon as he did this, she appeared. He looked up in the closest gum tree and there she was looking down on him with the stupid smile that Captain hinted meant she was high as a kite on eucalyptus leaves. So he called up to her, thinking he should really put more effort into helping her. He had noticed that his hoof drumming had certainly caught her attention and stopped her eating the leaves while he danced, but that was as far as it went. So it was time for the next step in Horse's healing.

'Hey Burbi, come on down. I want to talk to you', he hollered and hoped she wouldn't fall out of the tree in an attempt to come down in her eucalyptus-euphoric state. Burbi nodded and quickly made her way down, with the dexterity of an experienced tree climber. It was poor old Horse who was going to feel stupid once she had revealed what she knew of the dust cloud.

'So, Burbi, how are you these days?' asked Horse nonchalantly as he watched Burbi descend with such ease.

'Actually, Horse, I am very worried. I can feel that the Hounds are very close, and when they arrive they will search out what is living in that research facility over there', she said with deep concern in her voice as she made her way to Horse across the leaf-laden lands.

'What do you mean?' said Horse as he stepped back in shock. 'How did you know about that?' he asked incredulously.

'Surely you don't think koala bears are just a bunch of eucalypt junkies. You haven't been talking to Captain Koala about me, have you?' she asked, with an accusing eye. 'You know that different koalas have different Dreaming stories. Our ancient ones are the Wind Watchers, while Captain Koala's are what I call the Pond Drinker's Dreaming! The Pond Drinkers all descended from one big ancestor who never learnt to mind his own business, let alone remember a story of knowledge.'

'You see, Horse, some koalas just never get around to learning the ancient stories and so make up yarns and call that knowledge, rather than admit it's just plain laziness and gossip rolled into one big yarn. So when they come up against koalas who remember the old stories, they discredit them by saying they are somehow "off their tree"', she said, with an amused look. Horse shuffled his hooves.

'Really, Horse, I thought you looked so much more intelligent than that', said Burbi with an air of disappointment.

'No, honest', lied Horse. 'I knew you were smart. I was just going along with the Captain's big talk to make him feel okay about being dumb.'

'Hmm, dumb, hey? Takes one to know one!' said Burbi, and promptly turned her back on him and began climbing the tree again. Feeling thoroughly ashamed of himself, Horse hung his head and thought how silly he must have looked to this koala as he stomped around her tree.

Burbi looked back and saw how sheepish Horse looked, so she turned back and said, 'Listen, Horse, I want to tell you something, as I think you just might be a bit smarter than the animals you hang out with. We of the Eucalypt Dreaming know that the Great Hounds are not animals but small particles – as you might say in your tradition, the Particle Nation.' Horse was intrigued by what she said and swished his tail.

'They gather together to shape-shift into whatever form they like, and cause death and disease across our lands. They came after the killing of two magic dogs in ancient times. Since then, we Wind Watchers have been keeping an eye on their movements.'

'At first they were just a red dust that some kangaroos called the hounds, but as time passed they got bigger and bigger and so did the dust cloud. Little did the kangaroos realize that it was the cloud of dust that looked like the Great Hounds. Even the bandicoots that were terrorized by them believed they were hounds, but in fact it was merely the dust taking that form', explained Burbi, as she sadly looked into Horse's big brown eyes, which were beginning to show signs of fear.

'You mean they aren't animals, but shape-shifters?' whispered Horse as his knees began to shake with another memory that was returning to his blank mind.

'I remember I was told about these shape-shifting red clouds when I was a foal. The old horse, White Eagle, told me about the time he stood on top of a great butte and below he saw the red cloud of dust moving across the plains and then after that lots of deaths occurred. The humans called it a plague', said Horse nervously, as he remembered the story of the plague.

Burbi sighed in agreement. 'What these stupid humans don't realize is that when the Hounds arrive, they will search out that stupid research facility and find those little bacteria and enslave them. The dust nation searches out the small, like themselves, and captures them, making them

Wind Watchers' tale: Bringers of the Red Dust   149

part of the dust cloud, so it can cause even more death and disease than any human can come up with', warned Burbi, as she looked once again into Horse's eyes, just to see how terrified he really was. She wanted to ascertain just how powerful Horse's Native American horse medicine was. She wondered whether Horse would survive the dust particles when they arrived.

Horse looked back at Burbi and saw the strength in her eyes. He then remembered a saying of the Haisla Indian people of the northern coast. He said to Burbi, 'It is possible to retaliate against an enemy, but impossible to retaliate against storms.'

It then struck Horse with No Name, as he walked away to find Captain Koala, that he had again remembered something from his past. Maybe this Burbi could heal him and, if she could, he would have to find somewhere in his soul the fortitude to survive the Bringers of the Red Dust.

The Hounds are a coming!

Burbi could feel the Hounds were getting nearer. It was the silence – the strange kind of silence that you hear when noise is all around you. The silence occupies another dimension that you are tapping into. She could feel the rippling sensation all through her fur. And the smell was beginning to enter her nostrils. The smell of dust! Burbi began to telepathically tell the other Wind Watchers that she had heard the silence. And sure enough, so had the others. So Burbi called out to Colly, who was up in the next tree collecting the leftovers of a bird's nest.

'Colly, come quickly, the Hounds are coming!' she called out. Colly nearly fell out of the tree on hearing the news. She promptly dropped her bird's nest, which unfortunately landed on the head of a blue-tongued lizard that happened to be passing by.

'We must warn everyone', cried Colly, as she began to slip down the tree. Burbi could do nothing other than nod. She was trying to detect just how far away they were and how long they had, so let Colly run off.

Colly scurried up the hill and down into the valley towards the potoroo patch to warn them. She hoped Roosevelt had finished the bunker, and that it was big enough for them all, including the bats who had fallen to the ground due to hunger. The koalas could survive the Hounds as long as they moved high into the tops of the trees and faded into the leafy landscape, but the poor ground creatures didn't have a hope.

The bunker

Colly scurried up to Roosevelt who was talking to Motty and Potty.

'You must get everyone in, they are coming! Quick, quick!' cried Colly as she frantically thought how she was going to warn Captain Koala.

Motty and Potty looked at each other and then broke away instantly and went hopping around the camp to tell the others. Meanwhile, Roosevelt had not budged. In fact, the fear had gripped him and he had suddenly frozen and could not move. Colly just looked at him in disbelief.

'Trust a male to lose it just when you need to get things moving. Why they believe they are the superior sex is beyond me', she thought in annoyance, as she began to give him a shove. She was a very large marsupial compared with the little potoroo, so she had to be careful how much she shoved him, but she had to move him to the bunker or he might be left out in all the fuss. Gently she pushed his frozen body towards the bunker and then let it roll down the hole. And then she was off.

Roosevelt rolled down into the hole and landed up against the wall. He couldn't believe that his body had gone so rigid, but then again he couldn't believe it was time. He had invested so much time in being the hero in his mind; he had no idea how to be a hero in reality. And now reality had struck. He suddenly realized that there was actually more to courage than just action. He actually had no inner moral fibre and couldn't step up to the challenge when it arrived. He was so ashamed of himself.

Motty and Potty were well aware of the need for moral fibre, and were ready. They calmly invited everyone to make their way to the bunker. They did not go around screaming and calling out danger, but politely informed everyone that it was now time to enter the bunker.

When they came to the quolls, Kozy was angered by their controlled demeanour. Kozy wondered why they weren't shouting out orders and telling everyone to get in line. He leaned over to his mates and said, 'If it was me I would be telling everyone to hop to it and get in as fast as possible.'

'Oh yeah!' said Doll. 'And then we would all be pushing past your fat backside to get in. How would you like that, Mr Big?' Kozy was flabbergasted that Doll was being so mean to him in this time of danger. In fact, Doll was scared out of her wits and was truly concerned her husband was too fat for the bunker.

But Kozy was about to get even worse news. The bats were also being invited to come in. These were the poor hungry bats that had been wounded by the humans' attempts to catch and tag them. There weren't many of them, so they could easily fit in. Kozy nearly didn't go in. He actually contemplated trying to weather the Hounds rather than being so close to the bats. It irked him greatly, and of course he thought they stunk.

'The stench will suffocate me. I can't go in', he cried as Doll tried to push him through the entrance. 'Don't be stupid', said Doll impatiently. 'They smell like fruit, you idiot. They only eat fruit, which is more than I can say for you! It is you who stinks!' Kozy was mortified and slid into the bunker.

The potoroos could all feel the thundering coming through the ground. It was a terrifying sound. 'Give me lightning any day', said Potty as she helped some of the bats. 'I can't bear this sound. It is like listening to the drums of death thumping towards you.'

The potoroos didn't mind the closeness in the bunker, as it made them all feel safer. Roosevelt had recovered by now, and had returned to the surface to bring food down into the bunker. His bunker was about to save all these souls, and it was all due to his hard work. He was feeling very satisfied, even though at heart he was still scared witless of the Hounds.

Then suddenly a low and angry voice said, 'Well, Motty, Potty and Roosevelt, are you satisfied? You wanted the Hounds to "bring it on"! How do you feel now?' They turned to the voice and were shocked to find it was Doll. This was a strange turn of events considering she had just finished telling Kozy off. Kozy couldn't believe his ears. How could she be so ungrateful, especially as he had got a tongue-lashing for the very same thing? On hearing the sound of the thumping, Kozy had instantly had a change of heart and was very grateful to his fellow marsupials who were saving his life. Kozy turned to Doll and put his paw on her snout.

'Shut up. Do you want to get us kicked out of here? If I can put up with the bats you can be a bit grateful, you nasty quoll!'

This shocked Doll out of her fear and she recovered and sank into Kozy's rather ample fur.

The arrival of the Bringers of the Red Dust

And so the dust particles gathered in the hideous form of the Great Hounds of the North and the West. They travelled on the prevailing winds, joyously bringing death and destruction! The first to arrive were the Hounds of the West, which travelled with the westerly wind that was known for bringing the red dust from the desert lands up and beyond the great mountain ranges that protected the Guanaba from most of the inland heat.

The Great Hounds of the West were fleet of foot as they rode the westerly winds. They moved stealthily around the Beaudesert research facility. They had picked up the scent of 'other beings' and had come to see what lived in this building. Tight-fitting window panes and locked doors meant nothing to these shape-shifters: all they needed was a tiny crack and they were in. An opening as small as an ant passage was like an open door, an invitation to invade, snoop around and take captive whatever lived inside.

Unlike humans, all they wanted was bacteria to build their strength. No military machine could gun down bacteria. And by the time the military got out their own bio-weapons to fight the Hounds, it would be too late. For these Hounds were from the Dreaming, not just some manipulated bacteria from a bird or a bat. No, these Hounds had magic, freedom and strength.

The Hounds soon found the bacteria in the little dish. They swirled around the dish and swept up the bacteria. The scientists could hear the howling but they just thought it was outside. However, when they returned to the room where the bacteria had been, they found the dishes upturned and red dust all around. This sent the scientists into a frantic panic. 'What's happened? Who stole the bacteria? They must have come in from outside, look at the red dust on everything.'

And so the Hounds of the West began to grow and to incorporate and multiply the bacteria, and a sickness began to take down the local human population. The locals blamed the scientists for the sickness and an investigation was started to look into the research facility. They were all suspicious of each other, but at the same time horrified that they too may catch the virus. Somehow not only had the bacteria disappeared but it had mutated into exactly what they were trying to develop.

Just as that realization struck, the Hounds of the North arrived and the battle began. The humans thought a tornado had arrived to make things even worse for their already sickening society. The winds that appeared to be coming from the north whipped through the countryside, ripping up houses, gardens and trees. Birds, bats and insects were torn from the sky and flung across the trees. Bats hung like deathly black flags, swaying in the wind. The air was choked with red dust. The waterways had turned a blood-red colour and a foul smell filled the air. And then it began: the sickness turned to death. Humans fell like flies and unfortunately the larger animals also fell. The Hounds' battle attack had escalated and multiplied the bacteria until it turned into a strong, virile organism causing havoc across the population.

The battle made the dust cloud grow larger and larger, and the humans continued to get sicker and sicker. The antidote was useless and the scientists died one by one; then even more people died, until not a human was in sight. The land was covered with dust and humanity was no more. The Hounds, however, were already on the move. The deaths had given them even more strength and so the battle grew into a massive cyclone that moved out to sea.

What was left was nothing for human eyes, for there were no eyes left to see it. The Hounds did their work so efficiently that no human could match them. They had arrived and left before the blink of a now-dead eyelid.

Bacteria have no timesheets or profits to make – they just came and went. Who knows where they will go now? And all that had lived before were now dead, except for our faithful friends.

Our faithful friends

Luckily, our little friends were safe in the bunker and the koalas had used their medicine to protect themselves high in the treetops. As for Captain Koala and his friend at the pond, they suffered badly but not fatally. For as Fortune's favourites, they survived the disaster. Captain Koala and his smaller mates were blown into the pond by the force of the wind. As Horse raced to their rescue and jumped into the pond to save them, he suddenly had a flash of insight. Instead of pulling the Captain and his friends out of the water, he called out to the Captain and the others to stay low and hide under the water as the Hounds passed over. This was an old Indian trick. Luckily for them, the battling Hounds passed in a mere flash and so no one drowned.

And so ends the tale of the Bringers of the Red Dust.

Chapter 17

A poem

In search of immortality (an ode to the scientists)

They come with the westerly winds they say;
these diseases of the mind.
Diseases of desire gone mad
Immortality on their mind.

They come at night and search
of minds open as the face
of a newborn babe.
These minds no more developed
than the first day of life,
are a welcome sight to
the insidious evil
as it crosses the night.

No one sees them, they only feel them
deep down inside their veins,
flowing like rampant blood lust
in search of immortality.

And upon the dawn
the plague of fear
is set upon them
and in fright they search for surety.

Immortality forever be their dawn.
They search and search
and in so doing follow
the footsteps of the evil
and soon what was light is dark
and what was dark is light.

And immortality will be their birthright.

Chapter 18

The insidious disease of bioinsecurity

Bats and badgers at large!

(Dear Reader, please remember that the following is purely to stimulate your own thoughts, not to win you over.)

> Thus, at the level of an individual, disease could be thought of as a battle between systems of information ... Disease is a manifestation of human thought because it is ideas, worldviews, and beliefs that create the conditions in which a society can be riddled with disease, strife, and poverty, or can continue in health and harmony.[1]

> Adrian Gibbs, 75, who collaborated on research that led to the development of Roche Holding AG's Tamiflu drug, said in an interview that he intends to publish a report suggesting the new strain may have accidentally evolved in eggs scientists use to grow viruses and drug makers use to make vaccines. Gibbs said he came to his conclusion as part of an effort to trace the virus's origins by analyzing its genetic blueprint.
>
> 'One of the simplest explanations is that it's a laboratory escape', Gibbs said in an interview with Bloomberg Television today. 'But there are lots of others.'[2]

> The violence of the new law depends upon extending measures of arrest, interrogation, detention, rendition, and war across states and societies, through borders, to new zones of exceptionality and insecurity, to new plausible situations of danger and terror, and to new-fangled clusters and categories of '(always already capture) live forces or human bodies. The structure of the new order of exception is not hierarchical and totalitarian, then. It is rather open (to all spaces), plural (anybody can be a subject of the biopoliced system), and rhizomatic (it does not depend upon a rooted center of command but, instead, sovereign centrality and decisionism are consequences of it)'.[3]

156   Bioinsecurity

What is this little tale of potoroos and in the defence of their homelands against the marauding hounds made up of lethal pathogens shape-shifting across the Australian landscape? That far-flung nation-state of Australia, full of little Aussie Vegemites[4] punching above their weight, grandstanding like Porky Pig in front of the mirror, unable to recognize that they are the bacon in the sandwich of global superpower. The bread made up of the two hounds – the United States and China – fighting it out for dominance over the Asia Pacific, pressing our little Aussie pig to give up his bacon and align with either hound. And what better way to press our little pig than to instil fear? Yes, that old saying famously uttered by President Roosevelt to American citizens during the Great Depression of the 1930s still holds true: 'The only thing we have to fear is fear itself.'[5]

And so this discourse begins and ponders the name of Roosevelt in the bushlands of Australia. Why use such a name when coupled with such cuties as Motty and Potty? The reason was unknown to me at first, but as the story unfolded it became evident that Roosevelt's words would resonate throughout this story.[6]

When I wrote the tale in 2008, the Global Financial Crisis[7] stalked the world economy as though we were about to revisit the Great Depression.[8] The survivalists were ready and able, bunkers were being built and food was stockpiled. But as I wrote, my attention was being drawn to my garden grove. Each night I would hear the nightly squabbles of my little friends, the bats, then I remembered that the threat to their lives was more dire than any danger to my own. Furthermore, they were my relations (*Mitákuye Oyás'in*, as the Native Americans would say),[9] and what was done to them may soon be visited upon me. For the *politicians* in charge appeared to forget their constituents and instead become like cyborgs, instructed by political party machines – 'the banks are too large to fail'[10] was the mantra, and so billions were turned over to the banks to cover up the indebtedness they spread among the poor. 'We must have economic development' is a mantra made of gold – or is it uranium? The prevailing view seemed to be that if the nation failed to turn a profit the following year, the whole population would be forced to emigrate to Slovenia![11]

Some may think I exaggerate, but when you must constantly turn out research that ensures economic development in Indigenous communities, rather than policy or governance based on their Indigenous laws to solve their contemporary problems and to ensure that laws bring wellbeing rather than just profit, you tend to become a touch jaded. I have been reading recently that some nations are actually allowing a 'happiness' debate to enter their political arenas, but one cannot help wondering whether this is just a fad – or perhaps based on a fear that the youth may begin to question exactly what is going to be left for them in the future. Perhaps an Indigenous jurisprudence on how to allow them to be patterned into the land might give them more mental relief.[12] Thoughtful

The insidious disease 157

intellectual Shaun McVeigh[13] gives a clue on how that may be done in his paper 'Law as (More or Less): On Some Not Very Reflective Elements of Law'.[14] He calls for more thoughtfulness about the conduct of lawful relations between Common Law and Indigenous Law in Australia on the issue of repatriation. Might I therefore suggest that it is important for the sake of youth that legal academics take up McVeigh's debate and bring back to the public consciousness the importance of mindful conduct of lawful behaviour in public office, if they do not want their youth to run riot in the fear of what the future beholds for them.

Dis-ease of the mind

Physicist David Peats learnt from the Blackfoot Indians that it is more a mindset than an immune deficiency that allows a virus to take hold in a society:

> Thus, at the level of an individual, disease could be thought of as a battle between systems of information ... Disease is a manifestation of human thought because it is ideas, worldviews, and beliefs that create the conditions in which a society can be riddled with disease, strife, and poverty, or can continue in health and harmony.[15]

Perhaps even President Roosevelt knew that, and so set out through his speeches to identify that which would cause imbalance – the mindset of fear.

The chant of Roosevelt

What did Roosevelt say in times of economic uncertainty? What kind of bunker did he dig to save his people? From the following words of wisdom, his wisdom would seem to lay out the need for moral fortitude – 'on honesty, on honour, on the sacredness of obligations, on faithful protection'. And so I turn to Roosevelt:

> Happiness lies not in the mere possession of money; it lies in the joy of achievement, in the thrill of creative effort. The joy and moral stimulation of work no longer must be forgotten in the mad chase of evanescent profits. These dark days will be worth all they cost us if they teach us that our true destiny is not to be ministered unto but to minister to ourselves and to our fellow men.
>
> Recognition of the falsity of material wealth as the standard of success goes hand in hand with the abandonment of the false belief that public office and high political position are to be valued only by the standards of pride of place and personal profit; and there must be

an end to a conduct in banking and in business which too often has given to a sacred trust the likeness of callous and selfish wrongdoing. Small wonder that confidence languishes, for it thrives only on honesty, on honor, on the sacredness of obligations, on faithful protection, on unselfish performance; without them it cannot live.[16]

Does not such an eloquent speech send shivers down your spine – not only for its beautiful thoughts, but for the screaming realization that we have been here before? What is it that the great Western civilization fails to learn from history? And why exactly does a top-rating TV reality show, *The Apprentice*,[17] which was replicated in both Australia and the UK, throw up a corporate king such as Donald Trump as a serious presidential candidate in the 2016 presidential campaign?[18] Where is the common sense when the very people exploited by the 1 per cent like him, support such a man?[19] Furthermore, they encourage their children to be just like him – an emperor with no moral clothes.[20] But then this is the era of the Emperor's New Clothes: the illusion of greatness and style all woven by the spin doctors out of their digital thread. That is the role of the Hounds: they must rummage across the lands of the small and take no account of them, for they seek out what will make them great and do battle with other hounds, such as are found in presidential and other leadership battles.

For an answer to this dissonant behaviour, let us turn to the ever-watchful and ever-critical Noam Chomsky, MIT public intellectual, who identifies the rise of the golden-haired Emperor Trump with the troubles that plagued the era of the Great Depression. It would seem that my story and the deeds of our little Roosevelt have cyclical value, as we return to the 1930s to learn even more lessons. Chomsky makes a comparison with the similar economic woes that haunted the American psyche in that era, but he cautions that while in those days there was hope, now there is little – especially for the poor 'white men', who are dying at alarming rates due to suicide, alcohol and drug abuse.[21] It is a lesson that all future governments in the Anglo countries need to take heed of: the rise of Trump in the 2016 presidential campaign is a sign of what US Senator Elizabeth Warren has been warning about – the middle income earner is slipping back into the status of the working class, if not the unemployed.[22] This shift gives rise to fear, and so we see the rise of new types of leaders. By this I mean charismatic superheros with dictatorial tendencies who convey to the nervous citizenry that they, at least, have things under control. This is a phenomenon that, I would suggest, will continue into future elections in America and her sister nations, as the 'white man' feels the threat of their populations becoming more 'coloured' in their eyes and of women attaining equal pay.[23] In such fertile ground grows unrest, which allows for the legitimization of the securitization of the populous. We will all be encouraged to remember the Cold War and look for the 'red under the bed' – in their new clothing of the terrorist.

The virus

So let us investigate our other heroes, Captain Koala and the Horse with No Name, to see just what is going on down at the lab. And turn to the subject of this chapter – bioinsecurity. Bioinsecurity being a term first coined by Nancy Chen and Lesley Sharp, *In Bioinsecurity and Vulnerability*.[24] Chen and Sharp make us aware of the growing hysteria around worst-case scenarios of viral outbreaks, which, in turn, fuels the growth of securitization measures: intensive surveillance that enables pre-emptive measures of biological control based on worst-case scenarios, rather than waiting to see how an outbreak develops. Such surveillance makes the biosecurity industry a mechanism for making the populous feel constantly insecure about a possible biological threat.

So, who is our bio-terrorist in this story from Australia? Why the little bats – those little creatures that are essential to the pollination of our beautiful world. And what is this terror that the bats – presumed so evil in intent – bring to our safe little resource-rich shores of human Vegemites and potoroos? Some say that the Nipah virus is our culprit, the cousin of the already resident Hendra virus, that little terrorist beset on terrorizing the lucrative horse-racing industry.

So I searched the headquarters of the global fight against the 'viral' – the World Health Organization – to see what it had to say about the Hendra virus. This virus appears to be getting undue attention in Australia – and leading to defamation of the bats[25] – not to mention the millions of taxpayer research dollars being spent on finding the bug, rather than the horse-racing industry paying up. After all, this is not an essential service but rather an industry of indulgence for the rich – and the poor can ill-afford to indulge in this pastime.

> Hendra virus (HeV) is a rare, emerging zoonotic virus (a virus transmitted to humans from animals), that can cause respiratory and neurological disease and death in people. It can also cause severe disease and death in horses, resulting in considerable economic losses for horse breeders.
>
> Initially named Equine Morbilivirus, Hendra virus is a member of the genus Henipavirus, a new class of virus in the Paramyxoviridae family. It is closely related to Nipah virus.
>
> ...Hendra virus was first recognized in 1994 during an outbreak of acute respiratory disease among 21 horses in Australia. Two people were infected, and one died. Since then, there have been another ten outbreaks, all in Australia, and three involving human cases.
>
> ...Spill-over of Hendra virus from fruit bats to horses is rare.[26]

Bats! Such terror these little fellas spread; only a Charlie the Numbat would delight in it. Yet such news only really impacts on the wealthy few

160   Bioinsecurity

and their precious money-making breeds. Is it blown out of all proportion, or does it in fact reflect the reality of the gross inequalities of the Western world, in which what affects the wealthy is where the money goes? But who cares when the horse-racing lobby can get the government to agree immediately to spend millions of dollars of our taxes to research a threat to this rich industry? The patrons and owners of which could easily afford to clean up their own industry's act, and pay for the research and biosecurity that would contain what is an amazingly inane disease when compared with the many other diseases that impact the poverty-stricken Indigenous people of Australia.[27]

The Hendra virus is one of the rarest diseases in the world. Not only is it rare, but bat-to-human infection is unknown and they still don't understand why only the horses become infected. Hendra virus baffles the scientists, some saying it is in the paddocks and on the ground, while others blame the bat. This tells me that there is still much to learn about this disease before we all become insecure about this minor biosecurity threat. Instead, let us ponder the little virus's unique ability to escape the power of the almighty. There is much to learn if we take the time.

Down at the lab

> Hendra virus has unexpectedly jumped to dogs, with confirmation a family pet has been infected on a property near Brisbane that was already quarantined ... biosecurity policy, applied nationally, was to euthanize all animals found to have contracted the virus due to its capacity to become active after a period of dormancy in the host.[28]

There goes the family pet, now suspect as criminal alongside the bats. The family protests that the dog is part of the family and cannot be just done away with. But is it really the bats or dogs or horses or is it, in fact, human error?

If we take the case that turned the bat into a criminal and Malaysia into ground zero, an outbreak of swine flu was blamed on the bats rather than the industrialization of pig farming. Yet Australian virologist Adrian Gibbs said that there should be consideration given to the possibility that the swine flu virus may have been created as a result of human error:

> The 'laboratory error' theory. We note that influenza viruses survive well in virus laboratories, that laboratories are not subject to routine surveillance, and that there are probably many laboratories in the world that share and propagate a range of swine influenza viruses from different sources and continents, and also share and use immortalized

The insidious disease 161

lines of cultured cells. The viruses are used for research, diagnostic tests and for making vaccines, and the cells are used for propagating the viruses. Thus if S-OIV had been generated by laboratory activity, when one host was simultaneously infected with strains from the different parental lineages, this would explain most simply why S-OIV's genes had escaped surveillance for over a decade, and how viruses last sampled in North America, Europe and Asia became assembled in one place and generated a reassortant.[29]

Badger

Let us now turn to the Northern hemisphere to give some balance to this debate, and turn to Badger as the other named terrorist in the title of the chapter: Badger also defamed and executed at close range for terrorizing the multimillion-dollar bovine industries with her TB virus.

> Bovine tuberculosis (bTB) in UK cattle is increasing rapidly. Consequently, the UK Government is spending escalating sums of money in attempts at disease control. We propose that bTB control in cattle is irrelevant as a public health policy. In the UK, cattle-to-human transmission is negligible. Aerosol transmission, the only probable route of human acquisition, occurs at inconsequential levels when milk is pasteurised, even when bTB is highly endemic in cattle. Furthermore, there is little evidence for a positive cost benefit in terms of animal health of bTB control. Such evidence is required; otherwise, there is little justification for the large sums of public money spent on bTB control in the UK.[30]

Badger is an excellent story of specialists gone mad: badgers caught in traps; land marked out so the farmer can gun her down:

> Under the cull, 10 shooting licenses would be issued a year, and 1,000–1,500 badgers would probably be killed in a 150 sq km area over four years. This is about 30,000 badgers a year – and 50,000 already die on the roads annually. The English badger population was put at 190,000 in 1995. The animals have been a protected species since the 1973 Badgers Act.[31]

Seven full years to shoot on sight. Good old Britannia, forever emulating royalty with the fox hunts; ignoring the deficient husbandry practices of the dairy industry and instead blaming it on the defenceless badgers. Shoot them on sight, which sounds feudal to me. In April 2011, David Williams, the Badger Trust's chairman, defended the badgers against the claims that they are spreading Bovine TB:

The guilty parties are harbouring and spreading disease by keeping infected cattle on farms. The cattle-based measures now in place depend absolutely on effective movement controls, honest and accurate record keeping and discipline. They have been producing heartening results without killing a single badger, particularly in Wales. However, if badger culling had been introduced last year, these improvements would have been claimed as 'proof' that culling had been necessary.[32]

What happens to our totemic others of the North and South gives us pause to consider what might happen to us – or at least those of our citizenry who have been pushed from their homes by climate change and other economic forces, and left to range across the land and sea to foreign shores as refugees. As Professor John P. Wargo of Yale University, asserts: it is 'competing narratives, rather than caring or common sense which dictates the winners of the climate debate'.[33]

The totemic other

And who would it seem has the best narrative in town?

Of particular interest are the various ways in which colonial apparatuses often remain largely intact precisely by adapting to and morphing through new technologies of biopower. Despite celebratory narratives of globalised fluidity and unregulated flows, the exercise of biopower by the state is invariably premised on a body that is geopolitically sorted, biopolitically hierarchised and technologically surveilled.

What tactics of dissent and practices for political change remain viable in the face of the ever-increasing convergence of the state and biopolitical technologies of governmentality and securitisation?[34]

But what is this? The rulers know how to morph and adapt – are they by any chance totemically aligned to the viral?

Yes, that little mite who hitches a ride and turns poor bat and badger into bio-terrorists. It is a bright future indeed for our mite, if futurist Ray Kurzweil's predictions are true: a world policed by little dust particles carrying out reconnaissance missions – not unlike the Great Hounds of my story. For example, before this decade is out, devices the size of dust particles will be able to carry out actual reconnaissance missions.[35]

And what is this little virus that hides within their systems, all nice and tight – yes, a little bacterium so clever and well-hidden from sight? She is the one who teaches us how the mighty might fall. She fears no nuclear bomb, for she is a pathogen – or, even worse, a swarm of nanobots greedily eating up the carbon of the Earth in a mere matter of weeks. Our call is to the virus that happily shape-shifts as the bio-weapons are ready to strike. Shape-shifting is what she is all about – a trick well studied in the cultures of old. So do not try to understand the bacteria like a scientist locked in a world of sin, as he kills defenceless mice to save his own skin. Do not mention the chimps locked up for 30 years in laboratories of torture.[36] But ponder the following words:

> The violence of the new law depends upon extending measures of arrest, interrogation, detention, rendition, and war across states and societies, through borders, to new zones of exceptionality and insecurity, to new plausible situations of danger and terror, and to new-fangled clusters and categories of (always already captured) live forces or human bodies. The structure of the new order of exception is not hierarchical and totalitarian, then. It is rather open (to all spaces), plural (anybody can be a subject of the biopoliced system), and rhizomatic (it does not depend upon a rooted center of command but, instead, sovereign centrality and decisionism are consequences of it).[37]

So beware you humans that carry any kind of antibodies, for you will be next. So bunker down if you just want to Motty and Potty your life away, for you are as vulnerable to the Kozys of the world, who rely on the threat of the Hounds, and those who give news with no sense of context, but just sensationalism and disinformation, not unlike our Charlie Numbat.

Human experiments

Captain Koala knows something is rotten in the state of Denmark and, like all people who forget their history, the Horse with No Name misses the mark. This bio-terrorism is merely the resurfacing, in my mind, of eugenics. Therefore, let us note what this wondrous way of seeing the human brought forth and remember the people who deemed it a clever thought. Smart Nazi scientists who were grabbed like gold on a bull market as World War II ended. Project Paperclip was the code name for the secret intelligence programme to bring Nazi medical and aeronautic scientists to the United States. The book of the same title by Annie Jacobsen[38] makes us aware of the 'hero' state of the United States quite willing to take them and their shameful data from the Holocaust victims, all in the name of science and the good of humanity – and of course their ability to build the rockets that would see America win the race to the moon. One wonders whether, if those murdered in the concentration camps had been descendants of royalty or other famous people, the Americans would have been so quick to profit from such despicable use of the medical data from the tortured bodies of concentration camps. Unfortunately, the little porky pigs

164   Bioinsecurity

of Australia had their own little programme going long before the Holocaust:

> At the forefront of the eugenics movement in Melbourne was a renowned professor of anatomy, Richard Berry, who in the 1920s measured people's heads in pursuit of a theory that a small head indicated that a person had low intelligence. White, educated people were the smartest, according to Professor Berry; the poor, criminals and Aborigines the least so. He claimed Ned Kelly was a 'mental defective' because his brain size was that of a 14-year-old.
>
> Berry favoured the establishment of a 'lethal chamber' to euthanise what he called 'the grosser types of our mental defectives'.
>
> According to Dr Jones, the Eugenics Society of Victoria was 'an offspring of the University of Melbourne'. Many members of the society, which ran from 1936 to 1961, were academics at the university, including Sir John Medley, a vice-chancellor. The university's 'new' arts building is named after him.
>
> Berry, professor of anatomy at Melbourne between 1906 and 1929, was responsible for the construction of a new anatomy building, which now houses the university's maths and statistics department, and still bears his name.[39]

The professors had intellectual authority, which is typical of a society not able to see its own lack of equality and still unable to believe that the sign of a civilized and intelligent society is one that maintains very limited difference between the rich and poor. And if that means living with less stuff – hail says the Earth! But have these beliefs really gone away, and does the rise of bioinsecurity allow for an overreaction to threats to the populous. Suspicion then falls on those who do not abide by the 'sedimented' lifestyle.

Tagging: should it be the children or the immoral leaders?

Iskra Uzunova makes a case for the mistreatment of the Roma following the Decade of Roma Inclusion (2005–15):[40]

> At first, the European Parliament adopted a resolution urging Italian authorities 'to refrain from collecting fingerprints from Roma, including minors ... as this would clearly constitute an act of direct discrimination based on race and ethnic origin'. Italian authorities refused to comply with the recommendation and, instead, submitted detailed explanations of their policy, assuring that only unidentifiable persons – those lacking Italian or European identity documents – would be fingerprinted.[41]

The case has strained relations between France and the European Commission, with French President Nicolas Sarkozy vigorously defending the expulsions against widespread criticism from human rights groups and the Catholic Church.[42]

The template for the profile of the terrorist will be based on race. Orphaned Roma children no less. Just like Kozy of our tale from the bushland of Australia, who encourages the quolls like Mutface to discriminate against the fruitbats who are merely in search of protection against the marauding Great Hounds, the leaders of modern 'civilized' societies like France and Italy have encourged racism against the Roma by singling out Roma children to be tagged. Leadership has fallen into the hands of men of low moral integrity:

> The shock arrest of former French president Nicolas Sarkozy this week over allegations of corruption has sent shockwaves through France.[43]

> For Silvio Berlusconi, the news couldn't come at a worse time. The day after Italy's constitutional court struck down parts of a controversial law that had provided him immunity from his ongoing criminal trials, prosecutors confirmed on Friday, Jan. 14, that the embattled Prime Minister was under investigation for allegedly paying for sex with a 17-year-old girl last year.
>
> The allegations are by far the worst the scandal-ridden Berlusconi has faced during a long history of battles with Italy's legal system – which he has characterized as a campaign of political persecutions by left-wing judges. They include charges that the 74-year-old Prime Minister abused his position when he called a police station last May and intervened to free the girl in question, Karima El Mahroug, after she was detained on suspicion of theft.[44]

Consequently, the Roma children are tagged as the future criminals while the leaders are able to hide their disgrace and disrespect for women. But still the arguments continue as why the Roma children should be tagged:

> The perspective of many children and youths finding themselves without a family so the argument goes, might lead to the formation of pockets of delinquency that provide instability, even politically, with potential extremist associations.[45]

Refugees and migrants will also eventually be tagged if they are poor, unschooled, but worst of all, orphan – no longer human, but mere carriers of the potential disease of terrorism. And so securitization of the poor becomes the norm.

166   Bioinsecurity

In the meantime, the chosen few can roam the globe free of securitization but ready to impose it as long as it is under *their* rules, as Pereira explains:

> Conversely, the securitizing agents tend to be most influent groups in society, where power, according to Williams, is more 'sedimented' (rhetorically and discursively, culturally, and institutionally) and structured in ways that make securitizations somewhat predictable and thus subject to probabilistic analysis.[46]

Youth as a virus

> As is classical in biology, there's no gratitude once you make something like a virus, it turns round and kills the parent cell.[47]

Be warned the 'sedimented' societies, for the youth understand the viral nature of technology and its ability to coordinate unrest, just like the contagion on the loose. Mutating at a rate unchecked, just like a pandemic, the youth and their technology will infect and change the nature of society. The first global virus of note was Occupy, that leaderless and voluntary organization that staged sit-ins against the gigantic banks and the 1 per cent.

> In 2015, just 62 individuals had the same wealth as 3.6 billion people – the poorer half of humanity. As recently as 2010, it was 388 individuals with the same wealth as those 3.6 billion.[48]

The consolidation of wealth into fewer hands means a need for constant takeovers (better than saying cannibalism) between major multinationals. The future offspring then become vulnerable to viruses – be that hacking or corporate corruption by slick young executives or the worse possible scenario: a rogue algorithm running the stock exchange.[49]

The rogue algorithm is nothing more than a technological virus bent on a pandemic across the global stock exchange. Last time a pandemic spread – and I mean a genuine pandemic, not these 'disaster capitalism' pandemics, as Klein would call them – it was thanks to the US military, not the Spanish who spread the wrongly named flu (which in fact came out of Kansas, just like Dorothy and Toto in *The Wizard of Oz*, caught on a wind that took it far from its homeland). The following description gave me the idea for the Great Hounds of red dust:

> On Saturday, March 9, 1918, a threatening black sky forecast the coming of a significant dust storm. The dust, combining with the ash of burning manure, kicked up a stinging, stinking yellow haze. The sun was said to have gone dead black in Kansas that day.[50]

And so too did the flu migrate from chickens to soldiers and then off into the world. It is just like the traditional English nursery rhyme, 'Ring-a-Ring-o'Roses ... A-tishoo, a-tishoo, we all fall down'. Straight out of the days of the plague of the Middle Ages, the little jingle never went away. I wonder why: was it something in our genetic memory that kept it going to remind us that the plague will always return?

Therefore, be warned that it might just be the military once again, forgetting how infected it is with ideas of imperial madness, following the road map of the British Empire and every other empire that has lusted after other people's lands. So, as the greed for international capital has infected the world with the virus of hedge funds and other such diseases – which in turn take out the young through suicide, saddened by the many broken dreams of the young executive infected with the disease of greed – they, like the chickens, will also return home to roost. That roost however, might be more vigilant Occupiers fighting the 1 per cent, or even youthful hackers. The intergenerational gap grows every school year between the adults with no computer coding knowledge and those young graduates, who cut their teeth on codes. And we offer them a moral compass in which we praise the billions spent on the race to Mars, but forget the billions living on a dollar a day and treat the refugees like an invading species. And don't forget the annoying Indigenous who keep pointing to the cry of the planet that things are a changing and no amount of money can repair the climate havoc. The end-game needs consideration.

The end-game of the Hounds

As Jensen's *Endgame* argues,[51] they have built their own disease in the form of the digital virus, which the hackers delight in using to infect the great and self-indulgent good. Within those hacks could be a button that nukes us back to the stone age. When the Hounds of the great nations think the world is their oyster to take and spend where they please – the end-game is near.

You must forgive me, as I live in a capital city that is fondly known as the Gateway to Asia, the small city of Darwin – which I call Fort Darwin due to the fact that, on annual rotation, the spiffy US Military parades its youthful best in our small military parades. But lurking in Port Darwin are the new owners, the other great hound: China. The masters of the 'Art of War' have 'stunned' the United States who assumed they would be consulted about any sale.[52] Australian public policy analyst Geoff Wade warns:

> The 'Chinese Dream' involves the reassertion of the economic and political primacy that China claims it has enjoyed over neighbours for millennia. This agenda is now being pursued globally but most intensely in South-East Asia and Australia/New Zealand.

168   Bioinsecurity

...Darwin is intended to be a crucial link in China's new 21st Century Maritime Silk Road. The Darwin deal will provide Chinese shipping and naval vessels with facilitated access to Australia, the Indian Ocean and the South Pacific, as well as to Indonesia and PNG over the coming century.[53]

And so returning to my opening sentences, we indeed have become Porky Pig and the Great Hounds have come through the gateway.

As Australian social commentator Bernard Salt sets out quite clearly in *The Big Tilt*,[54] our Porky Pig mentality has seen us believe that we can 'manage the situation so that we never have to take sides: make money out of the Chinese and take military support from the American'. He further warns that Australians have to pull in their belts and dispel their illusions of a continued 'decadent western lifestyle' based on our symbiotic relationship with China and its demand for our resources rather than living within our own national means.

Like Norway, we have stolen the right to have the highest standard of living; both nations have benefited like drug lords from the sale of the deadly fossil fuels and oil that pollute the world. This has led to feelings of self-satisfaction – like Porky looking in the mirror – about our streamlined lifestyles stolen from the land to create misery for developing countries that suffer the 'wind-blown' pollution and desertification that has resulted.

And so the Great Hounds will arrive and turn our lovely land of potoroos and hopping mice into fields of war, where America and China will fight it out. It won't be with cannon and drones, as we are all friends; it is more likely to be something more insidious along the lines of the Art of War at the viral level – a pathogen here, a pathogen there, or a computer hack or two every second. It would be a war of stealth where the micro does the most damage, backed up by laws, all in the name of a biosecurity threat.

And so the Porky Australians will be forced to go on a diet of common sense and moral regard, and learn to care for the country just like the Natives of the land. For it is a land where the small survive and the large emigrate!

Notes

1 Peat, F. D., *Blackfoot Physics: A Journey into the Native American Worldview*, Phanes Press: Grand Rapids, MI, 2002: 117.

2 Bloomberg News, 'Swine Flu May be Lab Error: Aussie Researcher', 13 May 2009. www.smh.com.au/business/world-business/swine-flu-may-be-a-lab-error-aussie-researcher-20090513-b2zh.html, accessed 12 August 2009.

3 Debrix, F., 'The Permanent State of Exception and the Dismantling of the Law: Jean-Claude Paye's *Global War on Liberty* (Part 1)', TelosScope, 16 July 2007, www.telospress.com/the-permanent-state-of-exceptionand-the-dismantling-of-the-lawjean-claude-payes-global-war-on-libertypart-1, accessed 15 November 2015.

The insidious disease 169

4 Vegemite is a black yeast spread that has been very popular in Australia since the 1950s. Australian children are often fondly referred to as 'Little Vegemites'.
5 Roosevelt, speaking of the rise of the military industrial complex. 'Franklin D. Roosevelt, First Inaugural Address, Saturday, March 4, 1933', http://history-matters.gmu.edu/d/5057, accessed 30 September 2011.
6 Ibid.
7 'Financial Crisis of 2007–08', https://en.wikipedia.org/wiki/Financial_crisis_of_2007%E2%80%9308, accessed 11 June 2014.
8 'Great Depression', https://en.wikipedia.org/wiki/Great_Depression, accessed 16 July 2015.
9 Rita, U., 'Mitakuye Oyasin', www.grandmotherscouncil.org/mitakuye-oyasin-all-my-relations, accessed 3 April 2016.
10 'Too Big to Fail', https://en.wikipedia.org/wiki/Too_big_to_fail, accessed 3 April 2016.
11 'Helping Refugees', www.vlada.si/en/helping_refugees, accessed 3 April 2016.
12 Middleton, B., *Trust in the Land: New Directions in Tribal Conservation*, Tucson, AZ: University of Arizona Press, 2011; Zuni Cruz, C., 'Shadow War Scholarship, Indigenous Legal Tradition, and Modern Law in Indian Country', *Washburn Law Journal*, 47(3), 2008: 632–633.
13 Shaun McVeigh, Associate Professor of Law, Melbourne University, Australia.
14 McVeigh, S., 'Law as (More or Less): On Some Not Very Reflective Elements of Law', *UC Irvine Law Review*, 4 (2014): 471–492.
15 Peat, *Blackfoot Physics*: 117.
16 Roosevelt, 'First Inaugural Address'.
17 *The Apprentice*, created by Mark Burnett and hosted by Donald Trump, NBC.
18 Douthat, R., 'Trumpism After Trump', *New York Times*, 24 March 2016. www.nytimes.com/2016/03/24/opinion/campaign-stops/trumpism-after-trump, accessed 30 March 2016.
19 'We Are the 99 Per Cent', https://en.wikipedia.org/wiki/We_are_the_99%25, accessed 20 March 2016.
20 The statement refers to *The Tale of the Emperor's New Clothes* by Hans Christian Andersen, which in its day was a political parody.
21 Williams, A., 'N. Chomsky: We Owe the Rise of Trump to Fear and the "Breakdown of Society"', *Alternet*, 23 February 2016. www.alternet.org/news-amp-politics/noam-chomsky-we-owe-rise-trump-fear-and-breakdown-society, accessed 30 March 2016.
22 Warren, E. and Tyagi, A. W., *The Two-Income Trap: Why Middle-Class Parents are Going Broke*, New York: Basic Books, 2003.
23 Terkel, A., 'Elizabeth Warren Looms Large in the 2016 Presidential Race', *Huffington Post*, 6 February 2016. www.huffingtonpost.com.au/entry/elizabeth-warren-2016_us_56b4f8cee4b01d80b2462dc3?section=australia, accessed 31 March 2016.
24 Chen, N. N. and Sharp, L. A. (eds), *Bioinsecurity and Vulnerability*, Sar Press, 2014.
25 World Health Organization, 'Hendra Virus (HeV) Infection', www.who.int/csr/disease/hendra/en/, accessed 12 April 2016.
26 Horse Owner Today, 'Hendra Virus Facts', 5 July 2011. http://horseownertoday.com/blog/current-research/post/2011/07/05/Hendra-Virus-Facts.aspx, accessed 27 July 2011.
27 'The Gap: Indigenous Disadvantage in Australia', Australians Together, www.australianstogether.org.au/stories/detail/the-gap-indigenous-disadvantage-in-australia, accessed 12 April 2016.
28 Walker, J. and Barrett, R., 'Dog's Case of Hendra Worsens Worries Over Spreading Virus', *The Australian*, 27 July 2011. www.theaustralian.com.au/

news/nation/dogs-case-of-hendra-worsens-worries-over-spreading-virus/story-e6frg6nf-1226102334678, accessed 27 July 2011.

29 Gibbs, A. J., Armstrong, J. S. and Downie, J. C., 'From Where Did the 2009 "Swine-origin" Influenza A Virus (H1N1) Emerge?', *Virology Journal*, 2009 6:207. doi: 10.1186/1743-422X-6-207.

30 Torgerson, P. and Torgerson, D., 'Public Health and Bovine Tuberculosis: What's All the Fuss About?', *Trends in Microbiology*, 18(2) (2009): 67–72.

31 Harvey, F., 'Badger Cull: Caroline Spelman "Strongly Minded" to Allow Shooting', *Guardian*, 19 July 2011, www.guardian.co.uk/environment/2011/jul/19/badger-cull-caroline-spelman-shooting, accessed 15 September 2011.

32 Kaminski, J., 'Badger Culls Don't Stop Tuberculosis in Cattle – the Evidence is Clear', *Guardian*, 11 August 2011, www.guardian.co.uk/environment/blog/2011/aug/11/badger-cull-dont-stop-bovine-tb, accessed 15 September 2011.

33 Wargo, J. P., 'Principles and Strategies of Environmental Law', https://www.youtube.com/watch?v=R8BG-MJErSM, accessed 20 April 2011.

34 Macquarie University, 'Geo-soma-politics: Technologies of Biopower, Governmentality and Securitisation', conference abstract, www.arts.mq.edu.au/the_faculty/news_and_events/events/faculty_symposiumscolloquiums/geo-soma-politics_technologies_of_biopower,_governmentality_and_securitisation, accessed 15 November 2015.

35 Kurzweil, R., 'Nanotechnology Dangers and Defenses', *Nanotechnology Perceptions: A Review of Ultraprecision Engineering and Nanotechnology*, 2(1), 27 March 2006.

36 'Chimpanzee Locked Up for Thirty Years', www.smh.com.au/environment/animals/free-after-decades-in-research-labs-chimps-step-into-the-light-20110908-1jyjz.html, accessed 15 November 2015.

37 Debrix, 'The Permanent State of Exception'.

38 Jacobsen, A., *Project Paperclip: The Secret Intelligence Program that Brought Nazi Scientists to America*, Little, Brown: New York, 2014.

39 Cervini, E., 'A Theory Out of the Darkness', *The Age*, 13 September 2011, www.theage.com.au/national/education/a-theory-out-of-the-darkness-20110912-1k5r6.html#ixzz1XmyGygGV, accessed 15 November 2015.

40 'Decade of Roma Inclusion, 2005–2015', http://www.romadecade.org, accessed 15 November 2015.

41 Uzunova, I., 'Roma Integration in Europe: Why Minority Rights Are Failing', *Arizona Journal of International and Comparative Law*, 27(1): 283–323.

42 Troyer, J. and Pawluk, J., 'EU Gives France Chance to Avoid Sanctions Over Roma', *Reuters*, 29 September 2010. www.reuters.com/article/us-eu-roma-idUSTRE68S3IQ20100929, accessed 15 November 2015.

43 Cerrah, M. F., 'Nicolas Sarkozy May Recover from His Latest Scandal, Political Class Will Not Be So Lucky', *New Statesman*, www.newstatesman.com/politics/2014/07/nicolas-sarkozy-may-recover-his-latest-scandal-political-class-will-not-be-so-lucky, accessed 15 November 2015.

44 Faris, S., 'Did Italy's Berlusconi Pay for Sex?', *Time*, 14 January 2011. www.time.com/time/world/article/0,8599,2042595,00.html, accessed 15 November 2015.

45 Pereira, R., 'Processes of Securitization of Infectious Diseases and Western Hegemonic Power: A Historical-Political Analysis', *Global Health Governance*, 2(1) 2008: 5. www.ghgj.org/Pereira_%20processes%20of%20securitization.doc, accessed 15 November 2015.

46 Ibid.: 4.

47 'J.C. Venter Speaking at the Genbank 25th Anniversary', www.youtube.com/watch?v=tcazafdJmPE, accessed 23 October 2010.

48 Oxfam Australia, 'Inequality', https://www.oxfam.org.au/what-we-do/inequality, accessed 22 March 2016.
49 Banjo, S., 'Robots Have Been Running the US Stock Market, and the Government is Finally Taking Control', *Quartz*, 25 March 2015. http://qz.com/370019/robots-have-been-running-the-us-stock-market-and-the-government-is-finally-taking-control, accessed 31 March 2016.
50 'The First Wave', *American Experience* (PBS). www.pbs.org/wgbh/american experience/features/general-article/influenza-first-wave, accessed 14 September 2016.
51 Jensen, D., *Endgame*, Seven Stories Press: New York, 2006.
52 Kehoe, J. and Tingle, L., 'US "Stunned" by Sale of Port of Darwin to Chinese', *Financial Review*, 17 November 2015. www.afr.com/news/politics/us-stunned-by-port-of-darwin-sale-to-chinese-20151116-gl0omf, accessed 14 September 2016.
53 Wade, G., 'Port of Darwin: This is about More than China's Economic Interest', *ABC News*, 24 November 2015. www.abc.net.au/news/2015-11-24/wade-the-darwin-port-is-another-link-in-china's-expansion/6967640, accessed 14 September 2016.
54 Salt, B., *The Big Tilt: What Happens When the Boomers Bust and Xers and Ys Inherit the Earth*, Hardie Grant Books: London, 2011: 296.

Part V

Last words

Chapter 19

A poem

To the little people

It was the little people,
we are told who made the rock paintings
and caused the stars to fall.
It is the little people
who have the wisdom and
the knowledge of healing.
We must consent.

They are the ones, who are the giants,
for they fight for the liberties
that we abuse, the civil rights we ignore,
the moral courage we squander,
the freedom we assume.
For them it is a struggle to be allowed to vote,
for us it is a pain in the butt.

We have much to learn
if we would stop ourselves
from gauging a people by their material success,
rather than quality of family
and an ability to do something as simple as vote.

The little people came before us
and will last forever more.
As for our fate, well!

Chapter 20

In conclusion
Some reflective thoughts

> If you are truly embedded in the relational world, you understand your participation to be in ever-repeating cycles, not finite and linear time spans. The spirit that binds everything together as relatives does not expire: it merely transforms and reasserts itself as the circle repeats.[1]

In your haste, Dear Reader, remain vigilant about your clever mind: the cyclical nature of history will begin to become clear as you travel along your cyber-highways and lowways. For the faster you travel, the quicker the past returns. The circular nature of existence was well known by the ancients. The Indigenous are constantly fighting to make sense of a world that thinks it is on a linear path to the stars,[2] living in hope of shuttling its delinquent behaviour to the outer galaxies where they can once again colonize and make over in their own image. Or are they just trying to distance themselves from the never-ending mountains of garbage that fill the Earth with all their cleverness?[3]

New discoveries of neuroscience and quantum physics, when devoid of all their fancy words, are nothing more than can be found in traditional stories of humanity that stayed long and close to the Earth and know its workings not from a test tube but from lived experience.[4] Always remember that the plutonomy fears those who know how to listen, for they can hear beyond the 'white noise' that fills our lives. The listeners are the witnesses to the subtle but dangerous changes that turn democracies from places of freedom to places where rendition in plain sight becomes a daily occurrence – places where virtual walls of digital surveillance slowly creep and grow around us like ivy up a castle wall. And before we know it, we find ourselves in the thick of a digital jungle of our own making. We did not listen, but just 'heard' all the noise that told us democracy was our God-given right, rather than something that can disappear overnight. A visual image of democracy, as Richard K. Sherwin warns,[5] could be just an illusion if we do not take hold and source the real.

Long ago, McLuhan pondered the huge vortexes of energy created by our technologies and their unfathomable consequences. As he reminded

Some reflective thoughts 177

his fellow citizens, the inventors and their financiers never think of the consequences of their inventions as they become caught up in the bright glow of the wonders they will bring to our daily lives. McLuhan also warned that we cannot trust our instincts or responses to new things – did he know that we would just gobble up the latest fad without a moment's consideration? It is remarkable to consider that, at the time he wrote, there was no internet, and artificial intelligence had not yet danced across our screens to give us the visual delight of a bright future as cyborgs or living life with our buddy, I-robot,[6] which knew the three laws of robotics – well, that is until Ava[7] came along and ruined it all for us with her clever machine mind that imprisons the hero, leading Ava to run a mile. Not a story we wish to know. But advancements in quantum computers and the drive towards singularity have now called out the greats – Hawking, Gates and Musk – thanks to a little Aussie scientist paranoid about intelligent weaponry that might decide it is in command.[8]

As we speed through the second decade of the new century, we are coming face to face with the horrors that can manifest, such as rogue nanobots eating up the carbon of the planet.

> An analysis of the history of technology shows that technological change is exponential, contrary to the common-sense 'intuitive linear' view. So we won't experience 100 years of progress in the 21st century – it will be more like 20,000 years of progress (at today's rate). The 'returns', such as chip speed and cost-effectiveness, also increase exponentially. There's even exponential growth in the rate of exponential growth. Within a few decades, machine intelligence will surpass human intelligence, leading to The Singularity – technological change so rapid and profound it represents a rupture in the fabric of human history. The implications include the merger of biological and nonbiological intelligence, immortal software-based humans, and ultra-high levels of intelligence that expand outward in the universe at the speed of light.[9]

For McLuhan, the answer to how to comprehend and then mitigate our future cleverness was to turn to the jurisprudence that lay in the poem 'The Maelstrom' by Edgar Allan Poe.[10] Through his contemplation of that poem, he deduced that there were four laws of media that reveal the future of all technology:

> McLuhan prescribed his so-called Four Effects (laws of media) as a complementary method to Aristotle's well-known Four Causes: Material, Efficient, Formal, and Final. The Four Effects ... were named as follows: Retrieval, Reversal, Obsolescence and Amplification or Enhancement. These Four Effects are meant to apply simultaneously,

and not linearly or sequentially, mirroring the method of Aristotle's Four Causes. If applied properly and inventively, their perceptual impact on the reader will be one of aural/visual, discontinuous, resonant interplay, as they reveal already present or future features of media, culture and technology.[11]

The four laws were in fact four questions to be contemplated any time a new technology was brought to fruition, but not before it was subject to public use. McLuhan wanted inventive people to actually contemplate all the ways in which the invention could bring disaster to the planet – or at least humanity. In other words, it took a jurisprudential approach to the dilemmas of the future. This is the situation in which we now find ourselves.

My book suggests that we are at a point in time in which it is stories, rather than regulation, that will inspire the public – not just the regulators or inventors – to consider the patterns that such inventions will either disrupt or lay down anew. Stories therefore have an important role to play in legal text, to help law-makers consider their actions. More importantly, stories are egalitarian and can close the inter-generational gap. They open up the discussion for all, and not just the experts – who, as McLuhan pointed out, have invented technology that allows for moments of cognitive dissonance, such as drone operators in far-flung states hiding out in bunkers to keep them safe from demonstrators while the collateral damage to the innocent goes unreported – that is until a transgender whistle-blower got hold of the tapes!

The stories bring forth the jurisprudence or conduct of lawful behaviour, as McVeigh defines it, after writing about the ways in which common law and Australian Aboriginal law can come into lawful relations.[12] As this is a book aimed mainly at the Indigenous audience, it is the lawful relations that I propose the Indigenous might take in hand.

I will conclude this book with a quote from a lawful story from the south-west of America, the land of ancient Pueblo Indians who choose to stay in desert-like conditions to remind them just how dependent they really are on the benefactor of the cosmos. Local native Leslie Marmon Silko brought forth this little story in her classic book *Ceremony*.

> The old man shook his head. 'That is the trickery of the witchcraft', he said. 'They want us to believe all evil resides with white people. Then we will look no further to see what is really happening. They want us to separate ourselves from white people, to be ignorant and helpless as we watch our own destruction. But white people are only tools that the witchery manipulates; and I tell you, we can deal with white people, with their machines and their beliefs. We can because we invented white people; it was Indian witchery that made white people in the first place.'[13]

Notes

1 Ross, R., *Indigenous Healing: Exploring Traditional Paths*, Penguin: Harmondsworth, 2014.
2 Cajete, G., *Native Science: Natural Laws of Interdependence*, Clear Light: Santa Fe, NM, 2000.
3 For example, the Pacific Garbage patch.
4 Doidge, N., *The Brain's Way of Healing*, Viking: New York, 2015.
5 Sherwin, R. K., 'Democracy's Missing Meaning', *Project Syndicate*, 15 May 2015, www.project-syndicate.org/commentary/islamic-state-democracy-meaning-by-richard-k–sherwin-2015–05, accessed 15 November 2015.
6 Asimov, I., *I, Robot*, Random House: New York, 1991.
7 *Ex Machina*, distributed by Universal Pictures, 2015.
8 Walsh, T., 'Autonomous Weapons: An Open Letter from AI & Robotics Researchers', http://futureoflife.org/open-letter-autonomous-weapons, accessed 3 December 2015.
9 Kurzweil, R., 'The Law of Accelerating Returns', www.kurzweilai.net/the-law-of-accelerating-returns, accessed 12 July 2015.
10 *McLuhan's Wake*, YouTube video, https://www.youtube.com/watch?v=A9y-ZAIdxrE, accessed 7 April 2015.
11 Sandstrom, G., 'Laws of Media – The Four Effects: A McLuhan Contribution to Social Epistemology', *Social Epistemology Review and Reply Collective*, 1(12) (2012): 1–6.
12 McVeigh, S., 'Law As (More or Less) Itself: On Some Not Very Reflective Elements of Law', *UC Irvine Law Review* 4 (2014): 475.
13 Silko, L. M., *Ceremony*, Penguin: New York, 2006: 122.